Making Technology Standards Work for You

Second Edition

A Guide to the NETS•A for School Administrators with Self-Assessment Activities

Susan Brooks-Young

International Society for Technology in Education
EUGENE, OREGON • WASHINGTON, DC

Making Technology Standards Work for You

Second Edition

A Guide to the NETS•A for School Administrators with Self-Assessment Activities

Susan Brooks-Young

Director of Book Publishing: *Courtney Burkholder*
Acquisitions Editor: *Jeff V. Bolkan*
Production Editor: *Lanier Brandau, Lynda Gansel*
Production Coordinator: *Rachel Bannister*
Graphic Designer and Book Design: *Signe Landin*
Copy Editor: *Kärstin K. Painter*
Book Production: *Keith Van Norman*

Library of Congress Cataloging-in-Publication Data

Brooks-Young, Susan.
Making technology standards work for you : a guide to the NETS•A for school administrators with self-assessment activities / Susan Brooks-Young. — 2nd ed.
p. cm.
Includes bibliographical references.
ISBN 978-1-56484-253-4 (pbk. : alk. paper)
1. Educational technology—Standards—Handbooks, manuals, etc. 2. School administrators—Handbooks, manuals, etc. I. Title.
LB1028.3.B765 2009
371.33—dc22

2008042047

Second Edition
ISBN: 978-1-56484-253-4
Printed in the United States of America

International Society for Technology in Education (ISTE)
Washington, DC, Office:
1710 Rhode Island Ave. NW, Suite 900, Washington, DC 20036-3132
Eugene, Oregon, Office:
180 West 8th Ave., Suite 300, Eugene, OR 97401-2916
Order Desk: 1.800.336.5191
Order Fax: 1.541.302.3778
Customer Service: orders@iste.org
Book Publishing: books@iste.org
Book Sales and Marketing: booksmarketing@iste.org
Web: www.iste.org

The International Society for Technology in Education (ISTE) is the trusted source for professional development, knowledge generation, advocacy, and leadership for innovation. A nonprofit membership association, ISTE provides leadership and service to improve teaching, learning, and school leadership by advancing the effective use of technology in PK–12 and teacher education.

Home of the National Educational Technology Standards (NETS), the Center for Applied Research in Educational Technology (CARET), and the National Educational Computing Conference (NECC), ISTE represents more than 100,000 professionals worldwide. We support our members with information, networking opportunities, and guidance as they face the challenge of transforming education. To find out more about these and other ISTE initiatives, visit our website at **www.iste.org**.

As part of our mission, ISTE Book Publishing works with experienced educators to develop and produce practical resources for classroom teachers, teacher educators, and technology leaders. Every manuscript we select for publication is carefully peer-reviewed and professionally edited. We look for content that emphasizes the effective use of technology where it can make a difference—increasing the productivity of teachers and administrators; helping students with unique learning styles, abilities, or backgrounds; collecting and using data for decision making at the school and district levels; and creating dynamic, project-based learning environments that engage 21st-century learners. We value your feedback on this book and other ISTE products. E-mail us at **books@iste.org**.

About the Author

Susan Brooks-Young has been involved in the field of instructional technology since 1979. She was one of the original technology users in the district where she taught and has continued to explore ways in which technology can be used to facilitate student learning. She has worked as a computer mentor, technology trainer, and technology curriculum specialist. As a site administrator, Brooks-Young relied on technology developments to accomplish and expedite her work. In 1993, she founded Computer Using Educators' (CUE) Administrators' Special Interest Group, which still serves as a network and resource for school administrators across the country and in Canada. She has also served as co-chair for ISTE's Special Interest Group for Administrators.

Before establishing her own consulting firm, Susan was a teacher, site administrator, and technology specialist at a county office of education in a career that spanned more than 23 years. She now spends her time working with school districts and regional centers on technology-related issues, developing curriculum, presenting workshops, teaching online courses, and writing articles for a variety of education journals.

She is the author of the popular books *101 Best Web Sites for Principals* (ISTE, 2005) and *Digital-Age Literacy for Teachers* (ISTE, 2007).

Acknowledgments

I owe a great deal to Clint Taylor and Dick Archibald-Woodward for technical assistance in writing this book. Clint, a former district superintendent, and Dick, a technology coordinator for a local school district, provided invaluable information concerning the roles and responsibilities of district and cabinet leaders as they relate the ISTE NETS for Administrators.

I'd also like to thank Dick Archibald-Woodward and David E. Whale, of Central Michigan University, for taking the time to review the activities in this book. Their feedback and suggestions were very helpful in writing the final draft.

Introduction

In 1983, Apple announced the Kids Can't Wait program, in which approximately 10,000 Apple II computers were donated to California schools. The strategy was a brilliant move on the part of the company because for nearly 20 years afterward, Apple dominated the education market. Early computer users were certain that this new technology would sweep the schools and redefine educational practice, empowering teachers and students to attain greater heights of academic achievement. Twenty-five years later, schools are spending large sums of money yearly on various technologies, but the full promise of instructional technology has yet to be realized. A primary cause for this situation is that technology integration requires systemic reform, which must be supported by school and district leadership. The reality is that many school administrators do not have the necessary backgrounds in either system change or technology integration to make such reforms. The purpose of the ISTE NETS for Administrators (NETS•A) and the Technology Standards for School Administrators (TSSA), which form the core of the NETS•A, is to provide guidelines to administrators to assist in school reform, particularly as it relates to technology use.

Although reference is made to technology integration throughout the standards, the leadership skills described are not necessarily technology specific but identify current expectations for how school administrators need to approach all school reform. In a compilation of articles written for the Education Resources Information Center (ERIC) Clearinghouse on Educational Management and the College of Education at the University of Oregon, Larry Lashway, a freelance research analyst, points out that today's administrators have had little or no training in how to manage system change and that the current school reform movement does not clearly define the role of the administrator. Lashway states that although the school administrators who are publicly lauded for system changes typically are noted because they "came in and turned things around" (Lashway, 2003, p. 6) on their own, most reform movements suggest that the goal for districts sites is empowered leadership, in which decision making is shared throughout the district and site structure. These mixed messages leave administrators confused about how to approach any changes, let alone technology integration. For many school administrators who already feel stretched to their limits, the question becomes: How can I tackle an area such as instructional technology when I know true integration requires a kind of change that I don't know how to support and involves an approach to teaching that I'm not familiar with myself?

Becoming and remaining an effective leader in today's educational environment requires sustained effort on the administrator's part. It requires the ability to hold a global perspective of the school or district while being able to recognize and address all the pieces that affect programs, including technology, curriculum, instructional practice, staff and community members, and managerial tasks.

The TSSA were developed by the Technology Standards for School Administrators Collaborative (TSSA Collaborative), a group of educational organizations from across the United States, and published in November 2001. ISTE has adopted the TSSA as the core for its expanded National Educational Technology Standards (NETS) for Administrators. These standards represent a national consensus of the things PK–12 school administrators need to know and do to support technology integration effectively in schools and go beyond personal productivity or a technology plan. The six areas addressed in the standards provide a context that encourages administrators to use their leadership skills and expertise to promote instructional programs that support student outcomes, incorporating technology where appropriate.

The purpose of this book is to serve as a guide for site and district administrators as they review all aspects of planning, curriculum and instruction, assessment, staff development, and legal and social issues. The authors of the standards define three separate categories for school administrators. These are used in this book to describe the various responsibilities of educational leaders as they implement the standards in their differing roles. The categories are defined as follows:

- Campus Leaders—This group includes principals, assistant principals, deans, and other site-level administrators.
- District Leaders—This group is represented by coordinators, directors, assistant coordinators, assistant directors, and other district administrators who are not at the cabinet level.
- Superintendents and Cabinet Leaders—In addition to the superintendent, this group includes assistant and deputy superintendents.

Chapters 1–6 each address a separate standard and its performance indicators, which are statements that more specifically describe the skill set for each standard. The material in this book is presented in a consistent format designed to assist the reader in understanding the performance indicators. Individual performance indicators are discussed in a narra-

1. What Is Already in Place?—This section offers approaches to reviewing existing practices.
2. What Practices Demonstrate Successful Implementation of This Performance Indicator?—This entry defines implementation goals.
3. What Steps Lead to Successful Implementation of This Performance Indicator?—This section identifies tasks that will move you from where you are to where you want to be.

To reap the greatest benefit from this book, begin by reading the standards and their performance indicators carefully. This will give you an overview of the areas addressed by the standards. If you are looking for background information about a particular topic, the narrative for each performance indicator provides information and resources and will stand alone as a reference. If you are implementing a particular performance indicator, read both the narrative and the tasks and responsibilities described for the performance indicator as they pertain to your current position. Chapter 1 describes a model for planning, and the following five chapters address in-depth issues that pertain to planning, so it is likely that you will use Chapter 1 as an anchor point and refer to other chapters as needed.

As you cannot implement these standards in isolation, it is helpful to use the book as a reference for a group of leaders and the narratives as springboards for group discussions. However, you can also use the book on your own for background information and ideas to bring to the table for discussion with other educational leaders.

To assist readers further in implementing the NETS•A standards, this book provides entry-level self-assessment activities for each performance indicator—activities that may be completed as class assignments, as part of a professional study group, or by individuals writing their own professional growth plans or objectives. Begin by developing a global picture of where your skills and needs currently lie. Based on that self-assessment, you can develop an action plan that will bring your school or district into alignment with the standards efficiently.

Complete the *Individual Survey of NETS•A Skills for Site or District Level Leaders* found at the end of this Introduction. Your answers will provide a quick visual map of your own skill levels. Items that you mark Strongly Agree or Agree probably indicate areas where you are already implementing certain aspects of a standard. Areas marked Neither Agree nor Disagree, Disagree, or Strongly Disagree indicate areas where you may not be implementing a standard.

Think about the current needs at your site or within your district and any correlations you see between the school community's needs and your own technology strengths and weaknesses. Then, use the activities in this book to begin the process of learning more about specific standards, performance indicators, and activities to strengthen your skills in educational technology leadership.

The Action Plan included at the end of every chapter asks you to use the information you gather in these self-assessment activities to help you decide what to do next. Use the charts in each chapter to brainstorm ideas. Identify three steps you can take to further your school or district's implementation of that performance indicator. The Action Plan also prompts you to list the person(s) responsible for helping with the step, define how you will know when that step has been accomplished, and provide a timeline for completion.

to be used here. The language has been adapted to reflect the responsibilities of Site Leaders and of District Level Leaders.

Individual Survey of NETS•A Skills—Site Level Leaders					
Please mark the response number that best represents *your* level of *agreement* with the statement.					
Leadership and Vision	**Strongly Agree**	**Agree**	**Neither Agree nor Disagree**	**Disagree**	**Strongly Disagree**
1. I participate in an inclusive district process through which stakeholders formulate a shared vision that clearly defines expectations for technology use.					
2. I help to develop a collaborative, technology-rich school improvement plan grounded in research and aligned with the district strategic plan.					
Learning and Teaching	**Strongly Agree**	**Agree**	**Neither Agree nor Disagree**	**Disagree**	**Strongly Disagree**
3. I assist teachers in using technology to access, analyze, and interpret student performance data, and in using results to appropriately design, assess, and modify student instruction.					
4. I promote highly effective practices in technology integration among faculty and other staff.					
5. I collaboratively help to design, implement, support, and participate in professional development for all instructional staff that institutionalizes effective integration of technology for improved student learning.					
Productivity and Professional Practice	**Strongly Agree**	**Agree**	**Neither Agree nor Disagree**	**Disagree**	**Strongly Disagree**
6. I use current technology-based management systems to access and maintain personnel and student records.					

Continued

Continued

7. I use a variety of media and formats, including telecommunications and the school website, to communicate, interact, and collaborate with peers, experts, and other education stakeholders.					
8. I promote and model the use of technology to access, analyze, and interpret campus data to focus efforts for improving student learning and productivity.					
Support, Management, and Operations	**Strongly Agree**	**Agree**	**Neither Agree nor Disagree**	**Disagree**	**Strongly Disagree**
9. I allocate campus discretionary funds and other resources to advance implementation of the technology plan.					
10. I am an advocate for adequate, timely, and high-quality technology support services.					
Assessment and Evaluation	**Strongly Agree**	**Agree**	**Neither Agree nor Disagree**	**Disagree**	**Strongly Disagree**
11. I provide campus-wide staff development for sharing work and resources across commonly used formats and platforms.					
12. I implement evaluation procedures for teachers that assess individual growth toward established technology standards and guide professional development planning.					
13. I include effectiveness of technology use in the learning and teaching process as one criterion in assessing performance of instructional staff.					
Social, Legal, and Ethical Issues	**Strongly Agree**	**Agree**	**Neither Agree nor Disagree**	**Disagree**	**Strongly Disagree**
14. I secure and allocate technology resources to enable teachers to better meet the needs of all learners on campus.					
15. I adhere to and enforce among staff and students the district's acceptable use policy and other policies and procedures related to security, copyright, and technology use.					
16. I participate in the development of facility plans that support and focus on healthy and environmentally safe practices related to the use of technology.					

Leadership and Vision	Strongly Agree	Agree	Agree nor Disagree	Disagree	Strongly Disagree
1. I participate in an inclusive district process through which stakeholders formulate a shared vision that clearly defines expectations for technology use.					
2. I help to develop a collaborative, technology-rich district strategic plan grounded in research.					
Learning and Teaching	**Strongly Agree**	**Agree**	**Neither Agree nor Disagree**	**Disagree**	**Strongly Disagree**
3. I assist teachers and site administrators in using technology to access, analyze, and interpret student performance data, and in using results to appropriately design, assess, and modify student instruction.					
4. I promote highly effective practices in technology integration among faculty and other staff.					
5. I collaboratively help to design, implement, support, and participate in professional development for all instructional staff that institutionalizes effective integration of technology for improved student learning.					
Productivity and Professional Practice	**Strongly Agree**	**Agree**	**Neither Agree nor Disagree**	**Disagree**	**Strongly Disagree**
6. I use current technology-based management systems to access and maintain personnel and student records.					
7. I use a variety of media and formats, including telecommunications and the district website, to communicate, interact, and collaborate with peers, experts, and other education stakeholders.					
8. I promote and model the use of technology to access, analyze, and interpret district data to focus efforts for improving student learning and productivity.					

Continued

Continued

Support, Management, and Operations	Strongly Agree	Agree	Neither Agree nor Disagree	Disagree	Strongly Disagree
9. I allocate district discretionary funds and other resources to advance implementation of the technology plan.					
10. I am an advocate for adequate, timely, and high-quality technology support services.					
Assessment and Evaluation	**Strongly Agree**	**Agree**	**Neither Agree nor Disagree**	**Disagree**	**Strongly Disagree**
11. I provide district-wide staff development for sharing work and resources across commonly used formats and platforms.					
12. I assist in implementation of evaluation procedures for teachers that assess individual growth toward established technology standards and guide professional development planning.					
13. I include effectiveness of technology use in the learning and teaching process as one criterion in assessing performance of instructional staff.					
Social, Legal, and Ethical Issues	**Strongly Agree**	**Agree**	**Neither Agree nor Disagree**	**Disagree**	**Strongly Disagree**
14. I secure and allocate technology resources to enable teachers and administrators to better meet the needs of all learners in the district.					
15. I adhere to and enforce among staff and students the district's acceptable use policy and other policies and procedures related to security, copyright, and technology use.					
16. I participate in the development of facility plans that support and focus on healthy and environmentally safe practices related to the use of technology.					

Reprinted with permission from the author.

Lashway, L. (2003). *Role of the school leader: Trends and issues* [Online article]. Retrieved Jan. 22, 2009, from www.eric.ed.gov/ERICDocs/data/ericdocs2sql/content_storage_01/0000019b/80/1b/55/08.pdf

Tools

Whale, D.E. (n.d.) Individual Survey of NETS•A Skills. Available: www.sjbrooks-young.com/id15.html

(NETS•A) (2002)

All school administrators should be prepared to meet the following standards and performance indicators.

I. Leadership and Vision

Educational leaders inspire a shared vision for comprehensive integration of technology and foster an environment and culture conducive to the realization of that vision. Educational leaders:

- **A.** facilitate the shared development by all stakeholders of a vision for technology use and widely communicate that vision
- **B.** maintain an inclusive and cohesive process to develop, implement, and monitor a dynamic, long-range, and systemic technology plan to achieve the vision
- **C.** foster and nurture a culture of responsible risk-taking and advocate policies promoting continuous innovation with technology
- **D.** use data in making leadership decisions
- **E.** advocate for research-based effective practices in use of technology
- **F.** advocate, on the state and national levels, for policies, programs, and funding opportunities that support implementation of the district technology plan

II. Learning and Teaching

Educational leaders ensure that curricular design, instructional strategies, and learning environments integrate appropriate technologies to maximize learning and teaching. Educational leaders:

- **A.** identify, use, evaluate, and promote appropriate technologies to enhance and support instruction and standards-based curriculum leading to high levels of student achievement
- **B.** facilitate and support collaborative technology-enriched learning environments conducive to innovation for improved learning

- **C.** provide for learner-centered environments that use technology to meet the individual and diverse needs of learners
- **D.** facilitate the use of technologies to support and enhance instructional methods that develop higher-level thinking, decision-making, and problem-solving skills
- **E.** provide for and ensure that faculty and staff take advantage of quality professional learning opportunities for improved learning and teaching with technology

III. Productivity and Professional Practice

Educational leaders apply technology to enhance their professional practice and to increase their own productivity and that of others. Educational leaders:

- **A.** model the routine, intentional, and effective use of technology
- **B.** employ technology for communication and collaboration among colleagues, staff, parents, students, and the larger community
- **C.** create and participate in learning communities that stimulate, nurture, and support faculty and staff in using technology for improved productivity
- **D.** engage in sustained, job-related professional learning using technology resources
- **E.** maintain awareness of emerging technologies and their potential uses in education
- **F.** use technology to advance organizational improvement

IV. Support, Management, and Operations

Educational leaders ensure the integration of technology to support productive systems for learning and administration. Educational leaders:

- **A.** develop, implement, and monitor policies and guidelines to ensure compatibility of technologies
- **B.** implement and use integrated technology-based management and operations systems
- **C.** allocate financial and human resources to ensure complete and sustained implementation of the technology plan
- **D.** integrate strategic plans, technology plans, and other improvement plans and policies to align efforts and leverage resources
- **E.** implement procedures to drive continuous improvements of technology systems and to support technology replacement cycles

resources for learning, communication, and productivity

B. use technology to collect and analyze data, interpret results, and communicate findings to improve instructional practice and student learning

C. assess staff knowledge, skills, and performance in using technology and use results to facilitate quality professional development and to inform personnel decisions

D. use technology to assess, evaluate, and manage administrative and operational systems

VI. Social, Legal, and Ethical Issues

Educational leaders understand the social, legal, and ethical issues related to technology and model responsible decision making related to these issues. Educational leaders:

A. ensure equity of access to technology resources that enable and empower all learners and educators

B. identify, communicate, model, and enforce social, legal, and ethical practices to promote responsible use of technology

C. promote and enforce privacy, security, and online safety related to the use of technology

D. promote and enforce environmentally safe and healthy practices in the use of technology

E. participate in the development of policies that clearly enforce copyright law and assign ownership of intellectual property developed with district resources

This material was originally produced as a project of the Technology Standards for School Administrators Collaborative.

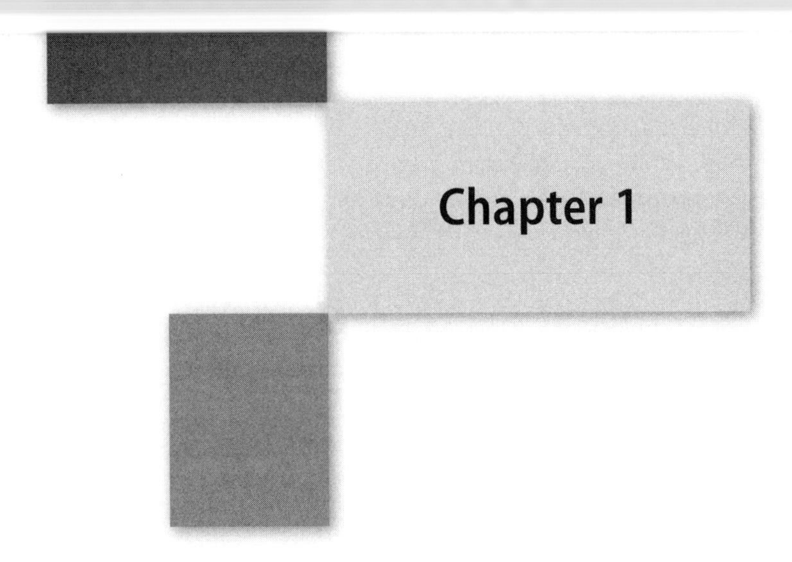

Standard I
Leadership and Vision

Educational leaders inspire a shared vision for comprehensive integration of technology and foster an environment and culture conducive to the realization of that vision.

Performance Indicators for Educational Leaders

I.A. Facilitate the shared development by all stakeholders of a vision for technology use and widely communicate that vision.

I.B. Maintain an inclusive and cohesive process to develop, implement, and monitor a dynamic, long-range, and systemic technology plan to achieve the vision.

I.C. Foster and nurture a culture of responsible risk-taking and advocate policies promoting continuous innovation with technology.

I.D. Use data in making leadership decisions.

I.E. Advocate for research-based effective practices in use of technology.

I.F. Advocate, on the state and national levels, for policies, programs, and funding opportunities that support implementation of the district technology plan.

Chapter 1 Overview

The days when many technology plans were the work of one or two highly enthusiastic teachers or not much more than shopping lists written outside the context of instructional programs are behind us. Glenn M. Kleiman (2000) writes, "*Only a clear-eyed commitment* to using technology to help meet central educational goals *will enable us to get a substantial return on our investment*" [emphasis mine]. Considering the dollars allocated for educational technology in 1999, an estimated $6.9 billion (Kleiman, 2000, p. 1), not only do educators owe it to themselves and their students to think carefully about how they approach integrating technology into our instructional programs, but they are now being held accountable by the public and funding sources to demonstrate that they have done so.

Technology is not a magic pill for school reform. The mere presence of technology will make no difference in student performance, particularly if it is unused or misused. Although your own personal productivity and modeling of technology use are a piece of the overall picture, simply becoming a "techie" is not the answer either. Many school administrators now have the latest, greatest gadgets in the office or on campus, and they have not made a bit of difference in students' academic achievement. What does make a difference is a school administrator at any level who is a thoughtful instructional leader.

The key to having a successful integrated technology program is developing a school or district instructional plan based upon input from the stakeholder groups within the school community in which appropriate technology use is infused throughout all programs. Although certain funding initiatives may request a separate technology plan, the information you present to meet this requirement needs to be drawn from the overall school plan. In those settings where technology plans are maintained as separate pieces, instructional technology continues to be viewed at some level as an optional, add-on program that may or may not be implemented depending upon other priorities.

As you look at Standard I and think about school planning, keep in mind that your ultimate goal is to weave technology use into the fabric of your educational program whenever doing so is appropriate and helpful for students. This does not mean that you swing to the extreme of technology for technology's sake, but rather, that you take a balanced, well-considered approach to its use.

Read through the information about the performance indicators with the understanding that they are not necessarily presented in the sequence you would use to implement the standard. The first two performance indicators address broad issues in planning: developing a vision statement and a plan. The next three performance indicators address creating a culture that supports risk taking, using data as a basis for decision making, and finding good examples of classroom technology use. Because of the relationships among the performance indicators, you will find it necessary to refer to the last three to implement the first two successfully. The final performance indicator addresses advocacy. Although many administrators find themselves taking on this role, the approaches are most often determined at a local level, as explained in the narrative for Performance Indicator I.F.

Performance Indicator I.A.

Educational leaders facilitate the shared development by all stakeholders of a vision for technology use and widely communicate that vision.

People often shy away from developing vision and mission statements as well as strategic planning because of previous unhappy experiences with the process. Consider hiring an outside consultant who can act as a facilitator and guide you through the steps leading to the development of meaningful statements and a dynamic plan.

Attempting to be completely inclusive by bringing in large groups of stakeholders often leads to becoming bogged down by the sheer size of the groups and in lengthy debates that almost always are based on questions of semantics. It is important to ensure that all stakeholder groups are represented, but it is equally important to contain the size of the group so reasonable progress can be made. It is also necessary to agree upfront to common definitions for terms you will use and not to get hung up on the wording of every sentence. If you can bring in a facilitator, identify a workable group, and agree to common definitions for planning terms, you will find that vision and mission statements will be useful tools for your site or district in strategic planning.

Begin by defining the groups that need to be represented. Typically this will include students, teachers, parents, community representatives, classified staff, and administrative staff. While some experts propose having large town meetings attended by 50 or more participants, at the school level, working with two representatives from each group keeps your planning group to a manageable size. One way to do this is to ask each stakeholder group to nominate its own representatives to participate in planning sessions and to communicate regularly with their constituents. For example, the full student council determines how to select student representatives who report back to the council. Class or grade-level representatives then share information with the full student body. Each group works with its own representatives to establish lines of communication. This serves two purposes: first, it maintains an open selection process; second, each group takes responsibility for sustaining communication in a way that best meets its needs. At the district level, more representatives are needed, but it is still important to limit group sizes and to work out plans for communication. Some school sites and districts are now using weblogs (blogs) or wikis to share planning information and solicit feedback.

Learn more about how these web-based tools can be used to facilitate communication in the planning process by viewing a presentation called Web 2.0 Tools for Busy Administrators, available at www.portical.org/Presentations/brooks-young/.

Once the planning group is identified, take the time to agree on working definitions for the terms *vision statement* and *mission statement.* You may decide that a vision statement expresses what you want your school community to look like in the future and that the mission statement explains what the organization does today to meet its goals. A perfect definition is far less important than a common definition. An example of one statement in a vision might be: "By 20XX, XYZ School will offer all students the option to use technology-based research and productivity tools in all academic core classes and electives." One statement in a mission could include: "At XYZ School, because we believe in preparing students to lead successful work lives, we offer opportunities for students to engage in technology-based school-to-work experiences through our partnerships with local businesses."

Definitions

Weblog or blog: Websites comprised of dated postings in reverse chronological order. Blogs often focus on a specific topic and are written by one or more contributors. Postings usually include links to other websites and may also feature images. Some blogs allow readers to add their own comments.

Wiki: A collaborative website where all the content can be edited by anyone. Some wiki sites limit editing permission using password protection or page locks.

Mission statements are not specifically addressed in this standard; however, you will want to develop a statement about the purpose of your organization (school, district) and how you achieve your current goals. This gives you a benchmark when developing your vision statement and also provides a framework for print versions of your statements. Easy-to-use guidelines are these: this is what we do and how we do it (mission); this is what we hope to do in the future and how we hope to do it (vision).

Performance Indicator I.A. talks about a vision for technology, but when you refer to Standard I, you see the wording "comprehensive integration of technology." Your purpose in developing a vision involves more than articulating how technology can support instructional programs. It describes an instructional program in which technology is present and regularly used as a teaching and learning tool. It is important to take your time developing the vision statement. Through discussions, group members will learn to articulate their own ideas and will also learn a great deal about the needs and expectations of other stakeholder groups.

Vision statements for educational settings are often written using one of two formats. You might choose to write the vision in a series of short scenarios that describe the kind of program you will strive to achieve. Or, you might write the vision statement based upon the critical issues facing the educational community. When using the latter approach, the group identifies and prioritizes the issues and includes possible solutions.

communicate that vision.

This section identifies strategies for educational leaders to assess current mission and vision statements, to identify what needs to be in place in the future, and to determine the necessary steps to accomplish their goals.

What Is Already in Place?

Review the current mission and vision statements for your educational community.

All educational leaders need to:

- Evaluate existing mission and vision statements to determine whether they address all major instructional strategies, including technology use.
- Review the process that was used to develop these statements to determine the level of participation of various stakeholders.
- Determine the means used to communicate these statements to the educational community.
- Conduct informal surveys or interviews to determine whether stakeholders are aware of the contents of current mission and vision statements.

What Practices Demonstrate Successful Implementation of This Performance Indicator?

Clearly communicate a mission and vision for instructional programs that include appropriate technology use.

All educational leaders need to:

- Support implementation of the planning group's dissemination plan through scheduling meetings, providing funds for printing and distribution costs, and so on.
- Use the mission and vision statements as the basis for ongoing discussion in writing and implementing the strategic plan.
- Formally adopt mission and vision statements using procedures identified by decision-making groups such as school site councils or school boards.
- Periodically remind stakeholders of the mission and vision of the site and district.

What Steps Lead to Successful Implementation of This Performance Indicator?

Develop or modify mission and vision statements to address all major instructional strategies, including technology use.

All educational leaders need to:

- Identify stakeholder groups in your educational community. Meet with these groups to determine a plan for selecting representatives to the planning committee.
- Schedule and plan agendas for meetings to develop mission and vision statements.
- Actively participate in the planning group to develop statements that address all major instructional strategies, including technology use.
- Develop an action plan and timeline for communicating mission and vision statements to the educational community.

Campus Leaders' Additional Responsibilities:	District Leaders' Additional Responsibilities:	Superintendents' and Cabinet Leaders' Additional Responsibilities:
• Work with site-based decision-making groups to decide whether to hire a consultant and how to fund the expense. • Make necessary provisions in the budget for release time for teachers and classified staff to participate in the planning process. • If requested, provide time for on-site meeting agendas for representatives to report the progress of the planning group. • Ensure that the site mission and vision statements are coordinated with the district mission and vision statements. • Identify ways you have successfully communicated with site stakeholders in the past and incorporate these strategies into your plan for disseminating the school's mission and vision statements.	• Contact the appropriate agencies to gather information about consultants who can act as planning facilitators. • Share information about consultants with site and cabinet leaders. • Offer assistance and support to campus leaders as they organize and implement the planning process. • Serve as active members of the district's planning group. • Work with cabinet members to decide whether to hire a consultant and how to fund the expense. • Work with campus leaders to ensure coordination of site and district mission and vision statements. • Work with cabinet leaders to identify ways the district has successfully communicated with stakeholders in the past and incorporate these strategies into your plan for disseminating the district's mission and vision statements.	• Actively participate in the planning process by having at least one representative on the district planning committee. • Monitor the progress made by the district's planning group to offer immediate assistance in avoiding potential problems or pitfalls. • Educate school board members about the value of fully integrated district and school plans. • Work with fellow superintendents and cabinet leaders in other districts to promote integrated planning to agencies that require separate plans for funding.

all stakeholders of a vision for technology use and widely communicate that vision.

Activity 1 • Articulating Your Personal Vision

The initial step in systemic change is the development of a vision statement that clearly describes what the school community will look like in the future. Before a leader can facilitate development of a shared vision for a site or district, he or she must be able to articulate his or her own personal vision clearly. This activity is designed to assist you in organizing and recording your own "big picture" about how technology can be used in your school or district to support instruction. The activity can also be used with larger groups to provide a springboard for discussion among stakeholders.

Activity 2 • Organizing Your Technology Planning Committee

The composition of any kind of planning committee is often based on who's willing to be there rather than who needs to be there. There's always the danger of creating a committee that is so large that little work can be accomplished. However, when a committee is too small, key decision makers are left out of the process, which inevitably leads to unrealistic plans with limited implementation. It's also important to remember that committee members need to cover a broad range of expertise in all areas of education.

Next Steps: After completing Activities 1 and 2, you may also need to complete other activities related to this Performance Indicator. Review the related Activity 2 for Performance Indicator I.A., and Activities 1 and 2 for Performance Indicator II.A. When you're ready to proceed, refer to the Action Plan at the end of this chapter to identify the steps that need to be taken next to develop and communicate a shared school or district vision for technology use.

Activity 1 • Articulating Your Personal Vision

Directions: Use this five-step process to develop a personal vision scenario for a technology-supported learning environment.

1. List in the first column the critical instruction-related issues facing your school or district.
2. Prioritize these issues by numbering each (1 = highest priority, 2 = medium priority, 3 = lowest priority). You may use each number more than once, but be honest—every issue cannot be your highest priority.
3. Review your list again.
    - Which issues are under your direct control and can be resolved by you alone? Mark these issues **D**.
    - Which issues can be indirectly controlled by you but would require assistance from others? Mark these issues **I**.
    - Which issues are completely out of your direct and indirect control? Mark these issues **N**.
4. Use the Possible Solutions column to write your ideas for solving each issue. Include technology use where appropriate. If an issue is marked **D**, write what you can do. If an issue is marked **I**, write what could be done and list those people whose support you need to make a change. If an issue is marked **N** and is truly outside your direct or indirect control, do not write a solution.
5. Use the information in the Critical Instruction-Related Issues and Possible Solutions columns to write in the last box a scenario that describes the kind of technology-supported learning environment you will strive to achieve.

Critical Instruction-Related Issues	Priority	Control	Possible Solutions
Personal Vision Scenario			

representation. For example, once you've entered district-level employees, make sure each division or department is represented by either an administrator or a classified employee and that equitable representation exists among administrators and classified staff.

Note: Review the teachers selected for committee participation to make sure all grade levels and each of the four main content areas (language arts, mathematics, social studies, and science) are adequately represented.

District-Level Employees	Major Divisions/Departments			
	Education Services	**Personnel**	**Finance**	**Maintenance and Operations**
Administrators				
Classified Staff				
School-Level Employees	**Grade Level Clusters**			
	K–2	**3–5**	**6–8**	**9–12**
Administrators				
Classified Staff				
Teachers (See note above)				
Parents				
Students	N/A	N/A		
Community Representatives	**Areas Within the Community**			
	Local Government Agencies	**Nonprofit Agencies**	**Local Businesses**	**Residents (Nonparents)**

Overview of Planning

Performance Indicator I.B.

Educational leaders maintain an inclusive and cohesive process to develop, implement, and monitor a dynamic, long-range, and systemic technology plan to achieve the vision.

Instructional plans for schools and districts are indispensable. These plans identify instructional priorities, provide strategies for implementing these priorities, list methods for evaluating progress and the success of implementation, name support resources, and identify those persons responsible for implementation and evaluation. A plan written by one or two people and left unused on a shelf is of no value to the educational community. Yes, writing and reviewing dynamic plans takes time and energy on the part of a lot of people, but you cannot expect to provide quality educational programs to your students without them.

Strategic planning and the concept of a shared vision find their roots in the business world. During the 1920s, members of the Harvard Business School developed the Harvard Policy Model. In the 1950s, businesses adopted strategic planning, an approach that grew in popularity through the 1970s. In the late 1980s, strategic planning began finding acceptance in academic circles. According to a compilation of studies done by the Northwest Regional Educational Laboratory in 1995 (Cotton), research on effective schools supports the strategic planning model by finding that a critical element in school restructuring is the ability of school administrators to articulate the mission of the school and establish a focus that unifies the staff. More than a decade later, these findings continue to hold true (Halfacre, et al., 2006).

Strategic planning differs from long-range planning, in that strategic planning is based upon the assumption that organizations are dynamic and must remain responsive to change. Long-range planning implies that identified goals will be accomplished over a period of several years because today's knowledge of the future will hold true over time. Of course, we know this is not the case. In strategic planning and leadership, it is expected that leaders will keep the big picture in mind and will continually ask if they are doing the right things to achieve the mission of the organization. Following a strategic plan is less comfortable than following a long-range plan, but the benefits are greater.

Unfortunately, educators do not have reputations for being good planners. There is a perception that educators tend to make decisions based upon what is needed at the moment without keeping the big picture in mind. This may be why there are now so many requirements for plans attached to funding sources. Do you want funds for E-Rate? Where's your technology plan? Do you need money to improve campus security? Where's your school safety plan? Do you want to implement an English language development program using federal monies? Where's your Title III plan?

work and also helps you become better organized and more accountable. Use the questions asked in the previous paragraph to develop a plan. Why do you want E-Rate funding? Gaining or enhancing Internet access isn't a good enough response. What is it about Internet access that will improve educational programs for your students, and how will you recognize success? How will providing a more secure campus or an English language development program affect students' academic performance? You should be able to write one plan for the school that addresses each of these questions to the satisfaction of any funding source.

The reality may be that you will continue to be required to produce individual plans for individual types of funding. However, if one comprehensive plan is written and implemented, today's office technologies make it simple to pull together those pieces of the plan specifically required for a particular funding source. The virtue of the comprehensive plan is that it forces you to look at how each program is woven into the fabric of the education you provide to students and helps you avoid writing technology plans that are nothing more than shopping lists. It causes you to recognize where programs overlap and support one another and to understand that no strategy or tool that you use, including technology, should be an add-on that can be stripped away without seriously affecting the work you do with students.

You may find yourself thinking, "This is all well and good; now please give me some practical suggestions for implementing this type of planning." Three of the remaining four performance indicators for this standard address ongoing systemic planning, risk taking, using data to make decisions about instructional programs, and finding examples of best practices for technology-based classroom instruction. You will look first at structuring the planning process and then at how Performance Indicators I.C. through I.E. can be used to support this planning.

Developing the Plan

Once your mission and vision statements are written, the next step is planning. In this process you need to gather data, identify, and prioritize instructional goals and then decide how you will meet your goals. There are numerous ways to approach this process, and one method is not necessarily better or worse than another. The important things to remember are that you need to continue to work with representative stakeholders and that the plan needs to be the result of work done by a group of people, not just one or two. It is also important for schools and districts to participate in ongoing discussions about decisions that affect everyone, including textbook selection, technology standardization, and the like. You will find it helpful to have a template for your plan available in electronic format so that it can be easily updated or modified. The district may have a form in place already.

Many plans require both a narrative and chart for each goal area. The narrative uses the data you have collected to explain why this goal area has been identified. You can also include detailed descriptions of instructional programs and strategies you will use to meet your goal, comments about making programs accessible to all students, an explanation about how you will monitor and evaluate progress, an explanation of staff development needs, and your plan for allocating resources. You might choose to include examples of best practices here as well. When considering strategies for infusing technology throughout your plan, you may want to refer to the following chapters in this book:

- Chapter 2 provides information on instruction and staff development.
- Chapter 4 covers total cost of ownership.
- Chapter 5 discusses assessment.
- Chapter 6 explores equity and social and legal issues.

A chart or table usually follows each narrative, offering an overview of the goal and how it will be addressed. Below is a sample chart. The structure of the sample allows for specific notations about instructional tools, such as technology use, and builds in staff development and funding needs.

Sample Planning Chart for School or District Goals	
Specific Goal: Identified area of need based on data collection	
Specific Desired Outcome: How students' academic performance will be improved by meeting this goal	
Specific Outputs	List of specific things that will be done to accomplish the goal
Specific Instructional Strategies	Corresponding list of instructional approaches to be used for each output
Specific Material to Use	Materials needed, including books, software, equipment, etc.
Assessment (Specific Measurements)	Specific student performance measures and documentation of steps taken by teachers and recorded in lesson plans or by other means
Staff Development	Specific training staff members need to implement each output
Budget	Funding sources and amounts
People Responsible	List may include certified and classified staff, business partners, outside agencies, and student groups
Timeline	When each output will be implemented and completed

people responsible for implementation; and your timeline. You also append documents provided by the district such as specifications for equipment and software, bids for renovations, and job descriptions for support personnel. Voila! You have a separate technology plan based upon the instructional plan in which technology has been infused.

Below is a sample chart for this step.

Sample Chart to Highlight Special Program Areas	
Integrated Technology Plan	
Purpose Statement: Briefly explain how technology is used to support the overall instructional program	
Related Goal and Specific Output	Refer to your overall instructional plan to identify those outputs that incorporate technology use in their implementation.
Specific Instructional Strategies	This section helps identify placement and types of equipment needed for implementation.
Specific Material to Use	This section identifies specific equipment, software, and technical support needs for each output.
Assessment (Specific Measurements)	Describe how success will be monitored and measured including student performance, teacher use, and so on.
Staff Development	Professional growth needs and opportunities as they pertain to technology use are identified.
Budget	Specific funding sources for equipment, software, technical support, and staff development are named.
People Responsible	List may include certified and classified staff, business partners, outside agencies, and student groups.
Timeline	Estimate the dates when each output will be implemented and completed. For technology, may also include purchasing cycles for equipment and software.

Good planning is an ongoing process. Even as you implement the current year's plan, you begin collecting data for evaluation and planning for the following year. The steps my staff and I used for writing the school plan included:

- Review data collected.
- Identify instructional goals based upon the data.
- Prioritize identified goals.
- Share information with stakeholder groups for input and modification.
- Form writing groups by goal and develop rough drafts of each section.
- Share information with stakeholder groups for input and modification.
- Write second draft for each section.
- Share information with stakeholder groups for additional input and modification.
- Publish and distribute final draft.
- Begin monitoring and data collection for evaluation and future planning.

Every teacher took part in writing the plan, and other stakeholders, including parents, students, classified staff, and community partners, were given multiple opportunities to read and comment on drafts of the plan as it was developed. When the final draft was published, all staff members, representatives in decision-making groups on campus, district and cabinet leaders, and school board members received copies of the plan. The plan was regularly referenced in meetings of all kinds, including staff, committee, grade level, leadership, and school-site council meetings.

and systemic technology plan to achieve the vision.

This section identifies the roles and responsibilities for educational leaders in reviewing current plans, identifying the desired end product, and taking steps to develop a comprehensive plan. Refer to the roles and responsibilities for Performance Indicators I.D. and I.E. for information specifically targeting use of data in decision making. Refer to the roles and responsibilities for Performance Indicator I.F. for steps in identifying research and best practices when using classroom technology.

What Is Already in Place?

Review existing school and district instructional program and technology plans.

All educational leaders need to:

- Be familiar with any existing plans that affect students' academic performance in any manner.
- Compare instructional program plans with technology plans, specifically looking for areas where the plans are aligned or misaligned.
- Find out who has copies of each plan and how plans are currently used.
- Identify the process used in the development of each plan.
- Identify current timetables for writing, implementing, and evaluating plans.
- Encourage staff members to identify areas of concern with instructional programs and technology and to explain their feelings.

Campus Leaders' Additional Responsibilities:	District Leaders' Additional Responsibilities:	Superintendents' and Cabinet Leaders' Additional Responsibilities:
• Compare site instructional program plans and technology plans with district instructional program plans and technology plans, specifically looking for areas where the plans are aligned or misaligned. • Describe how you monitor plan development, implementation, and evaluation at your site. • Clearly articulate how budgets are developed and monitored.	• Initiate discussions comparing district and site plans with both campus and cabinet leaders, addressing alignment and current levels of support. • Clearly describe how district plans are implemented and monitored and how this may be affected by implementation and monitoring practices on campuses. • Determine how district departments currently provide necessary assistance and support to school sites. • Review how budgets are allocated at the district and site levels.	• Identify how site and district plans are monitored in development, implementation, budgeting, evaluation, and reporting. • Determine how each division can provide support to schools and to individual district departments based upon this feedback. • Identify and clarify the types of support divisions need from sites and district departments.

What Practices Demonstrate Successful Implementation of This Performance Indicator?

Implement and maintain dynamic, long-range comprehensive program plans that incorporate technology use.

All educational leaders need to:

- Enforce and/or comply with agreed-upon timelines for implementing and maintaining the comprehensive plan.
- Provide copies of the plan to appropriate stakeholders and use it as a point of reference in meetings.
- Offer informational meetings to parents and community members.
- Implement ongoing monitoring and evaluation of the plan with the understanding that changes will be made as necessary.
- Revise and update the plan yearly.

Campus Leaders' Additional Responsibilities:	District Leaders' Additional Responsibilities:	Superintendents' and Cabinet Leaders' Additional Responsibilities:
• Monitor the plan to evaluate the success of implementation. • Refer to the district's comprehensive plan to ensure the proposed changes in site plan goals and strategies continue to be in alignment. • Refer to the district's comprehensive plan to ensure the proposed changes in site procedures for development, implementation, and evaluation continue to be in alignment.	• Continue to facilitate communication with both campus and cabinet leaders about plan alignment issues and current levels of support. • Monitor the implementation and evaluation of district plans and, if adjustments are made, consider the effect this may have on implementation and monitoring practices on campuses. • Document the kinds of support and assistance district departments are providing school sites. • Provide updated budget figures to campus leaders on a regular basis.	• Prepare and submit necessary board agenda items for presenting district and school plans. • Follow through on specified procedures for monitoring site and district plans during development, implementation, budgeting, evaluation, and reporting. • Document ways each division provides support to schools and to individual district departments. • Document the types of support divisions receive from sites and district departments.

All educational leaders need to:

- Identify all required plans that affect students' academic performance in any manner and consider ways to consolidate them into one comprehensive plan.
- Identify areas where school and district plans are not currently aligned and explore ways to correct this misalignment.
- Establish the purpose for each section of a comprehensive plan.
- Identify a process to be used in the development of comprehensive plans.
- Consider hiring a consultant to facilitate the planning process.
- Identify current timetables for writing, implementing, and evaluating plans.
- Identify stakeholders to be included in the planning process and invite their participation.
- Develop a budget that supports the comprehensive plan and can be easily monitored.
- Write a comprehensive plan in which technology use is embedded throughout.

Campus Leaders' Additional Responsibilities:	District Leaders' Additional Responsibilities:	Superintendents' and Cabinet Leaders' Additional Responsibilities:
• Refer to the district's comprehensive plan to ensure the proposed site plan goals and strategies are in alignment. • Refer to the district's comprehensive plan to ensure the proposed site procedures for development, implementation, and evaluation are in alignment.	• Facilitate communication with both campus and cabinet leaders about plan alignment issues and current levels of support. • Clearly describe requirements for the implementation and monitoring of district plans and how these may affect implementation and monitoring practices on campuses. • Clearly identify the kinds of support and assistance district departments are able to provide school sites. • Provide projected budget figures to campus leaders by early spring.	• Specify how site and district plans will be monitored in development, implementation, budgeting, evaluation, and reporting. • Determine how each division will provide support to schools and to individual district departments. • Clearly define the types of support divisions need from sites and district departments. • Educate board members concerning the value of developing a comprehensive school or district plan.

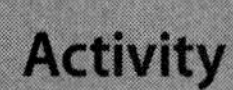

Activity

Performance Indicator I.B. Educational leaders maintain an inclusive and cohesive process to develop, implement, and monitor a dynamic, long-range, and systemic technology plan to achieve the vision.

Activity 3 • Independent Plan Review and Consolidation

Comprehensive, consolidated planning is one solution to reducing the mountain of paperwork faced by administrators and teachers. This approach also supports systemic planning. Begin this activity by reviewing the independent plans for educational technology, student achievement, school improvement, and so forth, that are in use at your school or in the district office. Then, note your findings in the Activity 3A table (you'll need to fill out a separate table for each plan). This task can be done by one person, but it's helpful to work with a leadership team and ask members to form small groups, with each group analyzing one plan. When the review is completed, meet and use Activity 3B to identify commonalities and differences among the plans and outline a strategy for consolidating these plans wherever possible.

Next Steps: Once Activity 3 has been completed, go to the Performance Indicator I.B. section of the Action Plan at the end of this chapter to identify the remaining steps to develop, implement, and monitor a dynamic, long-range, and systemic plan that is inclusive and cohesive and achieves your school's or district's vision for a technology-supported learning environment.

Number of years plan has been and will be in effect:
Directions: Use the space provided to note briefly the requested information for the individual plan. You may need to add information.
Stakeholder groups involved in developing this plan:
Process used to develop this plan:
Format for this plan:
Sections (e.g., curricular areas, professional development) included in this plan:
Goals and objectives included in this plan:
Required supporting documentation (e.g., research data, inventories):
Evaluation requirements for this plan:
Reporting requirements for this plan:
Revision cycle for this plan:
Funding sources to support this plan:
Additional important information about this plan:

 Activity 3B • Plan Commonalities and Differences

List all the plans reviewed here and the number of years each plan has been, and will be, in effect:
Directions: Use the space provided below to identify the *commonalities* among the plans reviewed. Topics are suggested, and you may add similarities.
Stakeholder groups:
Strategies for plan development:
Overall plan formats:
Plan sections (e.g., curricular areas, professional development):
Goals and objectives:
Required supporting documentation (e.g., research data, inventories):
Evaluation requirements for this plan:
Reporting requirements for this plan:
Revision cycle for this plan:
Funding sources to support this plan:
Additional similarities:

Continued

Stakeholder groups:
Strategies for plan development:
Overall plan formats:
Plan sections (e.g., curricular areas, professional development):
Goals and objectives:
Required supporting documentation (e.g., research data, inventories, etc.):
Evaluation requirements for this plan:

Continued

Activity 3B • Plan Commonalities and Differences

Continued

Reporting requirements for this plan:
Revision cycle for this plan:
Funding sources to support this plan:
Additional differences:
Directions: Use the space provided below to describe briefly ways you could consolidate work on developing, implementing, evaluating, reporting, and revising these plans.

Education leaders foster and nurture a culture of responsible risk-taking and advocate policies promoting continuous innovation with technology.

The systemic change required for technology integration is based upon a school culture that supports risk taking. *Fitting the Pieces: Education Reform That Works* (Klein, 1996), a report from the Office of Educational Research and Improvement, devotes an entire chapter to the need for educators to have adequate time for implementation and permission to take risks to see successful results in school reform. In today's climate, where instant success is the expectation, school administrators find themselves in a challenging position.

Educators are very successful in teaching some segments of the population. They do not do well with other groups. Your charge is to develop alternative strategies to meet the needs of those students who are underperforming. Persisting in the use of instructional programs that are inadequate for this part of the student population is not a reasonable option. However, the current pressure to fix things immediately is not reasonable either. Many school administrators believe they are currently in a no-win situation. If they choose to do nothing, they are in trouble. If they attempt reforms that are not immediately successful, they face sanctions. Before people are willing to take risks, there needs to be some hope that they will be successful (Klein, 1996). Most educators recognize that change is needed and are willing to do the necessary work. If they knew the answers, they would "fix" things tomorrow. Reform is often a process of trial and error. It is important to accept this fact and then plan reforms, such as technology integration, in such a way that educators know they will have a reasonable period of time for implementation, monitoring, and evaluation before a reform is declared unsuccessful.

What are strategies for creating an environment where educators feel free to take risks? There are several steps you can take, but there must be trust among all educators in the organization that people will work wholeheartedly to make changes that will benefit students. There are no instant solutions, no guaranteed pathways to success. Student performance will not improve simply because you say it will. Without the agreement that change must happen, that innovative approaches will be tried, that it will take two to three years before solid benefits will be apparent, and that initial approaches may need to be altered along the way, you are setting up yourself and your staff for failure. If your organization is incapable of functioning at this level of trust, you need to address the underlying reasons for lack of trust before you move into school reform.

Assuming your school or district is ready to tackle reform, here are some suggestions for making the work less stressful.

- Keep in mind the stages of concern and levels of use that occur during the change process. Chapter 2 includes specific information about the Concerns-Based Adoption Model and findings about change from the Apple Classrooms of Tomorrow (ACOT) project.

- Educate and inform stakeholders along the way. Be certain they understand the mission and vision for the organization, along with the goals. Also, take time to explain changes in procedures. For example, people may be very uncomfortable with increased data collection if they do not understand its purpose.

- Coordinate efforts as much as possible. If the district and individual schools are planning at the same time, share data collection responsibilities and be sensitive to meeting schedules so participants do not become overwhelmed.

- Find ways to guarantee small successes early in the process and celebrate them. A success could be bringing together a group to discuss a vision statement or implementing the use of student planners at targeted grade levels. Chapter 7 offers a brief discussion about the importance of sharing success stories in greater detail.

- Provide ample time for both planning and implementation. People will be more willing to accept change if they know that they will be held accountable, based upon reasonable expectations.

Technology integration requires a great deal of risk taking on the part of educators. Simply becoming personally proficient in its use will not guarantee its use as an instructional tool. To read more about the depth and breadth of adoption of technology in teaching, please refer to Chapter 2. The roles and responsibilities for Performance Indicator I.C. provides the steps educational leaders need to take to assess the current school culture and create an environment conducive to and supportive of change.

with technology.

Technology integration requires a great deal of risk taking on the part of educators. Simply becoming personally proficient in its use will not guarantee its use as an instructional tool. To read more about the depth and breadth of adoption of technology in teaching, please refer to Chapter 2. This section provides the steps educational leaders need to take to assess the current school culture and create an environment conducive to and supportive of change.

What Is Already in Place?

Assess existing school and district culture in relationship to risk taking and technology innovations.

All educational leaders need to:

- Identify the values, beliefs, and traditions that determine the current organizational culture.
- Articulate how the existing culture supports or discourages taking risks.
- Articulate how the existing culture supports or discourages use of technology innovations.
- Take time to learn about how the current culture of the organization developed.
- Learn about the relationship between schools and the district office to explore how the culture is affected by interactions.

What Practices Demonstrate Successful Implementation of This Performance Indicator?

Establish or maintain a school and district culture that supports responsible risk taking and innovations in technology use.

All educational leaders need to:

- Work with stakeholders to use gathered information to develop strategies for establishing or maintaining an organizational culture that supports risk taking and innovation.
- Develop and implement a plan of action that includes adequate time for planning and implementation, provisions for small success measures along the way, and a safety net for innovators.
- Identify types of support necessary to implement the plan and make them available.

- Demonstrate respect and trust toward all stakeholders and show through your behavior that you support their efforts and recognize their value.
- Be genuine in your dealings with each employee.
- Maintain your interest in innovative efforts and be available to individuals and stakeholder groups.

Campus Leaders' Additional Responsibilities:	District Leaders' Additional Responsibilities:	Superintendents' and Cabinet Leaders' Additional Responsibilities:
• Visit classrooms regularly and maintain high visibility on campus. • Ensure that important traditions and events continue to be recognized and celebrated, and initiate new celebrations.	• Maintain high visibility on school campuses and within the district office. • Attend celebrations on campuses and at the district office. • Educate board and community members about plans for innovations.	• Maintain high visibility on school campuses and within the district office. • Attend celebrations on campuses and at the district office. • Educate board and community members about plans for innovations.

What Steps Lead to Successful Implementation of This Performance Indicator?

Identify areas where the school or district culture could be strengthened to support responsible risk taking and innovation in technology use more effectively.

All educational leaders need to:

- Meet with appropriate stakeholders to discuss issues surrounding risk taking and technology integration.
- Use additional data-gathering strategies, including surveys, interviews, and observations.
- Identify areas where stakeholders feel comfortable with risk taking and where they are uncomfortable.
- Brainstorm possible strategies to raise the level of trust before attempting reforms.
- Increase knowledge and skill levels in creating a trusting environment through reading professional documents, attending workshops, and working with a coach or consultant.
- Provide information, training, and ongoing support to stakeholders.
- Model support of this process at every level within the organization.

risk-taking and advocate policies promoting continuous innovation with technology.

Activity 4 • School and District Support for Risk Taking

Use the questions to analyze the existing school and district culture in relationship to risk taking and technological innovations.

Activity 5 • Understanding Change and Technology Implementation

Overviews of the Concerns-Based Adoption Model (CBAM), the Stages of Educator Learning, and Apple Classrooms of Tomorrow (ACOT) are provided on pages 70, 72 and 104. Review these sections or access online information about each of these models. Web resources include:

- The Concerns-Based Adoption Model (CBAM), A Model for Change in Individuals: www.nas.edu/rise/backg4a.htm
- Traditions of Change Research: http://ide.ed.psu.edu/change/hall.htm
- Concerns-Based Adoption Model, Educators' Stages of Concern About Change: www.stlceo.org/InstructionalLeadership/CBAM.html
- Apple Classrooms of Tomorrow (ACOT) Library: www.apple.com/education/k12/leadership/acot/library.html
- Promising Practices in Technology: www.seirtec.org/ACOTstages.html
- What's so different about the 21st century?: www.metiri.com/features.html

After reviewing both the CBAM and ACOT models, use Activity 5 to reflect on the questions.

Next Steps: After completing Activities 4 and 5, you may also need to complete other activities related to this Performance Indicator. Review the related Activities 7 and 8 for Performance Indicator II.E., and Activity 2 for Performance Indicator V.B. When you're ready to proceed, go to the Performance Indicator I.C. section of the Action Plan at the end of this chapter to identify the steps that need to be taken next in your workplace to foster a culture of responsible risk taking and continuous technological innovation.

 Activity 4 • School and District Support for Risk Taking

Directions: Reflect on the items below and write your responses in the space provided to analyze the existing school and district culture in relation to risk taking and technological innovations.

1. List the values, beliefs, and traditions that determine the current organizational culture.
2. Describe which aspects of the existing organizational culture support risk taking and which discourage it.
3. Describe which aspects of the existing organizational culture support technological innovation and which discourage it.
4. How did the current organizational culture (with regard to risk taking and technological innovation) develop? Explain.

1. What are the commonalities in the CBAM and ACOT models?
2. What are the differences in the CBAM and ACOT models?
3. How does this information change and/or support your thinking about your school or district culture with regard to the way technological change and innovation are supported?
4. How can you use this information to support technological change and innovation at your site or within your district?

Data-Based Decision Making

Performance Indicator I.D.

Educational leaders use data in making leadership decisions.

One overwhelming factor for school administrators is the seeming conflict between traditional managerial responsibilities and the new demands of instructional leadership. A close friend reminds me often, "You can't keep doing things the same old way and expect different results." In general, the structure of school administration has not kept pace with the changes in administrative roles. This is an issue that each school district must address. In the meantime, start restructuring the way you do business by learning about the ins and outs of data-based decision making.

Begin by collecting the information that will provide a complete overview of the educational organization. Student achievement information is the type of data most educators think of first, and while performance data such as standardized test scores, grade-point averages, and scores on other multiple measures do provide some information, this is one small part of the overall picture. Many other types of data are available when developing plans for instructional programs that can be used as additional indicators to show what you are doing and how well students are performing. Use this additional data when making leadership decisions regarding instructional programs and technology or other scholastic tools.

An important step in gathering data is finding those artifacts that will help you understand the current situation, the whys and wherefores that have formed the existing culture. This information must reflect the entire instructional program and support systems and comes in several forms. In his article *Finding Your Way through the Data Smog,* Slowinski (2000) suggests identifying the data you will need to collect by asking the following questions:

- Why do you need to collect data? What is the purpose of data collection?
- What questions are you seeking answers to?
- What information is necessary to answer these questions?
- What method is best to collect this information without investing too much time on behalf of participants?
- Who should participate? Which variety of voices should be heard? When do I gather information from students, parents, and other community members?
- What questions did other schools or districts attempt to answer?
- What other research can I do to improve the quality of questions?

involved in the planning process, documents and information can be shared among the district office and school sites to reduce collection time. The initial site team might include the principal, assistant principal, and other campus leaders, while at the district level directors may choose to work together to divide tasks. The superintendent and cabinet members also need to be actively involved in making visits to sites and familiarizing themselves with written materials. As items are gathered mark them or organize them in files for later reference.

Roles and Responsibilities

Performance Indicator I.D. Educational leaders use data in making leadership decisions.

This section provides an overview of the kinds of data you may need to gather. It identifies six broad areas to address in your data collection: written documents, student data, existing technologies, funding resources, existing planning groups and resource people, and communication methods.

Data to Collect for Decision Making

Written Documents

All educational leaders:

Written documents to be collected include state standards and frameworks, inventories of equipment and instructional materials, current and past budgets, current and past years' staff development plans, academic calendars, and articles and research documents pertaining to student achievement and technology.

Campus Leaders Also Need to Collect:	District Leaders Also Need to Collect:	Superintendents and Cabinet Leaders Also Need to Collect:
• Current and past years' school plans • The site technology plan (if a separate document exists) • Curriculum guides and instructional materials • Program evaluations • Minutes from staff, site council, and committee meetings	• Current comprehensive plans for special projects • The district technology plan (if a separate document exists) • State and federal reports • Program reviews • Job descriptions • Employee association contracts • Grant proposals • District curriculum guides and instructional materials • School board policies and procedures • Minutes from administrative staff meetings	In addition to the documents listed for district leaders, bring out any other print materials you have access to that will help you better understand district policies, procedures, and practices. For example: • Building plans • Agreements with utility companies • Bidding procedures • Procedures for developing or modifying job descriptions or classifications

and graduation and dropout rates (high schools). In most cases, much or all of this information can be accessed through the district SIS.

Campus Leaders Also Need to Collect:	District Leaders Also Need to Collect:	Superintendents and Cabinet Leaders Also Need to Collect:
• Standardized test scores (individual and site), report cards, other achievement measures, and student and parent satisfaction surveys	• District reports for standardized test scores, Adequate Yearly Progress (AYP), graduation rates (if applicable), and dropout rates	• District reports for standardized test scores, Adequate Yearly Progress (AYP), graduation rates (if applicable), and dropout rates

Existing Technologies

All educational leaders:

When reviewing existing technologies, you need to explore the campus and district office to see whether the written material matches what actually exists. Do not assume that you know what is in place without actually looking and talking with staff.

Campus Leaders' Additional Responsibilities:	District Leaders' Additional Responsibilities:	Superintendents' and Cabinet Leaders' Additional Responsibilities:
Visit classrooms, the library or media center, the computer lab, and offices on campus to gather information. • What kinds of technology do you see in place? • How are the different technologies being used? • How old is the hardware? • Talk with staff members to find out how they use technology and what their successes and frustrations are. Visit the offices on campus and do the same thing.	Find out what technologies are available in your office and how they are used. In addition, visit school campuses to see what is in place, how it is being used, and why. • How is technology being used to support the special programs you oversee? • Has categorical money from your program been used to support technology? If so, how? • What grants are in place, and how are the funds being used? • Does the district make recommendations for standardized equipment and software configurations?	Find out what technologies are in place and how they are used throughout the district, both instructionally and as support for office staff. This involves visiting district offices and individual schools. • Talk with district technicians to learn about current hardware and infrastructure concerns. • Meet with district curriculum directors to learn about instructional technology use. • Interview site technicians, administrators, and teachers.

Funding Resources

All educational leaders:

What kinds of funds does your current budget include? How was this decided? What is the process for reallocation of monies? Does your district hire outside consultants for staff development and evaluation? What is your current financial situation?

Campus Leaders Also Need to Determine:	District Leaders Also Need to Determine:	Superintendents and Cabinet Leaders Also Need to Determine:
• How much control do you have over your site funds? • Are you required to have purchasing requisitions approved by someone in the district office? • How are budget decisions made at your site? • Who monitors the site budget?	• Do you control funds that sites do not have access to? • Do you monitor/approve site purchases? • Do you participate in allocating site funds? • Who monitors and approves your budget?	• What is the district's current financial situation? • How do you work with the board on budget planning and approval? • How are decisions made that affect financial impacts on sites and the district office?

Existing Planning Groups and Resource People

All educational leaders:

In reviewing existing groups and resources, make a list of existing committees and regularly scheduled meetings. Note the following for each: What committees and groups are currently in existence? Are all of them active? What do they do? How often do committees meet? How are staff meetings scheduled? Who attends these meetings? Are there contractual provisions that define meeting times and length? It is also important to review staff development plans to determine their appropriateness and effectiveness. Note the following: Who schedules staff development sessions? How are topics selected? How effective is staff development? How is it supported financially? Who presents workshops?

Campus Leaders' Additional Responsibilities:	District Leaders' Additional Responsibilities:	Superintendents' and Cabinet Leaders' Additional Responsibilities
• Develop a site master meeting calendar. Site experts: • Who are the content area experts on-site? • Who are the technology experts? • How were these people identified? • What support do they receive?	• Develop a meeting master calendar for your department or program. District experts: • Who are the content area experts within the district? • Who are the technology experts? • How were these people identified?	• Develop a district master calendar of meetings for sites and the district office. Site and district experts: • Review the lists of site and district experts in content and technology. How is this expertise tapped?

Continued

• Conduct staff surveys identifying professional development needs. • Does your site plan support the goals of the school plan? • Are individual teachers able to attend conferences or complete online courses at school expense? • Do teachers share what they learn with one another?	Staff development: • What kind of support does your department offer schools? • Who determines what you will offer? • Does your program or department have a staff development plan for its own staff?	they don't burn out? Staff development: • How does staff development affect student learning? • Do you have a master calendar of all staff development activities within the district? • When are activities scheduled? • How do you support staff development on site?

Communication

All educational leaders:

What processes for communication are in place? Who is included in the communication? When does communication occur within the decision-making process? How was this decided? How effective are the forms of communication currently in place? How do you measure the effectiveness?

Campus Leaders' Additional Responsibilities:	District Leaders' Additional Responsibilities:	Superintendents' and Cabinet Leaders' Additional Responsibilities:
List or find examples of each form of communication: • How do you provide information to site staff, the community, and to district staff? • How do you receive and handle information brought to you by students, parents, staff, and the district office?	List or find examples of each form of communication: • How do you provide information to one another, other district staff, the superintendent, and cabinet administrators? • How do you provide information to site administrators, staff, and members of the community? • How do you receive and work with information given to you by campus leaders, the superintendent, and cabinet members?	List or find examples of each form of communication: • How do you share information with district office staff? • How do you share information with site administrators and staff? • How do you share information with parents and community members? • How do you receive and act upon information brought to you by district and campus leaders? • How do you receive and act upon information brought to you by parents and community members? • How do you receive and act upon information brought to you by school board members?

Once the information has been collected, it is important to take time to review the materials carefully to develop an overview of current conditions within the district or at the site. Look for patterns or trends that surface. For example, you may find sharp increases or declines in attendance patterns at certain times of the year or note that some committees are virtually inactive while others carry a far heavier responsibility load. You may also find that schools throughout the district have embraced one textbook adoption but have failed to implement another successfully. It is possible that under close scrutiny the district ratio of five students per computer is actually 20:1 when you review inventories and discount obsolete equipment. This initial data search may also highlight areas in these standards where you currently lack expertise. If this is the case, refer to the chapter addressing the appropriate standard prior to working on a technology plan. For example, if you are not familiar with the term *total cost of ownership*, you need to refer to Chapter 4, or if you need an update on equity issues, refer to Chapter 6.

Roles and Responsibilities

Performance Indicator I.D. Educational leaders use data in making leadership decisions.

Chapter 5 takes a more detailed look at ongoing data collection and evaluation. This section identifies the steps educational leaders need to take to understand current local data collection processes and then to improve this practice to facilitate data-based decision making.

What Is Already in Place?

Assess ways administrators currently make leadership decisions based upon data analysis.

All educational leaders need to:

- Identify the types of data currently used when making leadership decisions.
- Describe how this data is collected.
- Explain how this data is analyzed.
- Clearly articulate how this data is used in developing mission and vision statements and strategic planning.
- Research how data is currently reported.

provided by the district office for data collection. • Clearly communicate concerns about data collection with the appropriate district offices.	collection. • Clearly define areas in which sites are asking for support in data collection. • Clearly define areas in which departments need support in data collection from sites and the type of support needed. • Work with cabinet leaders to find affordable solutions for data collection needs.	campus and district leaders regarding data collection. • Identify and clarify types of support divisions need from sites and district departments in data collection.

What Practices Demonstrate Successful Implementation of This Performance Indicator?

Ensure that administrators use data analysis in the decision-making process.

All educational leaders need to:

- Explain methods to be used in data collection and analysis to appropriate stakeholders.
- Follow through and collect the kinds of data identified for use in making leadership decisions.
- Use agreed-upon methods in data analysis.
- Adhere to recommended schedules for data collection and analysis.
- Use the data in developing mission and vision statements and in strategic planning.
- Participate in professional development opportunities designed to increase knowledge and skills in data-based decision making.
- Report findings from data to appropriate stakeholders.

Campus Leaders' Additional Responsibilities:	District Leaders' Additional Responsibilities:	Superintendents' and Cabinet Leaders' Additional Responsibilities:
• Use the support offered by the district office for thorough data collection. • Maintain regular, clear communication with the appropriate district offices about concerns related to data collection.	• Document the support offered to sites in data collection. • Document the system used for gathering needed data from school sites. • Work with cabinet leaders to support affordable solutions for data collection needs.	• Document the system used by divisions to collect needed data from sites and district departments. • Make budget allocations to support affordable solutions for data collection needs.

What Steps Lead to Successful Implementation of This Performance Indicator?

Create a system for ongoing data collection and identify areas where administrators could improve their skills in data analysis and decision making.

All educational leaders need to:

- Identify the types of data that will be used when making leadership decisions.
- Define methods for data collection.
- Define and explain methods to be used in data analysis.
- Establish recommended schedules for data collection and analysis.
- Clearly articulate how this information is to be used in developing mission and vision statements and strategic planning.
- Identify areas where leaders would benefit from additional professional development.

Campus Leaders' Additional Responsibilities:	District Leaders' Additional Responsibilities:	Superintendents' and Cabinet Leaders' Additional Responsibilities:
• Identify the kinds of support needed from the district office for thorough data collection. • Maintain regular, clear communication with the appropriate district offices about concerns related to data collection.	• Identify support that will be offered to sites in data collection. • Establish or refine the system for gathering needed data from school sites. • Work with cabinet leaders to implement affordable solutions for data collection needs.	• Educate school board members about data collection and analysis and their importance in providing an accurate picture of the educational organization. • Establish or refine the system for divisions to collect needed data from sites and district departments.

decisions.

Activity 6 • Data Library Master List

Use Activity 6 to create a master list of the types of data available to you and where this information is located.

Next Steps: Once a data library master list is established, you may also need to complete other activities related to this Performance Indicator. Review for relevance Activity 1 for Performance Indicator V.A., Activity 3 for Performance Indicator V.C., and Activities 1 and 2 for Performance Indicator VI.A. When you're ready to proceed, go to the Performance Indicator I.D. section of the Action Plan at the end of this chapter to identify the steps that need to be taken next to analyze data for decision making effectively.

Activity 6 • Data Library Master List

Directions: Create a master list of the types of data available to you and where this information is located.

Instructional Planning Data (e.g., State Standards and Frameworks, School Plans)		
Item Title or Description	Date	Location

Student Performance Data (e.g., Attendance Rates, Test Scores)		
Item Title or Description	Date	Location

Student Demographics Data (e.g., Ethnicity, Socioeconomic Level)		
Item Title or Description	Date	Location

Student Behavioral Data (e.g., Office Referrals, Parent Contacts)		
Item Title or Description	Date	Location

Continued

Item Title or Description	Date	Location
Financial Resources Data (e.g., Budgets, Purchasing Policies)		
Item Title or Description	Date	Location
Group and Organizational Data (e.g., Committee Rosters, Meeting Calendars)		
Item Title or Description	Date	Location
Communications Data (e.g., Newsletters, E-mail lists, Parent Meetings)		
Item Title or Description	Date	Location

Research and Best Practices

Performance Indicator I.E.

Educational leaders advocate for research-based effective practices in use of technology.

Much of the research on the effects of technology in classrooms is available to the public through various organizations such as Mid-Continent Research for Education and Learning, Research Center for Educational Technology, and Center for Children & Technology. You will find contact information for these agencies in the Resources section of this chapter.

Since the release of the Apple Classrooms of Tomorrow report in 1995, research indicates that, although technology use can have a positive effect on students, it is dependent upon the teacher's comfort in using it as an instructional tool (Apple, 2008). Another finding suggests that, while use of technology may increase student performance on tests of basic skills, "technology use is most powerful when used as a tool for problem solving, conceptual development, and critical thinking," skills not measured using standardized tests (Ringstaff & Kelley, 2002).

Finding research-based models of best practices is a challenge because much of the research has been conducted in classrooms where teachers have not yet adapted technology as an integrated instructional tool. Therefore, models presented in reports are often geared toward personal proficiency and entry-level skills rather than integrated instruction. Because teachers are still in a learning mode themselves, it will take time before there are widespread examples of teaching strategies that harness the potential for technology in classrooms. You will find some examples of classroom technology use at varying levels by visiting the following sites:

- Apple Learning Interchange. Teaching ideas and model lessons. http://edcommunity.apple.com/ali/
- Edutopia. This site offers articles and video clips that document various models for technology use with students. www.edutopia.org
- Technology Information Center for Administrative Leadership, TICAL Project. A portal for school administrators can be found at this location. http://portical.org

One model for technology integration that has withstood the test of time is the WebQuest, developed in 1995 by Bernie Dodge, a professor of educational technology at San Diego State University and long-time proponent of appropriate classroom technology use. Dodge, along with colleague Tom March, created the WebQuest approach to help the teachers he worked with support student learning through Internet use. WebQuests are designed using the inquiry approach to instruction. Students assume various working roles in small groups to solve an open-ended problem or complete a project through a series of activities that are both Internet-based and offline. Teachers may use WebQuests created and posted by other educators or can design their own. The WebQuest Portal (www.webquest.org) leads teachers step by step through the process of building an Internet-based lesson.

This section explains steps that must be taken by educational leaders to implement this Performance Indicator. Because so few leaders are currently familiar with research and models for technology use, at this time it is important that all educational leaders be involved in all aspects of reading, learning, and sharing their findings.

What Is Already in Place?

Review existing evidence that the school or district uses research-based models in technology implementation.

All educational leaders need to:

- Determine methods used to identify technology integration pieces in instructional plans through review of documents, interviews, and surveys.
- Review practices for selection of technology-based instructional materials.

What Practices Demonstrate Successful Implementation of This Performance Indicator?

Provide successful, research-based models for technology use.

All educational leaders need to:

- Share and discuss online and print material with site and district staff.
- Make professional growth opportunities for staff members a priority.
- Maintain contact with professional organizations, county and state departments of education, and local colleges and universities to get updated recommendations about successful technology integration programs.
- Continue to visit recommended school or district sites and take staff members and other stakeholders along.
- Encourage staff members to attend conferences, workshops, and online courses where technology integration issues are addressed.
- Formalize a process for staff members to share their findings and experiences with other educators.
- Apply information learned when planning the technology integration pieces in instructional plans and document their use.
- Identify practices for selection of technology-based instructional materials that will encourage a wide range of uses.

What Steps Lead to Successful Implementation of This Performance Indicator?

Find successful, research-based models for technology use in education.

All educational leaders need to:

- Engage in professional reading and growth opportunities geared toward finding research-based models for technology use.
- Contact professional organizations, county and state departments of education, and local colleges and universities to get recommendations about successful technology integration programs.
- Make visits to recommended sites and take staff members and other stakeholders along.
- Attend conferences, workshops, and online courses where technology integration issues are addressed.
- Communicate findings and experiences with other educational leaders.

practices in use of technology.

Activity 7 • Finding Sources for Research on Technology-Based Instruction

Demands for educators to cite research to support proposed instructional interventions are increasing. To meet those demands, administrators should take advantage of the numerous resources available on the Internet, with its easy access to research data and examples of best practices. In this activity, create an annotated Webliography of Internet sites useful to you and your staff members.

Once the initial list is completed, share these resources with colleagues and encourage them to add to the Webliography as appropriate. The list can be continually updated and modified to provide an ongoing tool for planning.

Note: This activity may be completed in one of three ways. The first method requires entry-level computer skills, the second requires intermediate skills, and the third requires advanced skills.

1. Using the format shown in Activity 7, create a table in a Word document and record the required information.
2. Use the Filamentality website (www.filamentality.com) to create a hotlist. Be sure to note the URL for your hotlist.
3. Create a free Backflip account (www.backflip.com) and make a folder for research on technology-based instruction. Add to this folder the sites you find and short descriptors. Make the folder public. Be sure to note your Backflip login information for later access.

Each of these formats enables you to access electronically the listed resources later (assuming that you have an active Internet connection). In the case of the Word document, you simply need to open the file and click on the URL (press Control and click when using the most recent versions of Word). The Filamentality hotlist will have its own URL, and you access your Backflip account by going to the Backflip website and logging in.

Next Steps: Once the Webliography has been created, go to the Performance Indicator I.E. section of the Action Plan at the end of this chapter to identify the steps that need to be taken next to ensure that research-based effective practices in technology use are considered and used in planning.

Activity 7 • Finding Sources for Research on Technology-Based Instruction

Directions:

- Before you begin your own search, you may want to visit the following sites, which are examples of sources that provide research on technology-based instruction:

  Center for Applied Research in Educational Technology: http://caret.iste.org

  The Metiri Group's research page: www.metiri.com/Solutions/Research.htm

- Your initial Webliography should include at least five resources.
- You may use traditional search engines, such as Google (www.google.com) or AltaVista (www.altavista.com), to find lists of sites that offer research on technology-based instruction or offer models of research-based best practices. If you need help refining your search, visit the Four NETS for Better Searching page at http://webquest.sdsu.edu/searching/fournets.htm.
- You may also want to try using a metasearch engine such as Vivisimo (http://vivisimo.com) or KartOO (www.kartoo.com). These search engines cluster your results into categories designed to help narrow your search.
- Record the name of each site and the URL in the form below, and write a one- or two-sentence description.

Site Name:	URL:
Description:	
Site Name:	URL:
Description:	
Site Name:	URL:
Description:	
Site Name:	URL:
Description:	
Site Name:	URL:
Description:	

Educational leaders advocate, on the state and national levels, for policies, programs, and funding opportunities that support implementation of the district technology plan.

This kind of activity is generally the responsibility of the district superintendent, cabinet members, and the school board. Policies and practices governing advocacy vary greatly from state to state as well as within communities. While administrators may take the lead in helping to develop state and federal policies, programs, and funding opportunities that support implementation of the district technology plan, it would not be possible for this kind of text to provide direction to administrators from across the nation. If this is an area of concern to you, begin by exploring district policies regarding advocacy as well as work done by professional organizations and past practices in your area.

Activity

Performance Indicator I.F. Educational leaders advocate, on the state and national levels, for policies, programs, and funding opportunities that support implementation of the district technology plan.

Activity 8 • Advocacy and Membership in Professional Organizations

Advocacy is generally the responsibility of the district superintendent, cabinet, and school board members. Because this is the case, this performance indicator is not addressed here.

However, individual school and district administrators may become involved in advocacy activities through the professional organizations they join and support. This activity will help you review the kinds of advocacy engaged in by professional organizations that you may already be a member of or might be interested in joining.

Next Steps: Once you have completed your research, go to the Performance Indicator I.F. section of the Action Plan at the end of this chapter to identify the steps that might be taken next to advocate for policies, programs, and funding opportunities that support implementation of the district technology plan.

American Association of School Administrators: www.aasa.org

Association of School Business Officials International: http://asbointl.org

National Association of Elementary School Principals: www.naesp.org

National Association of Secondary School Principals: www.nassp.org

Choose one of these organizations and visit its website to learn more about its advocacy efforts. If you're already a member of another organization relevant to your current position (e.g., a state-level professional group, or a technology-focused organization such as ISTE, www.iste.org), spend some time learning about its advocacy efforts.

After visiting the website, fill in the following sections.

Name of organization reviewed:
1. Which area(s) of the website address advocacy issues?
2. What kinds of advocacy activities are supported by this organization?
3. How does this organization advocate for policies, programs, and funding opportunities that support implementation of district technology plans?
4. Did the website provide information about advocacy that is new to you? Explain.

Action Plan

Standard I Educational leaders inspire a shared vision for comprehensive integration of technology and foster an environment and culture conducive to the realization of that vision.

Directions: Use the Action Plan to identify the steps that need to be taken to implement Standard I in your school or district.

Performance Indicator(s)	Next Steps	Person(s) Responsible	I Will Know This Step Has Been Achieved When ...	Timeline
I.A. Educational leaders facilitate the shared development by all stakeholders of a vision for technology use and widely communicate that vision.				
I.B. Educational leaders maintain an inclusive and cohesive process to develop, implement, and monitor a dynamic, long-range, and systemic technology plan to achieve the vision.				
I.C. Educational leaders foster and nurture a culture of responsible risk-taking and advocate policies promoting continuous innovation with technology.				
I.D. Educational leaders use data in making leadership decisions.				
I.E. Educational leaders advocate for research-based effective practices in use of technology.				
I.F. Educational leaders advocate, on the state and national levels, for policies, programs, and funding opportunities that support implementation of the district technology plan.				

[illegible] programs we offer to students. Here are some questions to ask yourself as you consider how to inspire a shared vision for comprehensive integration of technology and foster an environment and culture conducive to the realization of that vision:

- Does my school or district have one comprehensive vision statement that incorporates technology use as an administrative and instructional tool? If the answer is no, what is the process for revising the current vision statement?
- What steps are taken to share the vision with staff, students, parents, and the community?
- What plan development steps are in place, and how do we implement and monitor dynamic, long-range, and systemic plans to achieve our vision?
- How do the administrators in our school or district encourage and nurture a culture of responsible risk taking and advocate policies promoting continuous innovation with technology and other school reforms?
- How and when are data currently used in making leadership decisions, and how could the use of data be expanded or improved?
- What resources do we have to find examples of effective research-based practices in the use of technology, and how do we capitalize on these resources?

Carefully considered, consolidated planning based upon data analysis and the information we glean from research is critical in school reform today.

Resources

Projects/Internet Sites

Apple Learning Interchange. Teaching ideas and model lessons.
Available: http://edcommunity.apple.com/ali

Center for Children & Technology. Links to research on technology use in education.
Available: http://cct.edc.org

Center for Applied Research in Educational Technology: http://caret.iste.org

The Concerns-Based Adoption Model (CBAM), A Model for Change in Individuals:
www.nas.edu/rise/backg4a.htm

The Concerns-Based Adoption Model (CBAM), Educators' Stages of Concern About
Change: www.stlceo.org/InstructionalLeadership/CBAM.html

Education Leadership Action Network. Sponsored by the Wallace Foundation, this link leads to a series of recent reports about school leadership and data-driven decision making. Available: www.wallacefoundation.org/ELAN/TR/

Edutopia. Articles and video clips that document various models for technology use with students. Available: www.edutopia.org

The Metiri Group's research page: www.metiri.com/Solutions/Research/htm

Mid-Continent Research for Education and Learning. Technology use information. Available: www.mcrel.org/topics/EducationalTechnology/

Research Center for Educational Technology. Links to research on technology use in education. Available: www.rcet.org

Promising Practices in Technology: www.seirtec.org/ACOTstages.html

Quality Education Data. This organization regularly surveys schools and districts regarding technology planning and usage. Available: www.qeddata.com

Technology Information Center for Administrative Leadership (TICAL). Portal for school administrators. Available as a presentation or as a pdf: http://portical.org

Traditions of Change Research: http://ide.ed.psu.edu/change/hall.htm

Web 2.0 Tools for Busy Administrators. A Breeze presentation that describes how Travis Unified School District used several web-based tools while revising the district technology plan. Available as a presentation or as a pdf: www.portical.org/Presentations/brooks-young/

WebQuest Portal. Links to existing WebQuests and resources for creating your own WebQuests. Available: www.webquest.org

What's so different about the 21st century?: http://www.metiri.com/features.html

Search Engines

AltaVista: www.altavista.com

Four NETS for Better Searching: http://webquest.sdsu.edu/searching/fournets.htm

Google: www.google.com

Kart00: www.kartoo.com

Vivisimo: http://vivisimo.com

Apple. (2008, April). *Apple classrooms of tomorrow today: Learning in the 21st Century.* Available: http://images.apple.com/education/docs/leaders/Apple-ACOT2Whitepaper.pdf

BellSouth Foundation. (2000, May). BellSouth identifies best practices for professional development. (Abstract from *Professional Development Best Practices*) [Online report]. Available: www.eschoolnews.com/news/showStory.cfm?ArticleID=1472

Cotton, K. (1995). *Effective schooling practices: A research synthesis* [Online report]. Available: www.nwrel.org/scpd/esp/esp95toc.html

Klein, S. (1996, October). *Fitting the pieces: Education reform that works* [Online report]. U.S. Department of Education, Office of Educational Research and Improvement. Available: www.ed.gov/pubs/SER/FTP/title.html

North Central Regional Educational Laboratory. (1999, updated 2005). Critical issue: Using technology to improve student achievement. *Pathways to School Improvement* [Online document]. Available: www.ncrel.org/sdrs/areas/issues/methods/technlgy/te800.htm

Ringstaff, C., & Kelley, L. (2002). *The learning return on our educational investment. WestEd.* [Online report]. Available: www.wested.org/online_pubs/learning_return.pdf

U.S. Department of Education. (1996, July). *The role of leadership in sustaining school reform: Voices from the field* [Online report in archived information]. Available: www.ed.gov/pubs/Leadership/index.html

Valdez, G., McNabb, M., Foertsch, M., Anderson, M., Hawkes, M., & Raack, L. (1999). *Computer-based technology and learning: Evolving uses and expectations* [Online report]. North Central Regional Educational Laboratory. Available: www.eric.ed.gov:80/ERICDocs/data/ericdocs2sql/content_storage_01/000019b/80/16/23/c3.pdf

Weiss, S. (January, 2006). The progress of education reform 2006: Technology in education. *Education Commission of the States* [Online report]. Available: www.ecs.org/clearinghouse/67/10/6710.pdf

Articles

Halfacre, J.D., Lindsay, S.R., & Welch, F.C. (2005, March/April). Planning for strategic planning. *Principal-Closing the Gaps-Web Exclusives* [Online journal]. Available: www.naesp.org/ContentLoad.do?contentId=1544

Johnston, R. C. (2001, March). Central office is critical bridge to help schools. *Education Week* [Online journal]. Available (to subscribers): www.edweek.org/ew/ew_printstory.cfm?slug=25central.h20

Kaestner, R. (2006, March–April). Measuring the value of technology projects. *EDTECH: Focus on K–12* [Online journal]. Available: www.edtechmag.com/k12/issues/march-april-2006/measuring-the-value-of-technology-pro.html

Kleiman, G. M. (2000, April–June). Myths and realities about technology in K–12 schools. *LNT Perspectives* [Online journal], *14*. Available: www.edletter.org/dc/kleiman.htm. Also available at: www.edtechleaders.org/documents/myths.pdf

Lashway, L. (2003, July). Trends and issues: Role of the school leader [Online article]. ERIC Clearinghouse on Educational Management, College of Education, University of Oregon. Available: http://eric.uoregon.edu/trends_issues/rolelead/index.html#providing

McKenzie, J. (2000). Horse before cart. *From Now On* [Online journal], *10*(5). Available: www.fno.org/feb01/horsecart.html

McKenzie, J. (2002, Summer). Leading by example: The high touch high tech principal. *From Now On* [Online journal]. Available: http://fno.org/sum02/principal.html

Slowinski, J. (2000, September). Finding your way through the data smog: Enabling empowered decision making with free online tools. *From Now On* [Online journal], *10*(1). Available: www.fno.org/sept00/data.html

Print Material

Covey, S. R. (2004). *The seven habits of highly effective people.* 15th anniversary edition. New York: Simon & Schuster.

Fitzwater, I. (2001). *Time management for school administrators.* Rockport, MA: Pro>Active.

Kouzes, J. M., & Posner, B. Z. (2003). *The leadership challenge.* (3rd ed.) San Francisco: Jossey-Bass.

Wheatley, M. J. (2001). *Leadership and the new science.* San Francisco: Berrett-Koehler.

Professional Organizations for Administrators

American Association of School Administrators: www.aasa.org

Association of School Business Officials International: http://asbointl.org

National Association of Elementary School Principals: www.naesp.org

National Association of Secondary School Principals: www.nassp.org

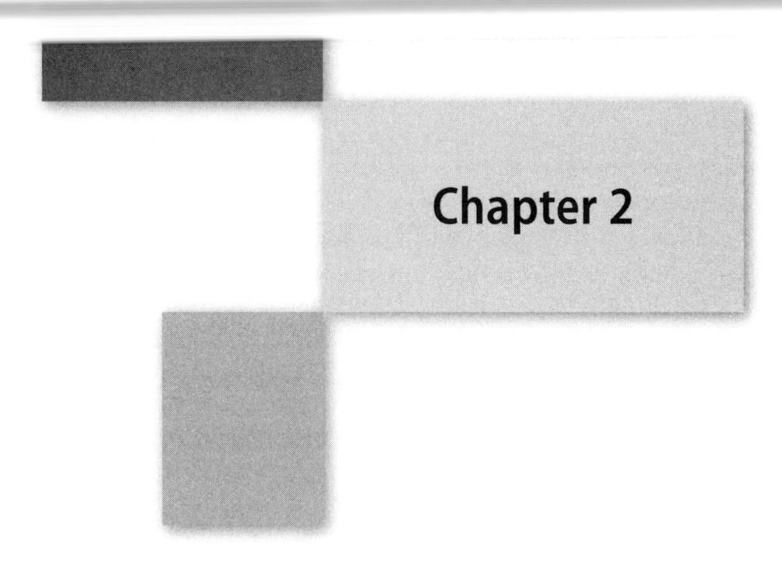

Standard II
Learning and Teaching

Educational leaders ensure that curricular design, instructional strategies, and learning environments integrate appropriate technologies to maximize learning and teaching.

Performance Indicators for Educational Leaders

II.A. Identify, use, evaluate, and promote appropriate technologies to enhance and support instruction and standards-based curriculum leading to high levels of student achievement.

II.B. Facilitate and support collaborative technology-enriched learning environments conducive to innovation for improved learning.

II.C. Provide for learner-centered environments that use technology to meet the individual and diverse needs of learners.

II.D. Facilitate the use of technologies to support and enhance instructional methods that develop higher-level thinking, decision-making, and problem-solving skills.

II.E. Provide for and ensure that faculty and staff take advantage of quality professional learning opportunities for improved learning and teaching with technology.

Chapter 2 Overview

When examining technology use as an instructional tool on your site or within your district, there are two questions you can ask. First: How is technology being used to support teaching and learning? Second: How well is technology being used to support teaching and learning? Although educators do not have all the answers to questions regarding how technology use best supports instruction, they do have access to studies showing certain factors must be present. For example, according to the Apple Classrooms of Tomorrow (ACOT) research (Apple, 1995), which reviewed classroom computer use from 1985 to 1995, and the *Lessons Learned* report, published in 2001 by the SouthEast Initiatives Regional Technology in Education Consortium (SEIR-TEC), leadership at all levels is a critical factor in implementation of successful educational technology programs. Additionally, though easy access to technology is important, these studies clearly show that without appropriate ongoing staff development and support, many teachers will not be willing, or able, to change their approach to classroom instruction.

To demonstrate the kind of instructional leadership necessary to create and sustain an environment that supports better technology use, you need to look at two specific elements: appropriate resources and training. Standard II helps administrators better understand how to evaluate current instructional technology use and then provide support to teachers as they improve their instructional practice. The first four performance indicators identify areas in the instructional environment that must be addressed, while the final performance indicator looks at perhaps the most important area of all, professional development.

> Educational leaders identify, use, evaluate, and promote appropriate technologies to enhance and support instruction and standards-based curriculum leading to high levels of student achievement.

Ask a roomful of educators to define the term *technology integration,* and it is likely each individual will give you a different response; yet most of them agree that this is their goal. Why is it difficult to come to a common agreement about what technology integration means, and how do school administrators provide leadership to implement integrated programs?

It may be that the scope of technology integration is difficult to define clearly because things change rapidly. New or improved technologies appear so quickly that even the most devout technology user has difficulty keeping up with what technologies can do and how they can support classroom instruction. In addition, there is a serious gap between the technologies accessed at home and the technologies available at school. Although technology use is pervasive in society, many people still question whether it has a place in schools. However, proactive school leaders recognize that the focus needs to shift to how technology can best be used in education, not why it should be there.

For the purposes of this book, when the term *technology integration* is used, it refers to an instructional program in which student outcomes are the focus and technology use is woven into the curriculum. In this type of program, technology is used on those occasions when it enables students to work with and understand a concept that might be too difficult, time consuming, or expensive to attempt otherwise. It is also a program in which teachers have ready access to the technologies they need and is structured to support teachers at various levels of expertise. It is an environment where simple competence is not enough, but where all educators are encouraged to look for innovative uses of technology that enable students to solve problems using a range of thinking skills and learning styles and where teachers ultimately change their approach to instruction through technology use.

It is important to note here that students' and teachers' ideas about when technology use is "appropriate" are becoming increasing divergent. Students often prefer to use a technology-based strategy even when a better alternative is readily available. Examples of this behavior include using cell phones in place of address books, turning to the Internet instead of a book when conducting initial research, or most students' preference to write at a keyboard instead of on paper. Teachers may view these behaviors as laziness, but students view them as natural—why would they want to behave differently when an easy solution is at hand? This doesn't mean that students should avoid doing things "the old-fashioned way," but it does mean that educators should regularly ask themselves if their planned technology use is designed to appeal to an adult's frame of reference or is designed to engage students.

Developing an instructional technology program on this scale requires a willingness to make mistakes and to learn how to do things differently. Change is often uncomfortable, but understanding the change process and recognizing that teachers must progress through a series of stages as they learn to use technology can help administrators to identify and implement meaningful models for instructional technology use. Before discussing performance indicators for Standard II, it is important to review the change process itself.

Concerns-Based Adoption Model (CBAM)

Several approaches have been used to explain the process of change. One well-known model, Concerns-Based Adoption Model, or (CBAM), is the result of work done by Gene E. Hall, Shirley Hord, Susan Loucks-Horsley, and Leslie Huling in the mid- and late 1970s. According to CBAM, change happens in seven stages and is reflected in seven levels of use, as shown in Table 2.1 and Table 2.2.

Change causes people to experience a sense of disequilibrium, which is usually very uncomfortable. Realizing that each new technology requires moving through these "stages of concern" and "levels of use" may highlight the scope of what is required for integration. It is also important to note that each innovation requires three to five years before individuals reach renewal and refinement. Keep these tables in mind as you read about each performance indicator for this standard.

Stages of Concern	Expressions of Concern
0. Awareness	The individual has no concern because there is no recognition of the innovation.
1. Information	There is awareness of the existence of the innovation and a realization that the individual needs information.
2. Personal	The individual wants to know how the innovation will affect him or her.
3. Management	The individual's focus is on the mechanics of coping with the innovation.
4. Consequence	The individual's focus is on how the innovation is affecting students and how it can be refined.
5. Collaboration	The individual's focus is on how his or her use of the innovation relates to others and their use.
6. Refocusing	The individual reaches a level of expertise that allows him or her to think about ways to make the innovation even better.

Source: Data adapted from S. Hord, W. Rutherford, L. Huling-Austin, and G. Hall. (n.d.) Taking charge of change. *Southwest Educational Development Laboratory.*

Table 2.2

Levels of Use for Change

Level of Use	Behaviors Associated with Levels of Use
0. Nonuse	Because there is no interest in the innovation, the individual is taking no action.
1. Orientation	The individual begins to gather information about the innovation.
2. Preparation	The individual begins to plan ways to implement the innovation.
3. Mechanical	The individual is concerned about the mechanics of implementing the innovation.
4A. Routine	The individual is comfortable with the innovation and implements its use as taught to him or her.
4B. Refinement	The individual begins to explore ways the outcomes of the innovation can be improved.
5. Integration	The individual views the innovation as an integral part of what he or she does, not as an add-on, and communicates with others about what they are doing.
6. Renewal	The individual explores new, better ways to implement the innovation.

Source: Data adapted from S. Hord, W. Rutherford, L. Huling-Austin, and G. Hall. (n.d.) Taking charge of change. *Southwest Educational Development Laboratory.*

Selecting Appropriate Technologies for Classroom Use

Remember that selection and evaluation of appropriate technologies for classroom use is a chicken-and-egg situation. You need to know the capabilities of various technologies as well as their effects on student learning to make informed decisions about their classroom use. By the same token, it is important to make sound curriculum and instruction decisions first and then choose effective technologies that will support your needs. When you look at technology first, the temptation is to mold your curriculum to fit the available hardware, software, and/or online resources. This negates the concept of technology as an instructional tool.

Unfortunately, many schools and districts continue to begin with the technology rather than desired outcomes for students. In part this may be because educators suffer from a sense that they are somehow always behind when it comes to technology. No sooner do they identify a use for a particular technology in classrooms than something faster, easier, cheaper, and better comes along. This is the nature of technology. Although it does not mean that it's OK to stick with outdated or less effective technology, it does mean that you need to take a balanced approach based upon what is best for students. When you bounce from one technology to another, you seldom achieve more than a low level of proficiency. As a result, many items disappear into closets or sit unused in classrooms and labs. When educators fail to keep up with advances in technology, they find that their equipment no longer supports new applications or online resources, and instructional time is wasted as they try to make outdated equipment or software function.

Having a vision for an instructional program that incorporates technology use and a plan for its implementation is critical. Once these are in place (refer to Chapter 1), it is necessary to decide how you will keep up with innovations in the instructional field. Though electronic newsletters and blogs, such as *eSchool News* (www.eschoolnews.com), the Association of Supervision and Curriculum Development (ASCD) *SmartBrief* (www.ascd.org), or *TechLearning* (http://techlearning.com) are helpful, it is important for administrators to realize that no individual, at any level, can do this on his or her own. Consider establishing leadership cadres at the district and site levels that meet regularly to discuss curriculum and instruction issues, whose roles are to research and review promising instructional practices along with new technologies and to share this information with administrators and staff. District cadres can conduct initial research, working with county and state offices of education, local colleges and universities, and other resources, and then share their findings with site cadres. These additional resources may include Internet sites that offer general research on the effects of technology on student learning. Examples include the Regional Education Laboratories (http://ies.ed.gov/ncee/edlabs/), SEIR-TEC (www.seirtec.org), and the ACOT project (www.apple.com/education/k12/leadership/acot/library.html). Once information is shared with campus leaders, it can be reviewed by the leadership cadre for its applicability to an individual school, which then makes recommendations that align with their common vision and plan.

When the staff selects a particular technology or strategy for further consideration, the cadre and administrator can arrange for time to use and evaluate the tool in question. When using and evaluating technologies, ask for time to allow both adults and students to work with the technology. Also ask for any research that specifically focuses on either the particular technology or similar technologies. Request references and contact sites where the technology is in place to discuss its effects with educators and students. Finally, consider where equipment will be placed and whether teachers will be able to have ready access to the technology. This approach increases opportunities for shared leadership and encourages collaborative planning.

standards-based curriculum leading to high levels of student achievement.

This section offers suggestions for reviewing your current process for selecting technologies as well as steps to take to identify and implement new strategies for this process. Review what is already in place, then define the ideal situation; finally, explore the steps you need to take to reach the ideal.

What Is Already in Place?

Assess existing methods employed at the site and district levels for identifying, using, and evaluating appropriate technologies to enhance and support curriculum and instruction.

All educational leaders need to:

- Identify existing documents that describe the vision and plan for technology use in classrooms.
- Identify existing procedures for selecting, using, and evaluating various instructional technologies, including who is involved in decision making.
- Articulate the current role for administrators in the process of selecting, using, and evaluating various instructional technologies.

Campus Leaders' Additional Responsibilities:	District Leaders' Additional Responsibilities:	Superintendents' and Cabinet Leaders' Additional Responsibilities:
• Review school site plans to see how instructional technologies are currently identified, used, and evaluated. • Review existing lesson plans and other documentation to determine types of technology use and level of use for students. • Review current committee structures to determine their focus and approaches taken to research and program improvement. • Review current equipment and software inventories, locations for equipment, and uses for the equipment and software. • Review web-based tools currently in use.	• Review district curriculum and technology plans to see how instructional technologies are currently identified, used, and evaluated. • Review existing departmental plans and policies that pertain to types of technology use and level of use for students. • Review current district committee structures to determine their focus and approaches taken to research and program improvement. • Meet with campus leaders about types of technology use and level of use for students. • Review current district equipment and software inventories, locations for equipment, and recommended uses for equipment and software. • Review web-based tools currently in use.	• Review existing board policies or regulations that address how instructional technologies are currently identified, used, and evaluated. • Obtain feedback from campus and district leaders regarding existing types of technology use and level of use for students. • Determine how each division can provide support to schools and to individual district departments based upon this feedback. • Determine whether existing policies and procedures provide for ongoing evaluation of how instructional technologies are currently identified and used.

What Practices Demonstrate Successful Implementation of This Performance Indicator?

Ensure that a process exists and is systemically implemented for identifying, using, and evaluating appropriate technologies to enhance and support curriculum and instruction.

All educational leaders need to:

- Determine whether current procedures are adequate.
- Determine whether current procedures are appropriately implemented and enforced.
- Participate in the process and follow newly established guidelines for selecting instructional technologies.

Campus Leaders' Additional Responsibilities:	District Leaders' Additional Responsibilities:	Superintendents' and Cabinet Leaders' Additional Responsibilities:
• Inform parents and staff members of the process for identifying, using, and evaluating instructional technologies and insist that the process be used. • Establish a leadership cadre or identify an existing group that will take responsibility for bringing information and recommendations to the site staff. • Update school plans and budgets to reflect ongoing costs of technology in all areas (see Chapter 4) and to allow for site visits to assess the effectiveness of various technologies. • Establish a plan for equipment placement that ensures ready access on an as-needed basis.	• Develop and present to both campus and cabinet leaders recommendations for implementation and enforcement of the process. • Establish a district leadership cadre or identify an existing group that will take responsibility for bringing information and recommendations to the site cadres. • Identify support that may be necessary for sites to ensure that the process is followed, including visits to sites using particular technologies, and make recommendations to the cabinet regarding who should be responsible for providing this support. • Consider the effect your recommendations will make on sites in terms of cost, training, and ongoing work required. • Communicate with site leaders prior to making final recommendations.	• Schedule time for campus and district leaders to discuss the technology selection and evaluation process and participate in these meetings. • Review recommendations for support and determine the ability of the district to provide this kind of support. • Share the selection and evaluation process recommendations with campus and district leaders prior to presenting them to the school board.

All educational leaders need to:

- Define the administrative role in the process for identifying, using, and evaluating instructional technologies.
- Bring a representative group of administrators, teachers, parents, and students together to make recommendations regarding policies and procedures for identifying, using, and evaluating instructional technologies.
- Develop an action plan and timeline for implementation of this process.
- Establish procedures for evaluation and modification of implementation.

Campus Leaders' Additional Responsibilities:	District Leaders' Additional Responsibilities:	Superintendents' and Cabinet Leaders' Additional Responsibilities:
• Identify ways existing committees or other decision-making groups will be involved in this process. • Provide information regarding the technology selection and evaluation process to all staff members and parents.	• Identify appropriate people to contact other districts, the county office of education, vendors, and professional organizations to gather information about technology selection and evaluation. • Identify ways existing district committees or other decision-making groups will be involved in this process. • Assist campus leaders in offering information to staff and parents regarding the technology selection and evaluation process. • Provide information to district staff, including cabinet leaders, regarding the technology selection and evaluation process.	• Participate in informational meetings concerning technology selection and evaluation. • Work with school board members to educate them on issues related to technology selection and evaluation. • Work with employee associations to restructure committees or other decision-making groups that meet regularly to support the formation of leadership cadres.

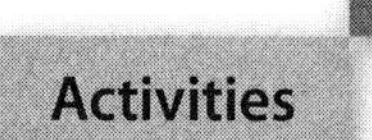

Activities

Performance Indicator II.A. Educational leaders identify, use, evaluate, and promote appropriate technologies to enhance and support instruction and standards-based curriculum leading to high levels of student achievement.

Activity 1 • Defining Technology Integration

The term *technology integration* means different things to different people. Before attempting to tackle this concept with the help of the school community, administrators need to have a clear idea of what they mean when they talk about technology integration. In preparation for working with teachers and planning committees, use this activity to develop a personal definition of technology integration. Like Activity 1 in Chapter 1, "Articulating Your Personal Vision," your definition will probably describe what *could* be done rather than the current state of technology integration in your workplace.

Activity 2 • Current Use of Technology

In addition to defining technology integration, it's important to analyze current practices at schools and within the district as they relate to technology use to enhance and support instruction and a standards-based curriculum. Several tools are available for this analysis. In this activity, you're asked to review three of those tools. Then, choose the one tool that's most appropriate for your school or district, and use it to complete your assessment of current practices. You may also decide to explore and use other tools instead of the ones listed.

Next Steps: You may need to complete other activities related to this performance indicator. Review for relevance Activities 1 and 2 for Performance Indicator I.A., and Activity 2 for Performance Indicator II.A. When you're ready, refer to the Action Plan at the end of this chapter to identify the steps that need to be taken next to ensure that technology integration in your school or district is effective and supports high levels of student achievement.

to write your own definition of the term *technology integration.*

Student Use of Technology

Record your thoughts about how technology can be used to support student achievement:

- What kinds of technologies are appropriate for classroom use?
- When is it appropriate to use technology-based instruction, and when are other strategies more appropriate?
- What kinds of activities would you like to see students engaged in when using technology?

Staff Use of Technology

Record your thoughts about how technology can be used to support the daily work of your teaching staff:

- What kinds of technologies are appropriate for teachers to use in the classroom?
- When is it appropriate for teachers to use technology-based instruction, and when are other strategies more appropriate?
- What kinds of activities would you like to see teachers engaged in when using technology?

Additional comments:

Write your definition of *technology integration.*

Activity 2 • Current Use of Technology

Directions: Review the three online tools listed below and decide which one is most appropriate for your school or district.

STaR chart: www.iste.org/inhouse/starchart/

Technology Integration Process Gauge:
www.seirtec.org/publications/ProgressGauge2000.pdf

Learning With Technology Profile Tool:
www.ncrtec.org/capacity/profile/profile.htm

1. Which tool did you select?
2. Why did you decide this tool was the most appropriate? Explain your reasoning.
3. Complete the assessment of current practice in your school or district and print a copy of your results.

Educational leaders facilitate and support collaborative technology-enriched learning environments conducive to innovation for improved learning.

Teachers who are comfortable with working collaboratively are more likely to encourage students to work in a project-based environment. Although the collaboration stage falls late in the change process continuum described in the CBAM model, administrators at all levels can take steps to encourage and support staff members new to innovations to work in groups rather than in isolation. As a consequence, not only will teachers be less reticent about using this instructional style in their classrooms, but a collaborative working structure can also become a foundation of your ongoing staff development program (see Performance Indicator II.E. later in this chapter).

Whether you are a cabinet leader who wants district and campus leaders to implement an innovation or a campus leader working with a school staff, there are almost always strategies you can use to reallocate time and resources to encourage collaboration and group work. For example, it is common to hold grade-level or departmental meetings at most school sites. Often these are business meetings used to provide information that can just as easily be distributed through bulletins, e-mail, online groups, blogs, or some other form of written communication. By clearing these items from the agenda, it is possible to redirect this time to focus on curriculum and instructional issues, making these meetings opportunities to provide information about innovations and to hold discussions about challenges as staff members work through stages of concern and levels of use. Other possibilities include utilizing restructured staff and leadership team meetings, using time on early release days, or offering stipends for regularly scheduled discussion groups outside the workday. Although it is also possible to set up and coordinate online discussions using tools such as chat rooms, blogs, or online groups, change at this level also requires face-to-face interaction.

Once you've found time, how do you structure the meetings to encourage collaboration? Assuming you are in a situation where multiple groups will be gathering, it's not possible or even desirable for you to try to participate in each group. One successful approach is to talk with the people who will attend meetings and develop a framework in which specified areas will be covered during each session; this work is tied into yearly school program goals or professional growth plans. Group members may bring sample technology-based lessons or articles about technology-related issues to read and discuss and schedule time to address mechanics and routine use issues. By including these areas, you ensure that people at each level of use walk away from every meeting with something they can use. Hold people accountable for this time. Request that agendas and minutes be provided to you for review and make yourself available to address questions or concerns.

Roles and Responsibilities

Performance Indicator II.B. Educational leaders facilitate and support collaborative technology-enriched learning environments conducive to innovation for improved learning.

This section suggests a process for administrators as they plan for collaborative, innovative learning environments where technology is fully integrated. Begin with reviewing the current status of learning environments within the school or district, identify your target goals, and decide what needs to be done to reach those goals.

What Is Already in Place?

Assess the current learning environment to determine the degree to which it supports collaboration and innovation through appropriate technology use.

All educational leaders need to:

- Articulate the current district and site vision for technology integration.
- Meet with staff members to discuss methods currently in place to ensure effective technology integration.
- Include parents and students in discussions about collaborative, technology-rich learning environments.

Campus Leaders' Additional Responsibilities:	District Leaders' Additional Responsibilities:	Superintendents' and Cabinet Leaders' Additional Responsibilities:
• Review school site plans to see whether collaboration and project-based learning are addressed. • Review the curriculum in place to see whether collaboration and project-based learning are addressed. • Review existing lesson plans, student work, and other documentation to determine how collaboration and project-based learning are addressed.	• Review district curriculum and technology plans to see whether collaboration and project-based learning are addressed. • Meet with campus leaders to gather input about collaboration and project-based learning in a technology-rich environment.	• Obtain feedback from campus and district leaders regarding existing instructional issues and concerns. • Determine how each division can provide support to schools and individual district departments based upon this feedback. • Determine whether existing policies and procedures support collaboration and project-based learning in a technology-rich environment.

All educational leaders need to:

- Assess findings from initial information gathering to determine whether the current learning environment supports collaboration and innovation.
- Decide whether further action needs to be taken.
- Develop and implement a plan to encourage and support this type of learning environment.
- Model the importance of supporting collaboration and innovation in their own behaviors, in planning, and through staff development sessions.

Campus Leaders' Additional Responsibilities:	District Leaders' Additional Responsibilities:	Superintendents' and Cabinet Leaders' Additional Responsibilities:
• Model support for collaborative, innovative learning environments through: design of site meetings and workshops, discussions of classroom visits and observations, written school plans and academic goals, and staff development plans. • Support teachers who strive to offer collaborative, innovative learning environments through incentives and recognition.	• Make recommendations to the cabinet regarding who would be responsible for providing support, both technical and financial. • Provide necessary support for sites to implement the plan. • Develop and present to both campus and cabinet leaders recommendations for strategies to implement and support collaborative, innovative learning environments. • Consider the effect your recommendations will make on sites in terms of cost, training, and ongoing work required. • Communicate with site leaders prior to making final recommendations.	• Review recommendations for support and determine the ability of the district to provide this kind of support. • Demonstrate support of collaboration and innovation by offering incentives and rewards to district and campus leaders who practice this approach themselves. • Support sites that strive to offer collaborative, innovative learning environments to all students through budget allocations, staffing, and other resources. • Update school board members on implementation of the plan, including successes and challenges. • Schedule time for campus and district leaders to engage in ongoing discussions about the learning environment and participate in these meetings.

What Steps Lead to Successful Implementation of This Performance Indicator?

Raise educators' comfort level with collaboration by using strategies that encourage and support group work and reward innovative thinking.

All educational leaders need to:

- Make the commitment of time and resources necessary to learn about the benefits and possible roadblocks to implementation of this type of learning environment.
- Develop a timeline for research and problem solving.
- Work together to develop recommendations concerning the learning environment.
- Develop an action plan and timeline for implementation of steps identified to raise awareness.
- Establish procedures for evaluation and modification of implementation.

Campus Leaders' Additional Responsibilities:	District Leaders' Additional Responsibilities:	Superintendents' and Cabinet Leaders' Additional Responsibilities:
• Write a personal professional development plan that includes learning how to create and sustain this kind of learning environment. • Seek out and share examples of instructional strategies that support this type of learning environment. • Provide information to all staff members and parents about the benefits of a collaborative, innovative learning environment. • Make provisions for equipment placement and materials availability that will encourage teachers to design lessons based on collaboration and innovation.	• Identify and contact other districts, the county office of education, vendors, and professional organizations to gather information about development of this type of learning environment. • Provide information to campus leaders and district staff, including cabinet leaders, regarding this type of learning environment, including research, educational opportunities, and model programs. • Include appropriate instructional design as a consideration when reviewing curriculum for adoption.	• Explore ways to model developing a collaborative, innovative learning environment for district and cabinet meetings and workshops. • Explore ways to model support of collaboration and innovation through incentives and rewards to district and campus leaders who practice this approach themselves. • Identify methods for supporting sites that strive to offer collaborative, innovative learning environments to all students through budget allocations, staffing, and other resources. • Work with appropriate employee associations to develop a model for evaluation that supports collaboration and innovation. • Work with school board members to educate them on issues related to learning environments that foster collaboration and innovation.

technology-enriched learning environments conducive to innovation for improved learning.

Activity 3 • Walk-Through Observations of Classroom Technology Use

Informal walk-through observations of actual classroom practice provide administrators with valuable information about how well a school's or district's planning and policy documents align with what is actually happening in classrooms. Walk-throughs should be brief: plan to spend no more than four to five minutes in each classroom. Because these are quick snapshots of what occurs in a classroom on a given day at a given time, it's valuable to conduct several walk-throughs, varying the day of the week and the time of day you visit. Walk-throughs may be conducted by administrators or by teams of educators.

A walk-through isn't meant to be an evaluation of the teacher. It's an opportunity to visit classrooms with specific questions in mind simply to see what's happening. Use the Activity 3 table to develop questions that will guide your informal observations of each classroom you visit. Once the walk-throughs are completed, use the data you've gathered as supporting documentation for Activities 4, 5, and 6.

Activity 4 • Collaborative Learning and Teaching

Creating an environment that supports collaborative learning and teaching is a challenge for some teachers, even when technology-based instruction isn't part of the mix. Teachers who struggle with this concept will not willingly embrace it simply because they're given access to technology that supports it. Use the Activity 4 table to identify current practices in collaborative learning and teaching in your school or district, with and without the use of technology. You may also want to use the information gathered in Chapter 2, Activity 3, as evidence.

Next Steps: After completing the activities related to this Performance Indicator, use the Action Plan at the end of this chapter to identify the steps that need to be taken next to encourage use of collaborative learning and teaching in a technology-enriched environment.

Activity 3 • Walk-Through Observations of Classroom Technology Use

Directions: Use the table below to develop questions that will guide your informal observations of each classroom you visit.

Before the Walk-Through
Determine the focus of the walk-through. What aspects of technology use are you concerned with? Read Performance Indicators II.B. through II.D. to decide what information you need. For example, you may want to focus on Performance Indicator II.B. to identify factors that encourage the use of collaborative learning and teaching in a technology-enriched environment. Write your focus here:
Develop your guiding questions. What is it you want to know or observe? To follow up on the example given above, what do you want to know about the factors that encourage the use of collaborative learning and teaching in a technology-enriched environment? For example, you might ask, "Are students working in collaborative pairs and small groups?" or, "What technologies are available to students when working in collaborative pairs and small groups?" Limit yourself to two or three questions. Write your guiding questions here:

Continued

Identify particulars that will help you answer the questions. The particulars might include the physical arrangement of the room, the presence of a variety of technologies, the level of student engagement, the teacher's behavior, etc. For the example given on the previous page, you might expect to see:

Furniture arranged to facilitate work in pairs and groups.

Adequate student access to a variety of technologies in the classroom.

Students using various technologies to complete projects.

Students working together and remaining on task.

The teacher acting as a facilitator.

Write your particulars here:

During the Walk-Through

Plan to spend no more than four to five minutes in each classroom. Using the guiding questions and particulars, take notes on index cards for later review. Be sure to document the date, time of day, grade level, type of class (when appropriate), room number, and content area being addressed, along with information about the environment, access to materials and equipment, and applicable student and teacher behavior. You may want to create a specific form for the walk-throughs. Remember your focus! Don't be distracted by things you see that are not directly related to the task at hand.

If teams are doing the walk-throughs, you'll need to set up a schedule and provide campus maps (if district administrators or other guests are assisting). Also, review the questions and particulars with visitors.

After the Walk-Through

Collect the comment cards and observation forms. Debrief with the team, if others were involved in observing. Write a nonevaluative summary of the data collected. Share this information with the staff, and use it as you complete other activities related to Performance Indicators II.B. through II.D.

Activity 4 • Collaborative Learning and Teaching

Directions: Read each statement and mark the rating that best reflects current practice in your school or district.

Student Learning	Never	Sometimes	Usually	Always
1. All students are provided opportunities to work in **heterogeneous** pairs.				
2. All students are provided opportunities to work in **homogeneous** pairs.				
3. All students are provided opportunities to work in small **heterogeneous** groups.				
4. All students are provided opportunities to work in small **homogeneous** groups.				
5. Student pairs/groups are responsible for their own goal setting.				
6. Student pairs/groups are responsible for designing their own learning tasks.				
7. Student pairs/groups are responsible for self-monitoring as they work.				
8. Student pairs/groups are responsible for assessing their own work.				
9. All students are encouraged to form study/ discussion groups to complete homework.				
10. While working at school, student pairs/groups have access to:				
computers				
digital cameras				
video cameras				
Internet				
handheld computers or PDAs				
calculators				
a monitor and VCR or DVD player, or both				
scanners				
printers				
robotics				
GPS devices				
other (please list)				
11. Students are encouraged to work collaboratively using:				
e-mail				
online discussion groups				
web logs or "blogs" (personal online journals that can be accessed by the public)				
WebQuests (inquiry-oriented activities where most or all information used by students is web-based)				
online projects involving other schools				

Continued

planning takes place.				
2. Teachers and the library media specialist plan together.				
3. Teachers share their successful instructional activities in meetings.				
4. Teachers participate in discussion groups.				
5. Teachers conduct peer observations.				
6. Teachers act as mentors or teaching buddies for one another.				
7. Time is scheduled regularly for teachers to engage in collaborative planning.				
8. Teachers have opportunities to share ideas with colleagues at other district schools.				
9. Teachers have opportunities to share ideas with colleagues in other districts.				
10. Teachers team-teach lessons with one another.				
11. Teachers team-teach lessons with the library media specialist.				
12. While working at school, teachers have access to:				
computers				
digital cameras				
video cameras				
Internet				
handheld computers or PDAs				
calculators				
a monitor and VCR or DVD player, or both				
scanners				
printers				
robotics				
GPS devices				
other (please list)				
13. Teachers are encouraged to work collaboratively using:				
e-mail				
online discussion groups				
web logs or "blogs"				
lesson-planning tools				
online professional development courses				

Student-Centered, Individualized Learning Environments

Performance Indicator II.C.

Educational leaders provide for learner-centered environments that use technology to meet the individual and diverse needs of learners.

One of the documented benefits of classroom technology use is that it lends itself to meeting individual student needs and results in teachers altering their instructional styles to a more student-centered approach as they reach higher levels of use. However, it is important that you continue to offer learning opportunities for those educators who have reached the stage of routine use in order for teachers to reach the point where they begin changing the ways they teach.

Educators who have achieved a level of routine *personal* technology use typically begin to explore individualized student learning through the use of commercially produced, content-oriented software or web-based activities. Some of the software packages are programs that can be used on individual, stand-alone computers, and others are kept on a file server on- or off-site. Web-based activities at this level may be free, require subscriptions, or include supplemental textbook offerings. These resources are aligned, to varying degrees, to state standards and often can be used to diagnose students' discrete skill levels in order to prescribe a series of lessons intended to increase student performance in the identified skills. These larger packages usually target mathematics and language arts most heavily, offer a management system that records student use and performance, and provide a variety of reporting options. Used judiciously, this kind of computer-assisted instruction (CAI) can show benefits for students. But CAI is only the tip of the iceberg when you consider how technology can be used to individualize instruction in a student-centered environment.

Imagine a classroom where students are working individually or in small groups on projects they have developed based on their own questions about the Industrial Revolution. Students have conferred with the teacher on the design of the projects, which will demonstrate what they learn. A variety of software and web-based tools are available for student use, including presentation applications, word processing programs, database products, spreadsheets, publishing programs, along with online and more traditional reference materials. Some students might use the Internet to research child labor laws and their origins for a multimedia presentation that will ultimately be an entry in a History Day event. Another group might write articles that will be published in a mock newspaper. One student might access materials for an advanced placement (AP) U.S. history course that is not offered at your site but is available online. The teacher moves around the classroom, commenting on work, asking questions, offering assistance. This is an environment where students are being encouraged to demonstrate learning through projects they have designed, some of which use technology as a tool. This is also a place where an individual student's needs are being met, not in remediation, but through access to an AP course.

Educators who have moved to more advanced levels of technology use recognize that great potential exists for individualizing instruction beyond a drill-and-practice strategy. Online courses, distance learning, and project-based learning are just a few of the possibilities. Again, it is difficult for one person to keep up with all the different promising practices in technology integration. This is another area where a district and site leadership cadre can provide a valuable service to the district and individual schools by reviewing and sharing information about these possibilities. Several resources for student-centered learning and distance learning are given at the end of this chapter.

learners.

Use this section as a guide for evaluating current instructional environments and for determining what you want to work toward. It provides steps to take to implement this change.

What Is Already in Place?

Assess strategies in place to meet the individual needs of learners in an environment that is student centered.

All educational leaders need to:

- Understand that this kind of environment is closely tied to each teacher's personal proficiency and confidence in technology use.
- Meet regularly with staff members to discuss how technology is currently used to meet individual student needs and assist in creating a student-centered environment.
- Include parents and students when soliciting feedback on meeting individual student needs and on student-centered learning.
- Assess the level and type of student-centered learning and individualized learning currently taking place.

Campus Leaders' Additional Responsibilities:	District Leaders' Additional Responsibilities:	Superintendents' and Cabinet Leaders' Additional Responsibilities:
• Review the school site plan and goals, individual student learning plans, lesson plans, and other documentation to assess the current level of student-centered instruction. • Visit classrooms to see the correlation between what is written and what is taking place. • Review student products and talk with parents and students to learn about how the work was done. • Review current equipment and software inventories, locations for equipment, and uses for the equipment, software, and online resources.	• Review district curriculum and technology plans to assess how student-centered instruction is currently addressed. • Review departmental plans and policies that include project-based learning and individualized student learning. • Meet with campus leaders to gather input about current levels of student-centered environments and technology integration. • Review current district equipment and software inventories, locations for equipment, and recommended uses for equipment, software, and online resources.	• Review the current district philosophy concerning meeting individual learning needs and student-centered learning. • Obtain feedback from campus and district leaders regarding current practices in these areas. • Determine how each division can provide support to schools and to individual district departments based upon this feedback. • Determine whether the existing philosophy and practice support this type of learning environment for students.

What Practices Demonstrate Successful Implementation of This Performance Indicator?

Ensure that all learners have opportunities for their individual learning needs to be met in a student-centered environment.

All educational leaders need to:

- Identify student groups that currently may not be having individual learning needs met and the level of student-centered learning available.
- Decide whether further action needs to be taken.
- Establish and implement policies and procedures regarding individual student learning needs for students of all academic abilities.
- Ensure that staff members, students, and parents are aware of options available to them to meet individual learning needs.

Campus Leaders' Additional Responsibilities:	District Leaders' Additional Responsibilities:	Superintendents' and Cabinet Leaders' Additional Responsibilities:
• Form a site-level leadership cadre to make recommendations to the staff about this type of learning environment. • Incorporate strategies and resources for addressing individual student needs in the school plan, individual learning plans, the school handbook, and other appropriate documents. • Review lesson plans, student work, and other documentation to ensure students are offered access to resources. • Use classroom visits and observations as opportunities to see evidence of student-centered learning and meeting individual learning needs. • Update budgets to reflect ongoing costs of individualized, technology-supported learning.	• Develop and present to both campus and cabinet leaders recommendations for policies or procedures to handle student-centered learning environments and meeting individual learning needs for all students. • Identify support that may be necessary for sites to implement this type of learning environment, including a district leadership cadre, and make recommendations to the cabinet regarding who would be responsible for providing the support, both technical and financial. • Consider the effect your recommendations will make on sites in terms of cost, training, and ongoing work required. • Communicate with site leaders prior to making final recommendations.	• Schedule time for campus and district leaders to hold ongoing discussions about student-centered learning environments and participate in these meetings. • Review recommendations for support and determine the ability of the district to provide this kind of support. • Share policy and procedure recommendations with campus and district leaders prior to presenting them to the school board.

All educational leaders need to:

- Bring a representative group of staff, parents, and students together to research the benefits and potential drawbacks of student-centered learning and targeting individual learning needs.
- Use feedback from this group to develop an action plan and timeline for raising awareness of this kind of learning environment.
- Establish procedures for evaluation and modification of implementation.

Campus Leaders' Additional Responsibilities:	District Leaders' Additional Responsibilities:	Superintendents' and Cabinet Leaders' Additional Responsibilities:
• Offer information, training, examples of promising practices, and site visit opportunities to staff members for professional development in student-centered learning environments. • Meet with staff members, parents, and students to discuss student-centered learning environments and possibilities for meeting individual learning needs. • Make provisions for equipment placement and replacement that will support student-centered learning environments. • Encourage staff, students, and parents to participate in alternative forms of learning, including online courses.	• Assist campus leaders in offering information to staff, parents, and students regarding student-centered learning and technology use. • Provide information to district staff, including cabinet leaders, regarding student-centered learning and technology use. • Support campus leaders in finding information, training, examples of promising practices, and site visit opportunities for staff members for professional development in student-centered learning environments. • Include student-centered learning projects using technology as a consideration when reviewing curriculum for adoption.	• Participate in informational meetings concerning student-centered learning and technology. • Support sites that strive to offer technology-supported student-centered learning environments to all students through budget allocations, staffing, and other resources. • Work with school board members to educate them about the benefits of student-centered learning environments and the effects of meeting individual student needs.

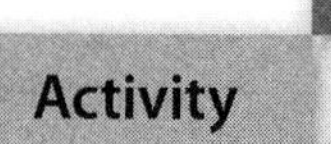

Performance Indicator II.C. Educational leaders provide for learner-centered environments that use technology to meet the individual and diverse needs of learners.

Activity 5 • Meeting the Needs of Diverse Learners

After completing Activities 3 and 4, use the Activity 5 tables to analyze the technology-based strategies used in your school or district to meet the needs of diverse learners. Site leaders should use Activity 5A, while district leaders should use Activity 5B.

While completing this activity, it's helpful to have a copy of the school's or district's curriculum and technology plans, sample lesson plans, individual education plans (IEPs), and other relevant documentation.

Next Steps: After completing the activities related to this Performance Indicator, use the Action Plan at the end of this chapter to identify the steps that need to be taken next to develop or enhance the use of technology to support the individual and diverse needs of learners. It's important to remember that implementation of this performance indicator is closely tied to each teacher's personal technology proficiency and the teacher's confidence in using it for instruction.

Site Leaders	Circle One	
Are student-centered or individualized learning issues addressed in your school-site plans, sample lesson plans, IEPs, and other relevant documentation?	**Yes**	**No**
If so, how?		
Are specific strategies for using technology-based individualized learning included in this documentation?	**Yes**	**No**
If so, how?		
Describe the technology access (hardware and software) provided to students at your school.		
When visiting classrooms, do you regularly see evidence of technology-supported individualized instruction?	**Yes**	**No**
Provide examples of typical technology-based individualized learning experiences taking place at your school.		
Provide examples of typical technology-based individualized learning experiences for special education students.		
Provide examples of typical technology-based individualized learning experiences for English language learners.		
Provide examples of typical technology-based individualized learning experiences for at-risk students.		
Provide examples of typical technology-based individualized learning experiences for high-achieving students.		
Summarize the current use of technology-supported individualized instruction on your campus. Where are your program's strengths and weaknesses?		

 Activity 5B • Meeting the Needs of Diverse Learners

Directions: The following table is for district leaders to use to analyze the technology-based strategies used in your school or district to meet the needs of diverse learners.

District Leaders	Circle One	
Are student-centered or individualized learning issues addressed in your district plans, sample lesson plans, IEPs, and other relevant documentation?	Yes	No
If so, how?		
Are specific strategies for using technology-based individualized learning included in this documentation?	Yes	No
If so, how?		
How does the district support schools in providing adequate student access to technology (hardware and software) for individualized learning?		
How do divisions or departments within the district office provide support to school sites implementing technology-based individualized instruction?		
Do existing policies and procedures provide adequate support for school sites implementing technology-based individualized instruction?	Yes	No
Explain.		
Summarize the current use of technology-supported individualized instruction in your district. What are your program's strengths and weaknesses?		

Performance Indicator II.D.

Educational leaders facilitate the use of technologies to support and enhance instructional methods that develop higher-level thinking, decision-making, and problem-solving skills.

For more than a decade researchers have discussed the relationship between thinking skills and the ability of people to function in a rapidly changing information- and technology-based world. In *Teaching Thinking Skills,* Cotton (1991) points out that, in general, students' thinking skills are not well developed, but they can be taught these skills directly or through lessons in which the opportunity to use thinking skills has been embedded in the curriculum. Cotton also cites research that indicates a correlation between learning thinking skills and gains in academic performance.

Fortunately, this approach to instruction directly supports student-centered learning environments that are capable of meeting individual learning needs as well. In fact, while it is possible to teach higher-order thinking skills directly through a separate curriculum, it is nearly impossible to have students engage in project-based learning without using critical-thinking skills.

Several instructional strategies, including inquiry and class discussions incorporating higher-level questioning, lend themselves well to the incorporation of technology to teach higher-level thinking skills through collaboration and project-based learning; however, the methodology alone is not enough. Teachers need to be skilled in these approaches, which requires time for them to learn the instructional strategies. They must also have administrative support when taking the necessary instructional time to implement fully thinking-based instruction. It is critical to invest time in developing a positive environment that supports students as they experiment with new ideas and approaches to learning.

In today's educational environment, teachers and administrators alike feel the pressure to demonstrate academic achievement as measured by standardized multiple-choice tests; thus some educators balk at moving away from direct instruction, particularly when these tests are not able to measure accurately students' problem-solving skills or other learning gained in a student-centered environment. Although this reaction is understandable, it also does a disservice to teachers and students.

Rote memorization may temporarily raise test scores, but it does not prepare students for collaborative work environments, where they will be expected to access and make sense of information using various technologies. Many teachers also express frustration about not having time to allow students to explore and create their own meaning through project-based learning activities. As a result, the joy of learning and teaching has been significantly diminished. Carefully designed standards-based activities can be the vehicle for ensuring that students have a command of basic knowledge and know how to apply it in real-life situations.

Roles and Responsibilities

Performance Indicator II.D. Educational leaders facilitate the use of technologies to support and enhance instructional methods that develop higher-level thinking, decision-making, and problem-solving skills.

This section charts factors to consider and steps to take when assessing current practices in instructional methods promoting higher-order thinking skills, deciding what the ideal environment would encompass, and achieving that goal. Because there is a close correlation with the steps taken to implement a student-centered learning environment, the roles and responsibilities for Performance Indicators II.C. and II.D. are very similar.

What Is Already in Place?

Assess ways technologies are currently used to guide and support instructional methods that promote higher-level thinking, decision-making, and problem-solving skills within the district or at the school site.

All educational leaders need to:

- Understand that this kind of environment is closely tied to each teacher's personal proficiency and confidence in technology use.
- Meet regularly with staff members to discuss how technology is currently used to promote higher-level thinking, decision-making, and problem-solving skills.
- Assess the level and type of higher-level thinking, decision-making, and problem-solving skills currently taught in classrooms.

Campus Leaders' Additional Responsibilities:	District Leaders' Additional Responsibilities:	Superintendents' and Cabinet Leaders' Additional Responsibilities:
• Review the school site plan and goals, individual student learning plans, lesson plans, and other documentation to assess the current level of use of higher-level thinking, decision-making, and problem-solving skills. • Visit classrooms to see the correlation between what is written and what is taking place. • Review student products and talk with parents and students to learn about how the work was done. • Review current equipment and software inventories, locations for equipment, and uses for the equipment, software, and online resources.	• Review district curriculum and technology plans to assess how higher-level thinking, decision-making, and problem-solving skills are currently addressed. • Review departmental plans and policies that include higher-level thinking, decision-making, and problem-solving skills. • Meet with campus leaders to gather input about current levels of higher-level thinking, decision-making, and problem-solving skills and technology integration. • Review current district equipment and software inventories, locations for equipment, and recommended uses for equipment, software, and online resources.	• Review the current district philosophy concerning higher-level thinking, decision-making, and problem-solving skills. • Obtain feedback from campus and district leaders regarding current practices in these areas. • Determine how each division can provide support to schools and to individual district departments based upon this feedback. • Determine whether the existing philosophy and practice supports the teaching of higher-level thinking, decision-making, and problem-solving skills.

the school site.

All educational leaders need to:

- Identify student groups that currently may not be exposed to higher-level thinking, decision-making, and problem-solving skills within the curriculum or classroom.
- Decide whether further action needs to be taken.
- Establish and implement policies and procedures regarding instruction in the use of higher-level thinking, decision-making, and problem-solving skills for students of all academic abilities.
- Ensure that staff members, students, and parents are aware that all students are to be offered instruction in higher-level thinking, decision-making, and problem-solving skills.

Campus Leaders' Additional Responsibilities:	District Leaders' Additional Responsibilities:	Superintendents' and Cabinet Leaders' Additional Responsibilities:
• Form a site-level leadership cadre to make recommendations to staff about this type of instruction. • Review lesson plans, student work, and other documentation to ensure students are receiving this type of instruction. • Use classroom visits and observations as opportunities to see evidence of teaching higher-level thinking, decision-making, and problem-solving skills.	• Develop and present to both campus and cabinet leaders recommendations for policies or procedures to promote teaching higher-level thinking, decision-making, and problem-solving skills for all students. • Identify support that may be necessary for sites to implement this type of learning environment, including a district leadership cadre, and make recommendations to the cabinet regarding who would be responsible for providing the support, both technical and financial. • Consider the effect your recommendations will have on sites in terms of cost, training, and ongoing work required. • Communicate with site leaders prior to making final recommendations.	• Schedule time for campus and district leaders to hold ongoing discussions about higher-level thinking, decision-making, and problem-solving skills and participate in these meetings. • Review recommendations for support and determine the ability of the district to provide this kind of support. • Share policy and procedure recommendations with campus and district leaders prior to presenting them to the school board.

What Steps Lead to Successful Implementation of This Performance Indicator?

Educate staff about the benefits of using technologies to guide and support instructional methods that promote higher-level thinking, decision-making, and problem-solving skills.

All educational leaders need to:

- Bring a representative group of staff members together to research the benefits and potential drawbacks of teaching higher-level thinking, decision-making, and problem-solving skills to all students.
- Use feedback from this group to develop an action plan and timeline for raising awareness of this kind of instruction.
- Establish procedures for evaluation and modification of implementation.

Campus Leaders' Additional Responsibilities:	District Leaders' Additional Responsibilities:	Superintendents' and Cabinet Leaders' Additional Responsibilities:
• Offer information, training, examples of promising practices, and site visit opportunities to staff members for professional development in teaching higher-level thinking, decision-making, and problem-solving skills. • Meet with staff members to discuss teaching higher-level thinking, decision-making, and problem-solving skills.	• Assist campus leaders in offering information to staff about teaching higher-level thinking, decision-making, and problem-solving skills and technology use. • Provide information to district staff, including cabinet leaders, regarding teaching higher-level thinking, decision-making, and problem-solving skills and technology use. • Support campus leaders in providing information, training, examples of promising practices, and site visit opportunities to staff members for professional development in teaching higher-level thinking, decision-making, and problem-solving skills. • Include lessons that teach higher-level thinking, decision-making, and problem-solving skills as a consideration when reviewing curriculum for adoption.	• Participate in informational meetings concerning teaching higher-level thinking, decision-making, and problem-solving skills and technology use. • Support sites that strive to offer technology-supported teaching of higher-level thinking, decision-making, and problem-solving skills to all students through budget allocations, staffing, and other resources. • Work with school board members to educate them about the benefits of teaching higher-level thinking, decision-making, and problem-solving skills and the effects of doing so.

to support and enhance instructional methods that develop higher-level thinking, decision-making, and problem-solving skills.

Activity 6 • Supporting Higher-Level Thinking, Decision-Making, and Problem-Solving Skills

Use the Activity 6 tables to analyze the technology-based strategies currently used to support all learners' higher-level thinking, decision-making, and problem-solving skills. Site leaders should use Activity 6A, while district leaders should use Activity 6B.

It's highly recommended that you complete Activities 3 and 5 before working on this activity. In addition to walk-through data and having Activity 5A or 5B filled out, it's helpful while completing this activity to have a copy of your school's or district's curriculum and technology plans, sample lesson plans, individual education plans (IEPs), and other relevant documentation.

Next Steps: Use the Action Plan at the end of this chapter to identify the steps that need to be taken next to develop or improve the use of technology to support and enhance higher-level thinking, decision-making, and problem-solving skills. It's important to remember that implementation of this Performance Indicator is closely tied to each teacher's personal technological proficiency and the teacher's confidence in using technology for instruction.

 Activity 6A • Supporting Higher-Level Thinking, Decision-Making, and Problem-Solving Skills

Directions: The following table is for site leaders to use to analyze the technology-based strategies necessary to support all learners' higher-level thinking, decision-making, and problem-solving skills.

Site Leaders	Circle One	
Using your responses to Activities 3 and 5A, other documentation you may have, and your own knowledge of the school, estimate the percentage of individualized instruction time currently devoted to remediation or rote memorization: enrichment activities:		
Are strategies to support and enhance higher-level thinking, decision-making, and problem-solving skills addressed in your school-site plans, sample lesson plans, IEPs, and other relevant documentation?	**Yes**	**No**
If so, how?		
Are specific technology-based strategies to support and enhance higher-level thinking, decision-making, and problem-solving skills included in this documentation?	**Yes**	**No**
If so, how?		
When visiting classrooms, do you regularly see evidence of technology-based strategies used to support and enhance higher-level thinking, decision-making, and problem-solving skills?	**Yes**	**No**
Provide examples of typical technology-based strategies used to support and enhance higher-level thinking, decision-making, and problem-solving skills at your school.		
Provide examples of typical technology-based strategies used to support and enhance higher-level thinking, decision-making, and problem-solving skills for special education students.		
Provide examples of typical technology-based strategies used to support and enhance higher-level thinking, decision-making, and problem-solving skills for limited English proficient (LEP) and English language learners.		
Provide examples of typical technology-based strategies used to support and enhance higher-level thinking, decision-making, and problem-solving skills for at-risk students.		
Provide examples of typical technology-based strategies used to support and enhance higher-level thinking, decision-making, and problem-solving skills for high-achieving students.		
What kinds of technology (hardware and software) are available at your school to teach higher-level thinking, decision-making, and problem-solving skills?		
Summarize the current use of technology-based strategies to support and enhance higher-level thinking, decision-making, and problem-solving skills on your campus. What are your program's strengths and weaknesses?		

necessary to support all learners' higher-level thinking, decision-making, and problem-solving skills.

District Leaders	Circle One	
Using your responses to Activities 3 and 5B, other documentation you may have, and your own knowledge of the district, estimate the percentage of individualized instruction time currently devoted to remediation or rote memorization: enrichment activities:		
Are strategies to support and enhance higher-level thinking, decision-making, and problem-solving skills addressed in your district plans, sample lesson plans, IEPs, and other relevant documentation?	**Yes**	**No**
If so, how?		
Are specific technology-based strategies to support and enhance higher-level thinking, decision-making, and problem-solving skills included in this documentation?	**Yes**	**No**
If so, how?		
How does the district support schools in providing adequate student access to technology (both hardware and software) to teach higher-level thinking, decision-making, and problem-solving skills?		
How do divisions or departments within the district office provide support to school sites implementing technology-based instruction to improve higher-level thinking, decision-making, and problem-solving skills?		
Do existing policies and procedures provide adequate support for school sites implementing technology-based instruction to improve higher-level thinking, decision-making, and problem-solving skills?	**Yes**	**No**
Explain.		
Summarize the current use of technology-supported instruction to improve higher-level thinking, decision-making, and problem-solving skills in your district. What are your program's strengths and weaknesses?		

Staff Development Opportunities

Performance Indicator II.E.

Educational leaders provide for and ensure that faculty and staff take advantage of quality professional learning opportunities for improved learning and teaching with technology.

The term *lifelong learners* frequently pops up in the literature, but if staff development programs are any kind of indicator, educators often do not do a very good job of offering sustained, effective learning opportunities to teachers or administrators. Learning to teach in a technology-supported environment requires time, practice, ongoing support, and then more time. This is a far cry from a single after-school workshop or a one- or two-day inservice. Educators also must expand the scope of staff development programs in educational technology. Too many programs continue to focus on the first four levels of use (nonuse, orientation, preparation, and mechanical), shown in Table 2.2, and offer little or no support to educators who are ready to move onto integration and renewal. While it is important to continue to offer learning opportunities to educators at the earliest levels of use, we must also recognize that many are ready to move on but cannot do so without assistance.

The Apple Classrooms of Tomorrow research (Apple, 1995), covering classroom technology use in targeted classrooms from 1985 through 1995, indicates that teachers learn in stages and that integration does not enter into the picture until later in the process. The stages identified in this research are shown in Table 2.3. These findings underscore the need to design staff development opportunities that reach beyond proficiency levels if technology integration is to be achieved.

Table 2.3

Stages of Educator Learning

Stage	Behaviors
Entry	Teacher is learning the basics of a technology, for example, how to set up equipment and operate it.
Adoption	Teacher begins to use the technology in management areas, for example, computer-generated quizzes or worksheets, gradebooks.
Adaptation	Teacher begins to use software and/or websites to support instruction, for example, a commercially produced content area program or productivity tools (word processor, database).
Appropriation	Teacher begins to focus on collaborative, project-based technology use and technology becomes one of several instructional tools.
Invention	Teacher begins to develop different uses for technology, for example, creates projects that combine two or more technologies.

Source: Data adapted from Apple. (1995). Changing the conversation about teaching, learning & technology: A report on 10 years of ACOT research [Online report]. Retrieved 2002: www.seirtec.org/ACOTstages.html

[illegible] well in an environment where they can make choices and take personal responsibility for their learning. Creating an environment that supports this kind of learning experience requires using a variety of approaches to staff development including:

- Written professional growth plans developed by individual teachers that target two to three areas and identify activities the teacher will use to foster growth.
- Self-selected teacher study groups that meet weekly to discuss common goals for professional growth and develop a plan for reaching these goals. This action plan may include site visitations, conference attendance, online courses, and tutorials, in addition to other learning opportunities.
- Formulation of curriculum development teams in which teachers meet to create standards-based lesson plans that incorporate technology use and will actually be used with students.
- Making skilled coaches and mentors available to teachers as they plan and implement their standards-based lessons.
- Offering just-in-time support through on-site staffing of technicians, mentors, and help lines.

Coordination and funding are perhaps the most important elements of this kind of staff development approach. This type of structure can be used to foster learning environments that focus on curriculum outcomes for students in all content areas and encourage educators to look at the big picture rather than compartmentalizing their own learning into "math inservice" or "language arts inservice." However, for this structure to work there must be support in terms of time, level of responsibility, and funding at all levels, including administrators, teachers, and professional associations. It also requires school districts and county or state departments of education to be more service oriented, and to design professional growth opportunities on a case-by-case basis.

It is helpful to have a measure for teachers and administrators to use in assessing their level of technology use. Although intended to be used as an overall gauge for progress in technology integration, section II of SEIR-TEC's Technology Integration Progress Gauge (www.seirtec.org) can be used to raise educators' awareness of their personal level of engagement. The Level of Technology Implementation (LoTi) Profile (www.learning-quest.com) is another tool, used to measure a teacher's use of instructional technology in three areas: technology implementation in the classroom, personal computer use, and current instructional practices. Additional resources are the *Promising Practices in Technology: Recognizing and Supporting Teaching with Technology* video clips (2000), which include examples of teachers using technology at various skill levels. These video clips can be downloaded at www.serve.org/seir-tec/ACOTstages.html. One task for a district leadership cadre may be to develop a rubric for technology integration within the district based upon research such as the ACOT report and the district's technology implementation plan.

The need for systemic, ongoing staff development is reinforced throughout this standard. Traditional delivery methods and schedules no longer work in today's educational environment. It is time to use alternative approaches designed to give educators more control of and responsibility for their own professional growth, to establish a more collegial learning environment for themselves, and to take advantage of technologies that can assist them in this process. This requires restructuring the system to permit formation of study groups, access to online content and groups, bringing long-term consultants on-site, and other innovative approaches. It also requires setting aside adequate funding (see Chapter 4) for professional growth activities and working with employee associations to renegotiate staff development programs.

improved learning and teaching with technology.

Use this section as a guide when reviewing your current staff development program and exploring ways to redefine professional growth to meet the current needs of educators.

What Is Already in Place?

Assess existing professional development opportunities.

All educational leaders need to:

- Review site and district documents that reflect current staff development policies and programs.
- Review site and district budgets to assess the current funding available to staff development programs.
- Review employee association contracts for language related to professional growth, objectives, meeting times, and staff development programs.
- Review staff objectives as they currently pertain to professional growth.
- Review evaluations of current staff development programs.

Campus Leaders' Additional Responsibilities:	District Leaders' Additional Responsibilities:	Superintendents' and Cabinet Leaders' Additional Responsibilities:
• Use classroom visits and observations to gauge the current implementation of techniques learned in staff development programs. • Consult site staff members about current staff development programs to identify strengths and weaknesses.	• Gather site data from campus leaders about staff development programs. • Gather input from district staff about staff development programs.	• Review existing board policies or regulations that address staff development. • Obtain feedback from campus and district leaders regarding existing staff development issues and concerns. • Determine how each division can provide support to schools and to individual district departments based upon this feedback. • Determine whether existing policies and procedures promote effective, timely professional growth opportunities.

What Practices Demonstrate Successful Implementation of This Performance Indicator?

Ensure that all staff members have access to professional development opportunities that both support them at their current level of use and encourage them to expand their knowledge and use to integrate appropriate technologies throughout the curriculum.

All educational leaders need to:

- Establish a professional development program that permits educators to define areas of growth that reflect school and district goals and to work in a collaborative environment to achieve these goals.
- Allocate adequate site and district funds to support ongoing, individualized professional growth opportunities (see Chapter 4).
- Align staff objectives to a professional growth plan.
- Monitor and evaluate professional growth on an ongoing basis, making adjustments as required.

Campus Leaders' Additional Responsibilities:	District Leaders' Additional Responsibilities:	Superintendents' and Cabinet Leaders' Additional Responsibilities:
• Meet with individuals and groups of staff to discuss professional growth plans that reflect individual needs and are aligned with school academic goals. • Assist staff members in implementation of their professional growth plans by restructuring meeting times and offering information about providers, models, sites to visit, conferences, and online opportunities.	• Develop and present to both campus and cabinet leaders recommendations for policies for staff development programs. • Maintain a database of resources for professional growth for sites and the district office. Include providers, models, sites to visit, conferences, online opportunities, and funding sources. • Consider the effect your recommendations will have on sites in terms of cost, training, and ongoing work required. • Communicate with site leaders prior to making final recommendations.	• Meet with campus and district leaders to discuss professional growth plans that reflect individual needs and are aligned with school and district academic goals. • Work with employee associations on contract language that permits a restructured professional growth model. • Inform school board members about progress made in implementation of a restructured professional growth program.

All educational leaders need to:

- Research professional development models that permit educators to define areas of growth that reflect school and district goals and to work in a collaborative environment to achieve these goals.
- Research the true cost of staff development to allocate adequate site and district funds to support ongoing, individualized professional growth opportunities.
- Ensure that all site and district employees are provided equal access to professional development support in terms of time and funding.
- Explore models for alignment of staff objectives with professional growth plans.
- Plan for ongoing monitoring and program evaluation.

Campus Leaders' Additional Responsibilities:	District Leaders' Additional Responsibilities:	Superintendents' and Cabinet Leaders' Additional Responsibilities:
• Include staff members in discussions about alternative forms of professional growth and share their input with district and cabinet leaders. • Share with the staff budget information regarding staff development cost.	• Assist campus leaders in offering information to staff regarding alternative forms of professional growth. • Provide information to district staff, including cabinet leaders, regarding alternative forms of professional growth. • Develop a database of resources for professional growth for sites and the district office. Include providers, models, sites to visit, conferences, online opportunities, and funding sources.	• Participate in informational meetings concerning equal access to technology. • Make restructured professional growth programs a goal in the district master plan. • Begin discussions with employee associations and other leaders about restructured professional growth. • Work to educate school board members on issues related to alternative forms of professional growth for all district and school staff.

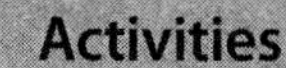

Activities

Performance Indicator II.E. Educational leaders provide for and ensure that faculty and staff take advantage of quality professional learning opportunities for improved learning and teaching with technology.

Activity 7 • Teacher Technology Use

Review Tables 2.1 and 2.2 on page 73 (CBAM Stages of Concern for Change and Levels of Use for Change) and Table 2.3 on page 104 (ACOT Stages of Educator Learning). Then answer the activity questions. You may also access this information online at:

- The Concerns-Based Adoption Model (CBAM), A Model for Change in Individuals: www.nas.edu/rise/backg4a.htm
- Promising Practices in Technology:www.seirtec.org/ACOTstages.html

Activity 8 • Technology Skills Self-Assessment for Teachers

In planning professional development programs that will help teachers integrate technology more readily into their instruction, it's important to have an accurate profile of their current skill levels. Certain funding sources require teaching staff to complete a self-assessment of their technological skill levels regularly. If this is the case in your school or district, print a copy of that profile. Review the results and use this information for this activity.

In districts where skills profiles are not regularly compiled, leaders can use the Internet to access self-assessment tools for teachers to evaluate their own proficiency levels. To complete this activity, review three of those tools, choose one that is most appropriate for your school or district, and then complete the assessment using the tool you've selected. You may also decide to explore additional tools on your own and select one of those.

Next Steps: When you've completed Activities 7 and 8, use the Action Plan at the end of the chapter to identify steps that need to be taken next to ensure that faculty and staff take advantage of quality professional learning opportunities for improved learning and teaching with technology.

1. Based on the information provided in those tables, what levels of technology use do you currently see in classrooms? Give specific examples.

2. Think about the technology-related professional development that has been offered to your teaching staff. Which of the ACOT Stages of Educator Learning have been targeted during those training opportunities?

3. What kinds of professional development opportunities could be offered to help teaching staff move further along the ACOT continuum?

Activity 8 • Technology Skills Self-Assessment for Teachers

Directions: Review the three online tools below and then answer the following questions.

- Teachers and Technology: A Snap-Shot Survey: www.tcet.unt.edu/research/online/snapshot.htm
- SEIR-TEC's Faculty and Staff Survey: www.seirtec.org/P2P.html, Chapter 7, p.198
- ProfilerPro Survey Library: www.profilerpro.com

1. After your review, decide which tool is most appropriate for your school or district. Explain your reasoning.
2. Ask the teaching staff to complete the tool you selected. Review the results. Remember, if your staff is already required to complete a survey of this type, you don't need to reassess; instead, use the results of that survey for the next step.
3. Write a summary of the survey results. How do they match up with your own answers to the questions in Activity 7? Did any results surprise you? Why?

Directions: Use the Action Plan to identify the actions that need to be taken to implement Standard II in the school or district.

Performance Indicator(s)	Next Steps	Person(s) Responsible	I Will Know This Step Has Been Achieved When ...	Timeline
II.A. Educational leaders identify, use, evaluate, and promote appropriate technologies to enhance and support instruction and standards-based curriculum leading to high levels of student achievement.				
II.B. Educational leaders facilitate and support collaborative technology-enriched learning environments conducive to innovation for improved learning.				
II.C. Educational leaders provide for learner-centered environments that use technology to meet the individual and diverse needs of learners.				
II.D. Educational leaders facilitate the use of technologies to support and enhance instructional methods that develop higher-level thinking, decision-making, and problem-solving skills.				
II.E. Educational leaders provide for and ensure that faculty and staff take advantage of quality professional learning opportunities for improved learning and teaching with technology.				

Conclusion

Simply reading about the scope of work necessary to successfully implement technology integration may be exhausting! However, if you remember that this is a long-term process that requires several years for full implementation, you may begin to plan accordingly. First, use your school or district academic plan and timeline for implementation as a guide. This plan should include references to learning environments and instructional strategies. Second, focus on working with staff members to raise their level of awareness and embark on professional growth plans that will facilitate implementation. Then begin to bring in technologies to support teacher growth, which will, in turn, promote student academic growth. It will take time, but it will be time well spent.

Resources

Projects/Internet Sites

International Review of Research in Open and Distance Learning. A refereed e-journal. [Online journal]. Available: www.irrodl.org/index.php/irrodl

Level of Technology Implementation (LoTi), Technology Use Profiles. Available: www.learning-quest.com/

North American Council for Online Learning (NACOL). This site offers online forums and resources related to online learning. Available: www.nacol.org

Regional Education Laboratories. Links to various resources that provide information about technology and learning. Available: http://ies.ed.gov/ncee/edlabs/

SouthEast Initiatives Regional Technology in Education Consortium. This site offers comprehensive information in various areas of instructional technology. Available: www.seirtec.org

Star Schools Program. These programs support improved instruction in mathematics, science, and foreign languages as well as increased literacy skills and vocational education. Using distance learning, high-need and at-risk students are targeted. Available: www.ed.gov/about/contacts/gen/othersites/star.html

Electronic Newsletters and Blogs

ASCD SmartBrief: www.ASCD.org

eSchool News: www.eschoolnews.com

TechLearning blogs: http://techlearning.com

This Week in Education: www.thisweekineducation.com

Tools

Learning with Technology Profile Tool: www.ncrtec.org/capacity/profile/profile.htm

STaR chart: www.iste.org/inhouse/starchart/

SouthEast Initiatives Regional Technology in Education Consortium. Various tools for observation and evaluation. Available: www.seirtec.org/eval.html

Technology Integration Process Gauge: www.seirtec.org/publications/ProgressGauge2000.pdf

Reports

Apple. (1995). *Changing the conversation about teaching, learning & technology: A report on 10 years of ACOT research* [Online report]. Original data: Retrieved 2002: www.apple.com/education/k12/leadership/acot/library.html Available: www.seirtec.org/ACOTstages.html

Culp, K. M., Honey, M., & Mandinach, E. (2003). *A retrospective on twenty years of education technology policy* [Online report]. U.S. Department of Education. Retrieved 2002: www.ed.gov/about/offices/list/os/technology/plan/2004/site/bb/edlite-Retrospective.htm

Partnership for 21st Century Skills. (2003) *Learning for the 21st century* [Online report]. Available: www.21stcenturyskills.org/downloads/P21_Report.pdf

Ringstaff, C., Kelley, L. (2002). *The learning return on our educational technology investment* [Online report]. WestEd. Available: www.wested.org/online_pubs/learning_return.pdf

State Educational Technology Directors Association (2007). *2007 National trends report* [Online report]. Available: www.setda.org/web/guest/2007NationalTrendsReport

SouthEast Initiatives Regional Technology in Education Consortium. (2001). *Lessons learned: Factors influencing the effective use of technology for teaching and learning* (2nd ed.) [Online report]. Available: www.seirtec.org/publications.html

Articles

Athena Curriculum. (1996). *What is student-centered learning?* [Online article]. Lake Washington School District. Retrieved 2002: http://vathena.arc.nasa.gov/curric/weather/adptcty/stcntr.html

Costa, A. (2001). *Components of a well developed thinking skills program* [Online article]. New Horizons for Learning. Available: www.newhorizons.org/strategies/thinking/costa2.htm

Cotton, K. (1991). Teaching thinking skills. *School Improvement Research Series* [Online research series]. Available: www.nwrel.org/scpd/sirs/6/cu11.html

Hord S., Rutherford W., Huling-Austin L., & Hall G. (n.d.) *Taking charge of change.* Southwest Educational Development Laboratory.

Horsley, D. L., & Loucks-Horsley, S. (1998) CBAM brings order to the tornado of change. *Journal of Staff Development 19*(4) 17–20 [Online journal]. Available: http://74.125.47.132/search?q=cache:t18Szn6CwlwJ:edweb.fdu.edu/faculty/GlickmanE/8704_SummerA_05/CBAM%2520%2520change.pdf+Loucks-Horsley,+CBAM&hl=en&ct=clnk&cd=3&gl=us&client=safari

Kleiman, G. M. (2004). *Myths and realities about technology in K–12 schools: Five years later.* [Online article]. Available: www.citejournal.org/articles/v4i2seminal2.pdf

Loucks-Horsley, S. (1996). The concerns-based adoption model (CBAM): A model for change in individuals. *National Standards & the Science Curriculum* [Online article]. Available: www.nas.edu/rise/backg4a.htm

McKenzie, J. (2003, Summer). *Stories of adult learning* [Online article]. Available: http://fno.org/sum03/adult.html

McKenzie, J. (2001). *How teachers learn technology best.* FNO Press. Available: http://fnopress.com/howlearn.html#Anchor

McKenzie, J. (2004, January). *How teachers learn* [Online article]. Available: http://fno.org/jan04/nsdc.html

Reese, J. (2005). Making a Difference One Student at a Time. *T.H.E. Journal,* Available: www.thejournal.com/articles/17328

Standard III

Productivity and Professional Practice

Educational leaders apply technology to enhance their professional practice and to increase their own productivity and that of others.

Performance Indicators for Educational Leaders

III.A. Model the routine, intentional, and effective use of technology.

III.B. Employ technology for communication and collaboration among colleagues, staff, parents, students, and the larger community.

III.C. Create and participate in learning communities that stimulate, nurture, and support faculty and staff in using technology for improved productivity.

III.D. Engage in sustained, job-related professional learning using technology resources.

III.E. Maintain awareness of emerging technologies and their potential uses in education.

III.F. Use technology to advance organizational improvement.

Chapter 3 Overview

The kind of change referred to in this standard requires that administrators have a general understanding of ongoing advances and new applications for technology use and model the use of technology. One easy way to stay on top of innovations in technology is through electronic newsletters and blogs. Three excellent no-cost resources for busy administrators are the *eSchool News* newsletter, published weekly and available at www.eschoolnews.com; the *ASCD SmartBrief*, published daily during the school year and available at www.ascd.org; and the *TechLearning* blogs, updated nearly every day and available at www.techlearning.com/blog/. When you subscribe to the electronic newsletters, they will automatically be e-mailed to you. When you subscribe to the blog, you will be notified of new posts through your RSS aggregator. It takes just a few minutes to scroll through the material to find articles of interest. While this won't make you an expert, it will give you a quick overview of current happenings in educational technology. Generally, the articles include additional links should you want to explore a topic in greater depth.

Another excellent resource is found at http://portical.org. This is an Internet portal designed specifically for school administrators through a California project called TICAL. By accessing this gateway, you will find articles, success stories, and a large database of Internet resources for administrators. There are many models for planning, surveys, best practices, and more.

Definitions

RSS Aggregator: A software application or web-based service that collects updated information from user-identified online sources and presents these updates in a consolidated view. Google Reader, Yahoo!, and Bloglines are popular aggregators.

Web-based application suites: Web-based versions of applications (e.g., word processing, spreadsheets, presentation) that allow users to create and share files easily. Simultaneous editing capabilities are especially useful for realtime collaboration. Examples include Google Docs, Zoho, and ThinkFree.

Luddite: Refers to a person who resists use of technology.

Online journals that target the business sector can also be valuable resources for school administrators. For example, articles found in *Wired* (www.wired.com) and *Entrepreneur* (www.entrepreneur.com) often address technology issues that impact educators.

Standard III addresses how educational administrators use technology to make positive changes in productivity for themselves and others. This chapter examines five areas: personal productivity; awareness of potential uses for emerging technologies in education; communication and collaboration; job-related professional development; and organizational improvement. Because modeling personal productivity and keeping up-to-date on recent technological developments are so closely related, two Performance Indicators, III.A. and III.E., are discussed in one narrative and displayed on one chart.

III.A. Educational leaders model the routine, intentional, and effective use of technology.

III.E. Educational leaders maintain awareness of emerging technologies and their potential uses in education.

Whether or not it's an accurate perception, school administrators are often regarded as Luddites when it comes to personal use of technology. However, a quick look around your office will reveal that you use a variety of technologies in your daily work: the telephone, a calculator, the copy machine, the fax, a computer system, or a two-way radio. You may also use a personal digital assistant (PDA), a cell phone, a microcassette recorder, or an MP3 player. For many administrators the question isn't whether they use technology, it's whether they use technology in a way that supports their work.

Choose Technologies Wisely

Technologies can become time wasters if not handled well, and some administrators abandon technology due to frustration or because they do not feel they can take the time to learn how personal technology use can help them function more effectively. This is one reason regular research about new products is valuable. When you are able to use electronic newsletters, blogs, and other resources to keep your technological knowledge up to date, you will be prepared to make better decisions about appropriate technologies for the office and classroom. Also keep in mind that the learning curve to implement new technology is not wasted time when the payoff is an improved working environment for yourself and your staff. Although there are still just 24 hours in each day, the demands on administrators' time and attention continue to increase, and most need assistance in learning how to handle additional expectations in different ways. What are some of the typical technologies administrators have at their disposal, and what are common uses and pitfalls?

The Paperwork Load

How many times do you get up daily to carry something out to your secretary? Using a web-based word processing or spreadsheet application such as Google Docs (http://docs.google.com) or Zoho (www.zoho.com) can save you many steps and streamline work. Unfortunately, many administrators fall into the bad habit of doing their own secretarial work when a computer is placed in the office. It seems easier to draft and edit that bulletin, letter, or memo than to rough it out and turn it over to a secretary to clean up and print. Try this instead. Sign up for a free account with one of the web-based application services mentioned above. Create a rough draft of the document and share it with your secretary by making her or him a collaborator. She or he will be notified about the document by means of e-mail and can access and edit the file. When it's time for a final review by you, she or he can send an e-mail notification from the document. Don't like some of the changes, or catch a mistake? Make a few revisions and send her or him an e-mail notification that the document has been revised and printed.

Another approach is to work with your secretary to set up templates for commonly used documents, which can also be stored online as master files using a web-based applications service. During your daily or weekly meetings with the secretary, give her or him changes for next week's bulletin or a memo that needs to go out. She or he can use the online template to draft a copy and share the document so you can review it prior to its being sent out. Still dealing with paper forms that are not available in digital format? Use a scanner to digitize forms that need to be completed regularly so the work can be done online. Another benefit is that once the form is completed, one needs only to go back and make the necessary updates the next time.

Keeping budgets, calendars, and student information electronically also saves time and improves your ability to work with information and communicate more effectively. When your secretary has access to this kind of data from her desk, she or he can often answer questions that would otherwise result in an interruption for you. It also is helpful to have up-to-date budget reports when planning, writing requisitions, and verifying expenditures; to have access to a school or districtwide calendar when scheduling events; and to be able to review a student's profile and history while meeting with a parent, the student, or another staff member.

Mobile Technology

Going back to effective school research published nearly 20 years ago, researchers regularly find that principal visibility and accessibility are key behaviors of leaders in successful schools. Mobile technologies make it easy for administrators to maintain high visibility and still be readily accessible to staff. Over the last five years it's become increasingly common for districts to issue notebook or tablet computers, PDAs, cell phones, and other portable technologies to members of the administrative team. Depending upon the equipment provided, it's possible to conduct a formal classroom observation and leave a copy of the evaluation form with the teacher before leaving the class, to verify a student's schedule while on campus rounds, or to make immediate contact with a parent during a medical emergency. If your district is not encouraging administrators to use mobile technologies, this is the time to discuss adopting these tools.

Performance Indicator III.E. Educational leaders maintain awareness of emerging technologies and their potential uses in education.

This section provides a framework for addressing the first and fifth Performance Indicators for Standard III. It details the roles and responsibilities for school administrators in assessing how they currently model the selection and routine, intentional, and effective use of technology; deciding what needs to be done; and determining how to accomplish this. In addition, you may want to refer to the narrative for Performance Indicator II.A. in Chapter 2, which discusses how to stay current on technology innovations in the classroom.

What Is Already in Place?

Assess personal technology use and how you model it for staff and students.

All educational leaders need to:

- Identify the technologies they regularly use to support their work and discuss examples.
- Regularly self-assess their technology skills to determine their effectiveness.
- Articulate ways they model technology use and provide examples.

Campus Leaders' Additional Responsibilities:	District Leaders' Additional Responsibilities:	Superintendents' and Cabinet Leaders' Additional Responsibilities:
• Ensure that teachers, students, and parents are able to identify ways that campus leaders use technology in their work.	• Ensure that campus and cabinet leaders are able to identify ways district leaders use technology in their work.	• Ensure that district and campus leaders are able to identify and cite examples of how the superintendent and cabinet leaders use technology in their work.

What Practices Demonstrate Successful Implementation of This Performance Indicator?

Model personal, routine use of technology.

All educational leaders need to:

- Access and use "infomation" tools, including student profile data, word processing, and spreadsheets. (For more information, see the Technology as a Tool for Organizational Improvement section in this chapter.)
- Identify those technologies most helpful in their daily work.
- Share information about technology with staff through articles, during discussions, and in staff development meetings.
- Make appropriate use of technology on a daily basis.

What Steps Lead to Successful Implementation of This Performance Indicator?

Choose one technology that could improve your work and publicly learn how to use it.

All educational leaders need to:

- Recognize that effective technology use requires ongoing education.
- Regularly choose an area of technology use for personal skill improvement.
- Seek out fellow educators who have similar interests and work collaboratively to improve skills.
- Willingly approach local experts for advice and assistance in improving skills.
- Self-evaluate your progress to determine whether new skills are benefiting you in your work.

Campus Leaders' Additional Responsibilities:	District Leaders' Additional Responsibilities:	Superintendents' and Cabinet Leaders' Additional Responsibilities:
• Encourage knowledgeable staff members to share information and ideas. • Share what you are learning with interested staff and fellow campus leaders.	• Provide support to one another and campus leaders by helping to find and organize training.	• Communicate your goals to campus and district leaders as well as your staff. • Offer incentives for campus and district leaders to improve their technology skills.

Performance Indicator III.E. Educational leaders maintain awareness of emerging technologies and their potential uses in education.

Activity 1 • Personal Technology Use

Because of the close relationship between staying current on emerging technologies and modeling their use, Performance Indicators III.A. and III.E. are paired.

Use Activity 1 to reflect on your own technology use in the workplace and the methods you use to maintain awareness of emerging technologies and their potential for use in education.

Next Steps: Use the Action Plan at the end of this chapter to identify the steps that need to be taken next in order for you to model your own use of technology in the workplace and to stay informed about emerging technologies.

Activity 1 • Personal Technology Use

Directions: Use the table below to reflect on your own technology use in the workplace.

Frequency of Use					
Which of the following technologies are available to you, and how often do you use them? This list includes technologies commonly found in school offices, but you may need to add additional items in the area marked "other."					
Technologies	**Not Available**	**Never Use**	**Sometimes Use**	**Frequently Use**	**Use Daily**
Desktop computer					
Laptop or tablet computer					
Internet and/or intranet connectivity					
Handheld computer or PDA					
Automated messaging system					
Cell phone					
Two-way radio					
Fax					
Videoconferencing equipment					
Other (list and rate):					
Of the technologies you use frequently, which are most helpful in your job? Why?					
Of the technologies you use frequently, which (if any) seem to be more trouble than they're worth in terms of productivity? Why?					

Continued

Which of the following technology applications are available to you, and how proficient are you in using them? This list includes applications that are commonly used in school offices, but you may need to add additional items in the area marked "other."

1 = I do not use this application.

2 = I can use this application with assistance.

3 = I can use this application on my own.

4 = I can teach others how to use this application.

Technology Applications	Not Available	1	2	3	4
Word processor					
Spreadsheet					
Database					
Presentation software					
Calendar					
E-mail					
E-mail lists					
Instant messaging (IM)					
Internet search engines					
School web pages					
Voice mail					
Student information system					
Other					

Of the applications you use, which are most helpful in your job? Why?

Of the applications you use, which (if any) seem to be more trouble than they're worth in terms of productivity? Why?

How do you currently model technology use in your workplace? Provide examples.

Continued

Activity 1 • Personal Technology Use

Continued

Emerging Technologies
What strategies do you currently use to stay abreast of emerging technologies and their potential uses in education?
Many professional organizations and publications offer free e-newsletters that include information about emerging technologies and education. For example: *ASCD SmartBrief:* www.smartbrief.com/ascd *eSchool News*: www.eschoolnews.com *Technology & Learning*: www.techlearning.com *The Doyle Report*: www.thedoylereport.com Visit these websites or search the Internet for other e-newsletters of interest to you. Subscribe to the e-newsletter that most interests you. After receiving and reviewing several issues, take a few moments to reflect on whether this electronic publication is helpful to you and why or why not.

Educational leaders employ technology for communication and collaboration among colleagues, staff, parents, students, and the larger community.

Communication and being available are good practices. Being bombarded by memos, faxes, e-mail, and telephone calls are not good practices. Think about the people with whom you need to communicate and the format that best supports that type of communication. As much as possible, choose one format for each group. For example, most communication between schools and the district office can take place through e-mail or a blog. If your site or office has a local area network, you may also be able to use an online group or blog for bulletins, reminders, distribution of meeting agendas or minutes, even individual messages. Let people know that you will pass along information using one consistent format as much as humanly possible, and then do it. Also let them know that you will not be sending more than one reminder about anything.

Do not double up on communication methods: If you have sent an e-mail, don't send a fax about the same thing or follow up with a telephone call. When you send too much information too often, people tend to become overwhelmed or to tune you out completely. They also learn to pay attention to your communiqués and respond in a timely way when they know you won't be sending multiple messages about every issue.

E-mail can become a trap if you end up checking it hourly, or worse yet, have your computer set up to make a sound every time you receive a new message. Check your e-mail no more than three times daily. Have one account for district e-mail and a different account for personal use. This will help you avoid the temptation of answering personal e-mails at the office or answering business e-mails from home. Try to keep your business e-mail box clutter-free by coping with e-mails as read. You need to decide whether the message can be deleted, should be printed or saved, or requires an immediate response. Follow the same one-time-only rule for e-mail that many administrators use for regular mail.

Most people realize that a hard line telephone can be a time waster and work with their secretaries, giving them the authority to screen and handle many calls. Often, however, the same administrators will fail to use the cell phone judiciously. Cell phones can be helpful because they enable office personnel to contact you in the event of an emergency when you are not in the office. This is fine, but thought needs to go into your use of the cell phone. Let staff know that you will set the phone on vibrate rather than ring so that incoming calls don't disturb meetings or classroom visits—voice mail can pick up messages for later response. Answering or making telephone calls when your focus should be directed elsewhere is a clear statement to the people you're with that you have more important things to do.

Text messaging may be the best way for staff to relay an urgent message, because a written message can be read and responded to fairly unobtrusively. But people define "urgent" differently—take the time to establish clear criteria for critical messages. Otherwise, text messages will quickly grow out of hand.

I've also noticed a suggestion in several time management books and articles that driving time is a great opportunity to catch up on phone calls and dictation. This is absolutely not true! It is downright dangerous to be distracted while driving, and you need some time to take your mind off the job and concentrate on getting yourself safely from one place to another. In fact, driver cell phone use is now illegal in some areas. Finally, unless you are at the top of the chain of command and must take work telephone calls at home, turn off your cell phone and spend a relaxing evening with your family, read a good book, or watch a movie to renew yourself for the next day.

Roles and Responsibilities

Performance Indicator III.B. Educational leaders employ technology for communication and collaboration among colleagues, staff, parents, students, and the larger community.

This section provides strategies for addressing this Performance Indicator for Standard III. It details the roles and responsibilities for school administrators in assessing how technology is currently employed for communication and collaboration among peers, staff, parents, and the larger community; deciding what needs to be done ; and determining how to accomplish this. In addition to providing items for which all administrators are responsible, this section offers a further breakdown for campus leaders, district leaders, and superintendents and cabinet leaders.

What Is Already in Place?

Assess existing forms of technology-based communication on site, within the district, and in the community.

All educational leaders need to:

- Recognize that there are various forms of technology-based communication systems.
- Understand that community demographics may dictate alternative forms of communication to reach all parents and community members.
- Be familiar with existing forms of technology-based communication on site, in the district, and within the community, and understand the various functions of each form.
- Effectively use various forms of technology-based communication.

technology-based communication. • Use communication methods that reflect community access and needs. • Know the proportion of families who have Internet access and telephones in their homes. • Know the kinds of Internet access available in the community. • Be aware of current Digital Divide issues as they relate to the school site.	methods that reflect community access and needs. • Be available to staff and community members.	board policies and regulations regarding various forms of technology-based communication. • Be familiar with policies regarding use of the Internet for students and employees. • Be available to staff and community members.

What Practices Demonstrate Successful Implementation of This Performance Indicator?

Use technology-based communication as a tool.

All educational leaders need to:

- Assess the effectiveness of current technology-based communication to determine strengths and weaknesses.
- Determine whether changes need to be made in the current system.
- Research various communication tools to determine their usefulness.
- Model effective personal use of technology-based communication.

Campus Leaders' Additional Responsibilities:	District Leaders' Additional Responsibilities:	Superintendents' and Cabinet Leaders' Additional Responsibilities:
• Establish clear lines of communication with staff and families and have shared expectations about staff and family communication. • Include methods of communication with families and community members in the school plan and school handbook. • Establish incentives for staff to use technology-based communication.	• Develop clear lines of communication among the district office, schools, and the community. • Publish and distribute information about various communication formats.	• Ensure that employees, students, and parents are aware of communication policies and that they are enforced.

What Steps Lead to Successful Implementation of This Performance Indicator?

Work with staff and the community to determine one way technology-based tools can be used to enhance communication.

All educational leaders need to:

- Use a shared decision-making model when making decisions affecting the school, the district, and the community.

Campus Leaders' Additional Responsibilities:	District Leaders' Additional Responsibilities:	Superintendents' and Cabinet Leaders' Additional Responsibilities:
• Work with staff and parents to establish communication needs and buy-in for use. • Develop an action plan and timeline for implementation. • Design a plan for evaluation of the implementation.	• Coordinate with campus and cabinet leaders to develop helpful communication methods that leaders agree to use and promote. • Obtain and respond to regular feedback about technology-based communication. • Support campus leaders in providing incentives to staff.	• Revise policies and regulations if necessary. • Educate the school board and community about technology-based communication. • Develop business partnerships to assist campus leaders in addressing Digital Divide issues. • Provide incentives to campus and district leaders to use technology-based communication.

and collaboration among colleagues, staff, parents, students, and the larger community.

Activity 2 • Communication Strategies

The ease with which a person can communicate using technology is a mixed blessing. Ready access to e-mail and cell phones often carries the implication that an administrator should be available 24 hours a day, 7 days a week. Overuse of these communication tools leads to information overload. On the other hand, when e-mail lists, fax machines, school websites, and automated messaging systems are underutilized, it creates frustration among stakeholders who expect to have access to current information.

Use the Activity 2 questions to examine your school's or district's current use of electronic communication and determine whether the strategies in place are effective.

Next Steps: Use the Action Plan at the end of this chapter to identify the steps that need to be taken next to improve communication among members of your school community.

Activity 2 • Communication Strategies

Directions: Use the following questions to examine your school's or district's current use of electronic communication and determine whether the strategies in place are effective.

1. What kinds of electronic communication are in use?
2. Which of these types of communication are underutilized? Explain.
3. Which of these types of communication are overutilized? Explain.
4. Do these forms of electronic communication accurately reflect community access and needs?
5. Which of these types of communication are most popular with your school community?
6. If you could focus your time and energy on improving your use of just one type of electronic communication, what would you choose? Why?

Educational leaders create and participate in learning communities that stimulate, nurture, and support faculty and staff in using technology for improved productivity.

Performance Indicator III.C. sums up what you hope to accomplish by implementing the first three performance indicators discussed for this standard (A, B, and E). Technology offers great potential for helping you to become more organized and to make better use of the information at your disposal. At the same time, you need to guard against creating an environment where faculty, staff, and leaders feel pressured to intensify or extend their workday simply because access to a computer, cell phone, or other device makes them more accessible.

If you're feeling overworked, chances are, you're right! Americans work more hours weekly than citizens of any other industrialized nation (Rosnick & Weisbrot, 2006). A survey conducted by Central Marketing, Inc., showed that 34% of the respondents have no down time at work during the day, and 32% work through lunch on a regular basis (HRM Guide Network, 2002). Improved productivity must not be equated with increased workload. An educator who is simply doing more is not necessarily an educator who is doing a better job. Responsible educational leaders do not want to promote an environment in which employees are overworked.

How then, do you create a learning community that supports faculty and staff in using technology for improved productivity? Alan November (1998), internationally recognized leader in the field of instructional technology, admonishes educators that the goal of productive technology use is to make better use of the information you have, not simply to do more of the same thing faster. Think about the ways increasingly sophisticated technologies have increased demands on your time because you have not learned how to manage them well.

Set realistic expectations for yourself and your staff. As you explore ways to improve organizational efficiency, take time to define your needs and establish a rationale for each of them. Collaborate with those people who will be directly affected to find solutions that will improve rather than intensify your work environment. You need to model the effective use of technology. Traveling between meetings with a cell phone clamped to your ear or answering business e-mail at midnight are not appropriate models! Using a laptop or handheld computer for note taking at a meeting or distributing staff meeting agendas online are good models.

Remember that everyone who works with information solutions needs access to sustained professional development opportunities to master technology resources. Collaborate with staff and faculty to create an environment where this kind of staff development can be successfully implemented. And finally, use technology to communicate, but don't allow it to become the tool for an information blitz.

Roles and Responsibilities

Performance Indicator III.C. Educational leaders create and participate in learning communities that stimulate, nurture, and support faculty and staff in using technology for improved productivity.

Use this section as a resource for strategies to employ as you evaluate the current learning community, identify what you want it to be, and then plan the steps to make it a reality.

What Is Already in Place?

Review current practice in your district for supporting staff and faculty as they learn to use technology.

All educational leaders need to:

- Examine current expectations for faculty and staff technology use to improve productivity.
- Identify ways leaders currently model the appropriate use of technology in their work.
- Identify existing professional development opportunities for faculty and staff.
- Identify the current use of technology-based communication.
- Describe how these expectations, models, and professional development opportunities were adopted.
- Identify potential obstacles to change.

What Practices Demonstrate Successful Implementation of This Performance Indicator?

Take steps to implement a district-wide support system for staff and faculty as they learn to use technology.

All educational leaders need to:

- Support the district-wide learning community by becoming an active participant.
- Facilitate staff and faculty participation in this learning community through release time or other incentives.
- Model positive technology use.
- Continue to have realistic expectations for yourself and others.
- Deal immediately with obstacles and issues that arise.

All educational leaders need to:

- Use a shared decision-making model when making decisions affecting the school, district, and community.
- Evaluate current expectations that are positive and need to be retained.
- Evaluate current expectations that are negative and need to be changed.
- Evaluate current leadership models of appropriate use of technology for work tasks, retaining those that are positive and changing those that are negative.
- Ensure that professional development opportunities for faculty and staff are designed to contribute positively to the district learning community.
- Evaluate current use of technology-based communication, retaining those methods that work well and changing or abandoning those that do not.
- Devise a plan to address potential obstacles to change.

Performance Indicator III.C. Educational leaders create and participate in learning communities that stimulate, nurture, and support faculty and staff in using technology for improved productivity.

Activity 3 • Supportive Learning Communities

Performance Indicator III.C. sums up what you hope to accomplish by implementing Performance Indicators III.A., III.B., and III.E. If you haven't already completed Activities 1 and 2, it would be useful to work through those exercises before tackling this activity.

Improved productivity must not be equated with increased workload. Use the guiding questions in Activity 3 to reflect on your understanding of how technology is currently used to improve faculty and staff productivity.

Next Steps: Use the Action Plan at the end of this chapter to identify the steps that need to be taken next to create or sustain learning communities where faculty and staff are encouraged and supported in their use of technology for improved productivity.

1. In general, how is technology used in your workplace to improve productivity?
2. What process is used to select technologies designed to improve productivity?
3. How is technology used in your workplace to collect data such as attendance, test scores, grades, expenses, and so on?
4. How is technology used in your workplace to analyze the data collected?
5. How is technology used to support communication and collaboration among members of the school community?
6. How do you model appropriate use of technologies that improve productivity?
7. Which of the uses described above work well and need to be retained?
8. Which of the uses described above do not work well and need to be modified or stopped?
9. What challenges do you face in providing a learning community where faculty and staff use technology for improved productivity?

Using Technology to Enhance Professional Practice: A Resource and a Delivery System

Performance Indicator III.D.

Educational leaders engage in sustained, job-related professional learning using technology resources.

In his article *Secrets of Success: Professional Development That Works,* Jamie McKenzie (1998) writes about the importance of giving teachers something worthwhile to accomplish in staff development: "When you engage teachers in the search for answers to essential questions, they acknowledge the power of information." Knowledge Loom's Spotlight on Professional Development, based upon the National Staff Development Council's Standards for Staff Development (revised 2001), and other subsequent writings support McKenzie's position. Provide staff development that offers participants opportunities to explore issues surrounding the effectiveness of technology as both an instructional and productivity tool and gives models for successful implementation. Information about these topics can be found at Internet sites, including the U.S. Department of Education (www.ed.gov/Technology), the North Central Regional Educational Laboratory (NCREL, www.ncrel.org/sdrs/areas/issues/methods/technlgy/te1000.htm), and the George Lucas Educational Foundation (www.edutopia.org/instructional-modules).

Experts recommend 15–60 hours of staff development annually to assist educators in effective technology use. Most school districts are not able to schedule this kind of time. Explore alternative forms of content delivery, including online courses, self-paced content on video or CD, or teleconferencing. Technology is not just an effective tool for students; adults can benefit from using it as a learning tool as well.

This section provides a framework for addressing the fourth Performance Indicator for Standard III. It details the roles and responsibilities for school administrators in assessing how technology is currently used to engage in sustained, job-related professional development, deciding what needs to be done, and determining how to accomplish this. In addition to providing responsibilities for all administrators, this section offers a further breakdown for campus leaders, district leaders, and superintendents and cabinet leaders.

What Is Already in Place?

Assess current staff development plans to see where technology has been incorporated as a resource or delivery system.

All educational leaders need to:

- Review feedback regularly about staff development, both positive comments and concerns.
- Recognize that in addition to technology training, various technologies should be used to support staff development in other areas.
- Determine whether technology is currently in use on site or within the district for sustained, job-related professional development.
- Learn about various technology delivery methods for staff development.

Campus Leaders' Additional Responsibilities:	District Leaders' Additional Responsibilities:	Superintendents' and Cabinet Leaders' Additional Responsibilities:
• Explore ways technology resources could be used for on-site inservice and in meetings for staff, parents, and community members. • Identify existing resources on campus.	• Gather input from campus and cabinet leaders about current delivery of district staff development programs and suggestions for their improvement or enhancement. • Identify existing resources within the district and through county or regional offices of education.	• Review current staff development policies to determine whether they meet current needs for the district. • Discuss policies with campus and district leaders to gain their perspectives. • Identify issues that may be contract items that would require negotiation.

What Practices Demonstrate Successful Implementation of This Performance Indicator?

Identify areas where technology can be incorporated as a resource or delivery system.

All educational leaders need to:

- Research alternative delivery methods for staff development, including online courses, self-paced video or CD-based classes, and teleconferences.
- Become familiar with service providers, including consultants, county or regional offices of education, and commercial staff development firms.
- Learn about the content of these courses or trainings.
- Match existing services to existing needs.

Campus Leaders' Additional Responsibilities:	District Leaders' Additional Responsibilities:	Superintendents' and Cabinet Leaders' Additional Responsibilities:
• Determine which technology resources would be cost effective for an individual site. • Explore partnerships with other sites or the district for funding and support. • Determine space and time requirements.	• Act as liaisons for campus leaders and staff development providers. • Make recommendations to the superintendent and cabinet based upon the needs of schools and departments and the availability of providers.	• Provide the services of a grant writer or fund-raiser to help meet the costs of staff development. • Make budget allocations for cost and support. • Work with professional associations to redefine staff development if necessary.

All educational leaders need to:

- Assess staff needs to determine the most useful delivery systems for staff development.
- Insist on staff development at all levels for all employees.
- Develop an action plan and timeline for implementation.
- Provide for regular evaluation and monitoring of implementation.
- Participate in trainings.

Campus Leaders' Additional Responsibilities:	District Leaders' Additional Responsibilities:	Superintendents' and Cabinet Leaders' Additional Responsibilities:
• Ensure that staff development offerings support the school plan and identified staff needs. • Communicate the benefits of a redesigned program to staff.	• Assist in coordinating and scheduling trainings. • Meet regularly with campus leaders to collect feedback and to monitor implementation.	• Monitor the calendar to ensure that scheduling is realistic. • Educate the school board about alternative forms of staff development.

Performance Indicator III.D. Educational leaders engage in sustained, job-related professional learning using technology resources.

Activity 4 • Technology Resources to Support Professional Development

Use Activity 4 to explore the ways technology resources are used in your school or district to provide sustained, job-related professional development opportunities. It may be helpful to have for reference a copy of your school's or district's professional development plan.

Next Steps: Use the Action Plan at the end of this chapter to identify the steps that need to be taken next to ensure that technology resources are being used to support professional development.

	Circle One	
Does your school or district professional development plan provide for sustained professional learning for you and your staff, as well as the time necessary to take advantage of it?	**Yes**	**No**
Explain.		
Is use of technology resources addressed in your school or district professional development plan?	**Yes**	**No**
Explain.		
Is content-based professional development provided in an environment where you and your staff have access to technology and can use appropriate hardware and software to explore technology resources?	**Yes**	**No**
Explain.		
Is productivity-based professional development provided in an environment where you and your staff have access to technology and can use appropriate hardware and software to explore applications?	**Yes**	**No**
Explain.		
Are you and your staff encouraged to engage in professional development through online courses?	**Yes**	**No**
Explain.		
Are you and your staff provided opportunities to engage in professional development through videoconferencing?	**Yes**	**No**
Explain.		
Are you and your staff encouraged to engage in professional development in your school or district? Where are your program's strengths and weaknesses?	**Yes**	**No**
Explain.		
Summarize the current use of technological resources in professional development in your school or district. What are your program's strengths and weaknesses?		

Technology as a Tool for Organizational Improvement

Performance Indicator III.F.

Educational leaders use technology to advance organizational improvement.

In 1998, Alan November suggested that technology has not been fully integrated into the education environment because its use is viewed as an additional layer over what is already done rather than as an information and communication tool that can change the structure of the organization. All too often this continues to be the case. However, there is great potential for organizational change through the use of technology tools, and administrators need to be active players in technology integration.

November also differentiates between "automating," that is, what happens when technology is layered on the existing system, and "informating," what occurs when systemic change is achieved using information and communication. November suggests that doing the same old thing faster should not be your goal. Instead, aim for making better use of information, which may, in turn, lead to increased efficiency. (See also Shoshana Zuboff, 1988, *In the age of the smart machine.*)

Student information management systems have become widely accepted over the last few years. These systems make it easy for office staff and administrators to create master schedules, track student attendance, and maintain individual student records in areas such as grades, health, and discipline—features that enable you to work more quickly and efficiently. These systems also enable administrators to access and aggregate or disaggregate student test data, create portfolios of student work, and generate reports that ask "what if" kinds of questions as student performance and participation in school are examined. See Chapter 5, Performance Indicator V.A., for a complete discussion about using technology to gather and analyze data.

Most districts have wide area networks (WANs) that allow schools and central offices to share data, which is often extremely helpful in areas where transience is high and records are shuffled often. Use of integrated office software and web-based applications is also helpful in decreasing workload through use of word processing, spreadsheets, and similar programs. Time not spent on creating documents or manually tracking budgets is time that can be devoted to students, staff, and parents.

Although you cannot take on sole responsibility for identifying the information needed and the means by which it will be communicated, you cannot simply rely on staff members to handle these decisions for you. To bring about systemic change, you need to make sure the staff sees that you value information and the technology that enables access to it and that you are willing and able to use technology yourself.

This section provides guidelines for addressing the last Performance Indicator for Standard III. It details the roles and responsibilities for school administrators in assessing how technology is currently used to improve the organization, deciding what needs to be done, and determining how to accomplish this. In addition to providing responsibilities of all administrators, this section offers a further breakdown for campus leaders, district leaders, and superintendents and cabinet leaders.

What Is Already in Place?

Assess existing information tools in the school and district to determine where they could be enhanced or improved.

All educational leaders need to:

- Be aware of information tools currently in use at the site or in the district office.
- Meet periodically with the office staff to discuss technologies currently in place.
- Encourage staff members to identify information tools that work well and explain why.
- Encourage staff members to identify areas of concern with information tools and explain why.
- Understand that in a networked environment some decisions about information tools can be site based, but others must include all network users.
- Use a proactive approach when addressing areas of concern and be sensitive to the needs of all users.

Campus Leaders' Additional Responsibilities:	District Leaders' Additional Responsibilities:	Superintendents' and Cabinet Leaders' Additional Responsibilities:
• Meet periodically with teachers to discuss information tools that assist them in their work. • Clearly communicate concerns in a timely manner with the appropriate district offices.	• Solicit regular feedback from sites regarding information tools. • Clearly define areas where sites are asking for support. • Determine how departments can provide necessary assistance and support to school sites. • Clearly define areas where departments need support from sites and the type of support needed. • Work with cabinet leaders to find affordable solutions to information needs.	• Obtain regular feedback from campus and district leaders regarding information tools. • Determine how each division can provide support to schools and to individual district departments based upon this feedback. • Identify and clarify types of support the divisions need from sites and district departments.

What Practices Demonstrate Successful Implementation of This Performance Indicator?

Use technologies to informate basic tasks and increase efficiency in daily routines.

All educational leaders need to:

- Define target audiences for information tools and determine who should be involved in problem solving and research.
- Decide whether further action needs to be taken.
- Develop a timeline for research and problem solving.
- Based upon regular feedback on current conditions of information throughout the school and district, identify site and district issues and research possible solutions for concerns.
- Identify the appropriate people to contact other districts, the county office of education, vendors, and professional organizations to gather information.

Campus Leaders' Additional Responsibilities:	District Leaders' Additional Responsibilities:	Superintendents' and Cabinet Leaders' Additional Responsibilities:
• Determine the impact your choices may have on other network users, both on your site and others. • Determine the level of support you will need for each possible solution and from where that support will come. • Consider budget issues: Will funding come from the site or district? • Determine the ongoing costs. • Determine the levels of training required for each solution.	• Communicate with both campus and cabinet leaders about choices under consideration. • Identify support that may be necessary and make recommendations to the cabinet regarding who would be responsible for providing the support, both technical and financial. • Consider the effect your decision makes on sites in terms of cost, training, and ongoing work required. • Communicate with site leaders prior to making final recommendations.	• Ensure that campus and district leaders regularly discuss needs and constraints during decision making. • Review support needs and the ability of the district to provide this support. • Avoid making final decisions about information tools prior to communicating with campus and district leaders.

All educational leaders need to:

- Use gathered data to define one area where information would positively affect productivity and could be implemented within a reasonable time frame.
- Develop an action plan and timeline for implementation.
- Establish procedures for evaluation and modification of implementation.
- Attend training sessions.

Campus Leaders' Additional Responsibilities:	District Leaders' Additional Responsibilities:	Superintendents' and Cabinet Leaders' Additional Responsibilities:
• Establish procedures for technical support. • Release appropriate staff for training. • Make necessary provisions in the budget for technical support and staff development. • Communicate regularly with staff (and the community, if appropriate) about implementation.	• Assist campus leaders in defining procedures for technical support. • Assist in scheduling and providing staff development at mutually convenient times. • Communicate regularly with campus leaders regarding implementation.	• Support technical assistance and staff development through budget allocations.

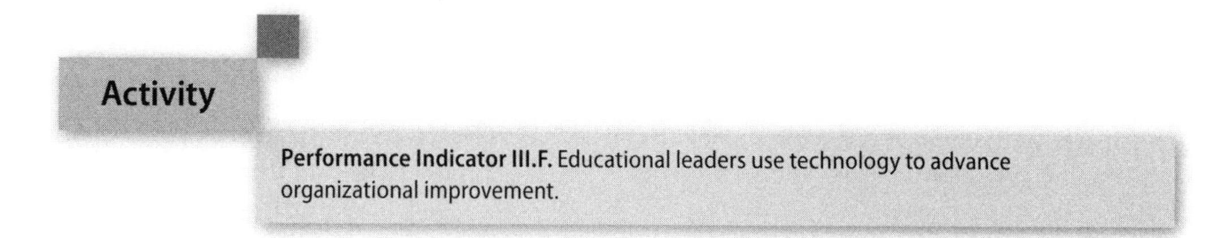

Activity 5 • Technology and Organizational Improvement

Use the questions in Activity 5 to describe how technology is currently used in your school or district to support organizational improvement.

Next Steps: Use the Action Plan at the end of this chapter to identify the steps that need to be taken next to support organizational improvement.

1. Read Section 5, "Automating vs. Informating," of Alan November's "Creating a New Culture of Teaching and Learning," accessible at http://novemberlearning.com/resources/archive-of-articles/creating-culture/. How does this concept apply to the idea of using technology as a tool for organizational improvement?

2. What technology tools are currently available to you that could be used to inform as well as to automate?

3. Are you using these tools for this purpose? Explain.

4. Are teachers and office staff using these tools to inform as well as to automate? Explain.

Action Plan

Standard III Educational leaders apply technology to enhance their professional practice and to increase their own productivity and that of others.

Directions: Use the Action Plan to identify the actions that need to be taken to implement Standard III in the school or district.

Performance Indicator(s)	Next Steps	Person(s) Responsible	I Will Know This Step Has Been Achieved When ...	Timeline
III.A. Educational leaders model the routine, intentional, and effective use of technology. **III.E.** Educational leaders maintain awareness of emerging technologies and their potential uses in education.				
III.B. Educational leaders employ technology for communication and collaboration among colleagues, staff, parents, students, and the larger community.				
III.C. Educational leaders create and participate in learning communities that stimulate, nurture, and support faculty and staff in using technology for improved productivity.				
III.D. Educational leaders engage in sustained, job-related professional learning using technology resources.				
III.F. Educational leaders use technology to advance organizational improvement.				

tion and collaboration within the educational community. The process for accomplishing this requires that leaders first be willing to examine their expectations for themselves and their staff honestly in terms of work ethic and workload. Second, leaders need to develop an accurate picture of how technology can be employed to improve both the kind of work done and the environment in which the work takes place. Finally, leaders must do all they can to support and nurture a healthy work environment.

Resources

Electronic Newsletters and Blogs

ASCD SmartBrief: www.smartbrief.com/ascd

The Doyle Report: http://thedoylereport.com

eSchool News: www.eschoolnews.com

TechLearning blogs: www.techlearning.com/section/Blogs

Technology & Learning: www.techlearning.com

Web Portals and Internet Sites

George Lucas Educational Foundation (GLEF): www.edutopia.org/instructional-modules

In the Classroom: www.nea.org/classroom/aol.html

Knowledge Loom Spotlight on Professional Development: http://knowledgeloom.org/practices3.jsp?t=1&location=1&bpinterid=1034&spotlightid=1034

North Central Regional Educational Laboratory: www.ncrel.org/sdrs/areas/issues/methods/technlgy/te1000.htm

Technology Information Center for Administrative Leadership (TICAL): http://portical.org

U.S. Department of Education. Office of Educational Technology (OET): www.ed.gov/about/offices/list/os/technology/index.html

Online Journals

Entrepreneur: www.entrepreneur.com

TechLearning: www.techlearning.com/section/Magazine

T.H.E. Journal: www.thejournal.com

Wired: www.wired.com/wired

Books

Zuboff, S. (1988). *In the age of the smart machine: The future of work and power.* New York: Basic Books.

Articles

Blomeyer, R. (2001). *Effective use of online educational resources at NCREL: A WebQuest on locating and using new web-based technology professional development resources* [Online article]. North Central Regional Educational Laboratory. Available: http://task.ncrel.org/tech/tpd/

Cunningham, J. (2003). *Between technology and teacher effectiveness: Professional development* [Online article]. Available: www.techlearning.com/story/showArticle.php?articleID=10810511

HRM Guide Network. (2002, May 13). *Overworked Americans can't use up their vacation* [Online article]. Available: www.hrmguide.net/usa/worklife/unused_vacation.htm

McKenzie, J. (1998, March). Professional development that works. *eSchool News* [Online journal]. Available: http://staffdevelop.org/secrets.html

November, A. (1998, February). *Creating a new culture of teaching and learning* [Online article based on a presentation at the Asilomar Symposium on Standards, Students, and Success]. Available: http://novemberlearning.com/resources/archive-of-articles/creating-culture/

Rosnick, D. and M. Weisbrot. (2006, December). *Are shorter work hours good for the environment? A comparison of U.S. and European energy consumption.* Center for Economic and Policy Research [Online report]. Available: www.cepr.net/documents/publications/energy_2006_12.pdf

Salpeter, J. (2003). *Professional development: 21st century models* [Online article]. Available: www.techlearning.com/showArticle.php?articleID=13000492

Web-Based Applications

AirSet: www.airset.com

Google Docs: http://docs.google.com

Think Free: http://www.thinkfree.com

Zoho: www.zoho.com

Standard IV

Support, Management, and Operations

Educational leaders ensure the integration of technology to support productive systems for learning and administration.

Performance Indicators for Educational Leaders

IV.A. Develop, implement, and monitor policies and guidelines to ensure compatibility of technologies.

IV.B. Implement and use integrated technology-based management and operations systems.

IV.C. Allocate financial and human resources to ensure complete and sustained implementation of the technology plan.

IV.D. Integrate strategic plans, technology plans, and other improvement plans and policies to align efforts and leverage resources.

IV.E. Implement procedures to drive continuous improvements of technology systems and to support technology replacement cycles.

Chapter 4 Overview

Until recently many school administrators did not realize the importance of the needs addressed in Standard IV in terms of successful technology integration. Questions about equipment compatibility, long-term sustainability, large-scale information, and replacement cycles don't arise when your initial focus is acquiring the basics for technology. Because of initiatives such as E-Rate that make it possible for schools to install larger, up-to-date networks and Internet connections, educators now find themselves confronted with ongoing, large-scale implementation issues.

The overriding theme for this standard falls under the umbrella of total cost of ownership (TCO) and value of investment (VOI). The term TCO appeared in the business world nearly 20 years ago, when it became apparent to automated companies that increasingly sophisticated and widespread technologies required expanded, ongoing support, such as software upgrades; staff training; network maintenance personnel; and updates for infrastructure, connectivity, and equipment replacement. Most businesses now have fairly reliable figures for TCO, but this tends not to be the case for schools. It is difficult to make an accurate estimate for costs because schools do not always use standardized configurations for local area networks, routinely use computers five years or longer, purchase less expensive equipment and software at discounted prices, and benefit from undocumented technical support provided by teachers and students. The current best guesses for actual TCO in schools run somewhere between one-fifth and one-half of the original cost of each computer. Based upon the U.S. Department of Education recommendations of setting aside 30% of a school's total technology budget for staff development alone, realistic figures most likely fall within the range of 40% to 50% of the original cost.

An excellent TCO resource for school administrators is *Taking TCO to the Classroom,* published by the Consortium for School Networking (CoSN, 2001) and available on the Internet: www.classroomtco.org. In addition to an explanatory guide, this site offers a series of checklists or comprehensive descriptions of areas where TCO must be considered, including professional development, support, connectivity, software, replacement costs, and retrofitting. Also available on the website are a chart for districts to use in assessing where they currently stand in controlling TCO and a PowerPoint presentation (updated in 2003) to explain TCO issues to leaders and decision makers.

The idea of VOI is also based on a business concept called return on investment (ROI). TCO encompasses the costs associated with purchasing and using technology, but the focus of VOI is more comprehensive. While VOI includes projected costs for TCO, it also incorporates the anticipated benefits of specific technology projects. School leaders who have done a VOI survey of a proposed technology project are able to justify decisions to proceed with (or suspend) plans based upon a comparison of the costs and benefits. CoSN offers more information about this critical concept at its Value of Investment Leadership Initiative site: www.edtechvoi.org/.

The performance indicators in this chapter examine areas vital to the ongoing success of your technology program: technology compatibility, implementation of technology-based managerial and operations systems, financial and human resources for full program implementation, integration of financial resources through planning and policies, and continuous system improvements and replacement cycles.

Educational leaders develop, implement, and monitor policies and guidelines to ensure compatibility of technologies.

I frequently witness fairly heated debates between classroom teachers and network technicians. These discussions focus on standardization of equipment specifications for hardware and software purchased by the district. Teachers want the freedom of accessing multiple platforms for different instructional needs. Technicians argue that each additional nonstandard piece of equipment increases the difficulties they face in keeping the networks up and running. The underlying thread of these conversations is: Which of these needs are most important? Is it up to technicians to figure out how to maintain more flexible networks, or is it up to teachers to conform to certain hardware and software standards? Unfortunately, the answer is not based upon a simple either/or proposition. Each group has valid points and concerns that require the ability to work together to find common ground and ways to make jobs in each area easier.

Complicating the compatibility issue further is that in the past many educators were, for the most part, free to purchase any equipment and software they favored. This resulted in districts supporting multiple computer platforms and a myriad of software programs, often on the same school campus. While this approach encourages site users to introduce equipment and software they know how to operate, therefore ensuring a level of technology use that might not exist otherwise, problems with connectivity and compatibility are a prevalent result. Administrators often find themselves caught in the middle as they attempt to plan for networks that both run efficiently and meet instructional needs, all while countering a natural resistance to change.

Roles and Responsibilities

Performance Indicator IV.A. Educational leaders develop, implement, and monitor policies and guidelines to ensure compatibility of technologies.

The first step toward resolving compatibility problems is to review existing policies and guidelines regarding technology purchases to determine their effectiveness or to develop such documents. This section addresses the first Performance Indicator for Standard IV, identifying the roles and responsibilities of educational leaders as they assess current policies and guidelines, decide what modifications are required to resolve compatibility issues, and determine how this can be accomplished.

What Is Already in Place?

Assess existing policies and guidelines in the school and district to determine what is currently in place. Identify areas where policies or guidelines do not exist.

All educational leaders need to:

- Be aware of existing policies and guidelines regarding hardware and software purchases for sites or the district office.
- Be aware of monitoring practices for policies and guidelines regarding hardware and software purchases for sites or the district office.
- Understand the basis for current policies and guidelines and be able to explain the underlying reasoning.
- Encourage staff members to identify and explain areas of concern with existing policies and guidelines regarding hardware and software purchases.
- Understand that in a networked environment some decisions regarding hardware and software purchases can be site based but that others must include all network users.
- Use a proactive approach when addressing areas of concern and be sensitive to the needs of all users.

Campus Leaders' Additional Responsibilities:	District Leaders' Additional Responsibilities:	Superintendents' and Cabinet Leaders' Additional Responsibilities:
• Meet with site staff to discuss current hardware and software compatibility issues. • Clearly communicate concerns in a timely manner with the appropriate district offices. • Support current policies and guidelines when working with appropriate decision-making groups to plan purchases.	• Solicit feedback from sites regarding hardware and software compatibility issues. • Identify areas not addressed by current policies and guidelines. • Identify areas where departments currently provide assistance and support to school sites in policy implementation. • Identify areas where departments need to provide assistance and support to school sites in policy implementation. • Clearly define areas where departments need support from sites and the type of support needed. • Work with cabinet leaders to identify current issues with policies and guidelines.	• Obtain feedback from campus and district leaders regarding policies and guidelines for hardware and software compatibility. • Determine how each division can provide support to schools and to individual district departments based upon this feedback. • Identify and clarify types of support divisions need from sites and district departments. • Identify current needs within the district for compatible equipment and software.

All educational leaders need to:

- Educate themselves about the issues surrounding technology compatibility.
- Review data gathered about the effectiveness of existing policies and guidelines and decide whether further action needs to be taken.
- Identify those stakeholders at the site and district levels who make technology purchasing recommendations and decisions. Draw from this pool of people when deciding who should be involved in reviewing and/or modifying policies and guidelines for future purchases.
- Use feedback on current implementation of policies and guidelines throughout the school and district, identify site and district issues, and research possible solutions for concerns.
- Identify the appropriate people to gather information from other districts, the county office of education, vendors, and professional organizations.
- Develop a timeline for modification of current policies and guidelines.

Campus Leaders' Additional Responsibilities:	District Leaders' Additional Responsibilities:	Superintendents' and Cabinet Leaders' Additional Responsibilities:
• Research the impact hardware and software selections may have on other network users both on and off the site. • Determine the level of support needed for each possible option and where that support would come from. • Identify levels of training required for each solution.	• Specify areas where current policies and guidelines are lacking support from sites and district offices. • Specify areas where current policies and guidelines receive support from sites and district offices. • Communicate with both campus and cabinet leaders about hardware and software guidelines under consideration. • Consider the effect district decisions make on sites in terms of cost, training, and ongoing work required. • Communicate with site leaders prior to making final recommendations.	• Ensure that campus and district leaders regularly discuss needs and constraints during decision making. • Review support needs and the ability of the district to provide this support. • Educate school board members regarding technology compatibility issues. • Formalize and present policy and guideline documents for public meetings and board approval.

What Steps Lead to Successful Implementation of This Performance Indicator?

Develop an implementation plan for policies and guidelines that clearly delineates site and district decision-making responsibilities. Disseminate this information to garner support from staff based upon understanding of the issues.

All educational leaders need to:

- Share information with all staff members affected by policies and guidelines.
- Develop an action plan and timeline for implementation.
- Incorporate procedures for ongoing evaluation and updating of policies and guidelines.

Campus Leaders' Additional Responsibilities:	District Leaders' Additional Responsibilities:	Superintendents' and Cabinet Leaders' Additional Responsibilities:
• Communicate regularly with staff (and the community, if appropriate) about implementation of new policies and guidelines. • Restrict purchases to hardware and software that meet guidelines. • Establish procedures for installing appropriate equipment and software on site.	• Monitor purchases of hardware and software to ensure that they meet guidelines. • Assist campus leaders in defining procedures for technical installation and monitoring. • Communicate regularly with campus and cabinet leaders regarding implementation.	• Offer incentives for sites and district offices that support and follow policies and guidelines. • Maintain open lines of communication with school board members and the community to keep them informed about implementation progress.

policies and guidelines to ensure compatibility of technologies.

Activity 1 • Equipment Compatibility

Use the questions in Activity 1 to review existing policies and guidelines related to technology compatibility and to reflect on whether they are effective in supporting a stable infrastructure that lends itself to the use of technology-based instructional strategies.

Next Steps: Use the Action Plan at the end of this chapter to identify the steps that need to be taken next to ensure that policies and guidelines for compatible technologies are developed, implemented, and reviewed regularly.

Activity 1 • Equipment Compatibility

Directions: Use the questions below to review existing policies and guidelines related to technology compatibility and to reflect on whether they are effective in supporting a stable infrastructure that lends itself well to the use of technology-based instructional strategies.

	Circle One	
Does your school or district have policies or guidelines that regulate hardware purchases?	Yes	No
Explain.		
Does your school or district have policies or guidelines that regulate software purchases?	Yes	No
Explain.		
Describe how and why these policies or guidelines were developed and their impact on your workplace. If such policies or guidelines do not exist, describe the impact this has on your workplace.	Yes	No
Explain.		
On a regular basis, do you discuss hardware and software compatibility issues with your staff?	Yes	No
Describe the compatibility issues of which you're aware.		
Are you usually able to resolve conflicts between instructional needs and compatibility issues?	Yes	No
Explain.		
Summarize the current hardware and software compatibility issues in your school or within the district. What are your program's strengths and weaknesses?		

Performance Indicator IV.B.

Educational leaders implement and use integrated technology-based management and operations systems.

Schools and districts collect mountains of data about students but often do little with what has been gathered. In part, this is because until recently it has been difficult for those people who needed the information to have ready access to it. Now there are a variety of software solutions districts and state agencies can use to make data available to educational leaders, teachers, and other staff members. Performance Indicator III.F., found in Chapter 3, discusses the philosophy behind choosing automated student record systems, and Performance Indicator V.B., in Chapter 5, presents the case for using automated data retrieval systems in designing and monitoring program evaluation.

Many districts have also been slow in adopting technology-based operations systems. Although the capability for automating basic business practices, including purchasing, warehouse inventories, work orders, and so on, has been available for some time, problems with district-wide networks, hardware and software compatibility, budgets, and staffing have been impediments. Steps for monitoring this kind of system once it is in place are addressed in Chapter 5, Performance Indicator V.D. Performance Indicator IV.B. looks at the practical steps in choosing and implementing technology-based management and operations systems.

Management: Data Retrieval and Reporting Systems

Student record-keeping systems have been available for some time, but access has often been limited to office staff. In part, this is because it was difficult to manipulate data and get reports that would be useful to anyone else. This is no longer the case. There are now many different software solutions ranging from relatively simple record-keeping systems that can be expanded to generate various reports through additional software modules to data warehouses, modeled after business data management systems, that import and standardize data from district operational systems. Data warehouses can also integrate the imported data. The sophistication level of the system you buy is basically limited by your imagination and your budget.

Prior to shopping for a software solution, educational leaders need to take the time to identify their needs. This is a task that requires input from those people who will enter and use the data and from the technicians who must maintain the system once it is in place. Committee work is definitely called for, considering the scope of this kind of project.

Why is information needed? What kinds of data are needed? What will be done with the information once it is accessible? These are just a few of the questions the committee needs to ask. Here are a few resources for laying this groundwork:

- Student Data Handbook for Elementary, Secondary, and Early Childhood Education (U.S. Department of Education, National Center for Education Statistics, Updated 2001; http://nces.ed.gov/pubsearch/pubsinfo.asp?pubid=2000343rev)
- Building an Automated Student Record System: A Step-by-Step Guide for Local and State Education Agencies (U.S. Department of Education, National Center for Education Statistics, National Forum on Education Statistics, 2000; http://nces.ed.gov/pubs2000/building/)
- Buried Treasure: Developing a Management Guide from Mountains of School Data (Center on Reinventing Public Education, January 2005; www.crpe.org/pubs/pdf/BuriedTreasure_celio.pdf)

Once the reasons for data collection, the types of data needed, and reporting requirements are identified, the committee must focus on more technical issues surrounding database records design, data entry, access to records, security, report format design, and so on. Budget, current hardware and software, and current data storage and retrieval capabilities must also be considered at this point. During this process it is helpful to begin meeting with vendors to find out what they can offer. Do not limit your search to one or two companies. Spend time not only interviewing multiple vendors, but also visiting sites where their software is in place to speak with current users and determine their level of satisfaction with various products.

This is going to be a large, expensive project that can take anywhere from three to six months to prepare to implement after you have selected a vendor. Many districts choose to pilot this kind of system on a small scale prior to using it district-wide. Although this delays full implementation, it is a wise intermediate step. It is also commonplace for districts to plan their full implementation in incremental stages both for purposes of trouble-shooting and so users have time to learn each part of the system gradually. Because your ultimate goal is to provide a system that is easy to use and immediately valuable to stakeholders, this approach also makes sense.

including transportation chores such as bus routes and schedules, cafeteria menu planning and food inventories, and online procurement of goods and services. Although these programs can save both time and money in the long run, initial installation and operation can be rocky. Preplanning with ongoing monitoring and evaluation of the system is necessary. If you are considering automating operations on a large scale, here are some points to consider:

- What has led to the decision to automate or to expand automation?
- Are new modules or programs compatible with existing software?
- How secure are the data?
- How are mistakes in data entry handled?
- Can software be tailored to meet the district's specific needs?
- Can software be modified to meet the district's existing reporting requirements?
- Can software be expanded or upgraded at a later date? At what cost?
- Who will need access to the system?
- What kind of training is necessary for users?
- What kind of trouble-shooting support does the vendor offer?
- What are additional costs beyond the software?
- What are the projected long-term savings?

When the decision to implement an automated program is made, select only those modules that will provide useful information or services. For example, if your district owns just three school buses, you probably don't need to automate transportation services, but if your bus fleet is large and schools follow multiple schedules, an automated transportation system may be needed. Then, plan for a temporary period when both the old and new systems are running concurrently. This will help alleviate problems that arise in the event that a new application is not working properly.

Roles and Responsibilities

Performance Indicator IV.B. Educational leaders implement and use integrated technology-based management and operations systems.

This section presents strategies for leaders at different levels as they review current student record-keeping systems, build a vision of the ideal system, and identify the steps to be taken to make that vision a reality.

What Is Already in Place?

Assess existing technology-based management and operations systems.

All educational leaders need to:

- Review existing policies and procedures for management and operations systems.
- Assess the capabilities of the current management and operations systems.
- Identify current hardware and software used for management and operations systems.
- Identify staff members who have the background and training to assist with design of technology-based management and operations systems.

Campus Leaders' Additional Responsibilities:	District Leaders' Additional Responsibilities:	Superintendents' and Cabinet Leaders' Additional Responsibilities:
• Identify the kinds of data collected on site and how it is used. • Survey faculty and staff on their data needs and the ability of the current management system to meet these needs. • Meet with staff to discuss issues with data retrieval and reporting. • Share surveys with district and cabinet leaders. • Identify ways technology-based operations are used on site and evaluate their effectiveness.	• Identify the kinds of data collected within the district and how it is used. • Survey district staff on their data needs and the ability of the current management system to meet these needs. • Meet with district staff to discuss issues with data retrieval and reporting. • Share surveys with campus and cabinet leaders. • Check district automation software agreements for information about expansion and compatibility issues. • Identify types of technology-based operations currently in place in the district and evaluate their effectiveness.	• Form a district committee to complete the assessment of existing management and operations systems. • Provide necessary resources and time to review the existing management and operations systems. • Review existing board policies or regulations that address reporting format requirements.

All educational leaders need to:

- Educate staff about new policies and procedures for technology-based management and operations systems.
- Educate staff about the capabilities of the new or upgraded management and operations systems through informational meetings and professional growth opportunities.
- Purchase necessary upgrades or replacement needs for hardware and software used for management and operations systems.

Campus Leaders' Additional Responsibilities:	District Leaders' Additional Responsibilities:	Superintendents' and Cabinet Leaders' Additional Responsibilities:
• Make data easily accessible to staff and faculty. • Streamline operations procedures, such as warehouse ordering, for ease of use by staff. • Provide easy access to equipment for faculty and staff. • Support implementation by making arrangements for faculty and staff to attend training on the use of the new or upgraded systems. • Make necessary budget allocations.	• Make data easily accessible to staff. • Streamline operations procedures, such as warehouse ordering, for ease of use by staff. • Provide easy access to equipment for staff. • Coordinate training schedules with campus and cabinet leaders. • Support implementation by making arrangements for faculty and staff to attend training on the use of the new or upgraded systems. • Make necessary budget allocations.	• Based on input from all education leaders, develop and submit formal policies and procedures for technology-based management and operations systems. • Educate the school board and community on progress made in implementation of the upgraded or new management and operations systems. • Support sites and district divisions in implementation through provision of time and resources.

What Steps Lead to Successful Implementation of This Performance Indicator?

All educational leaders need to:

- Have a representative on the district committee and use a shared decision-making model when making decisions affecting the schools and the district.
- Identify areas where existing policies and procedures for technology-based management and operations systems need to be written or revised.
- Identify areas where the existing technology-based management and operations systems need to be upgraded or modified, such as necessary upgrades or replacements for hardware and software.
- Develop an implementation plan and timeline.

Campus Leaders' Additional Responsibilities:	District Leaders' Additional Responsibilities:	Superintendents' and Cabinet Leaders' Additional Responsibilities:
• Identify the kinds of data that need to be collected on site and how the information will be used. • Identify the operations procedures that could be automated to improve productivity at the site. • Work with staff to establish buy-in for new policies and procedures. • Support new policies and procedures through planning and budget development.	• Identify the kinds of data that need to be collected within the district and how the information will be used. • Identify the operations procedures that could be automated to improve productivity within the district. • Clearly delineate financial responsibilities for system improvements. • Coordinate with campus and cabinet leaders to promote buy-in for new policies and procedures. • Obtain and respond to regular feedback about system improvements.	• Develop recommendations for revisions and additions to policies and procedures for technology-based management and operations systems. • Educate the school board and community on the need for technology-based management and operations systems.

technology-based management and operations systems.

Activity 2 • Technology-Based Management and Operations Systems

Use Activity 2 to analyze the management and operations systems currently used, identifying the strengths and weaknesses of those systems.

Next Steps: Use the Action Plan at the end of this chapter to identify the steps that need to be taken next to implement and use integrated technology-based management and operations systems.

Activity 2 • Technology-Based Management and Operations Systems

Directions: Answer the following questions to analyze the management and operations systems you use, identifying the strengths and weaknesses of those systems.

1. List the technology-based management and operations systems currently available for your use.
2. How were these systems selected?
3. What kind of training did you receive on how to use these systems, and was it effective?
4. Which of these systems do you use regularly? Why?
5. Which of these systems do you use infrequently or not at all? Why?
6. Which of these systems are used by certificated or classified staff?
7. What kind of training did certified and classified staff receive on these systems?
8. Do parents have access to information on any of these systems (e.g., student grades)?
9. If so, what kind of training did parents receive on how to use the system?
10. Summarize the strengths and weaknesses of the existing technology-based management and operations systems used by you and staff members.

Educational leaders allocate financial and human resources to ensure complete and sustained implementation of the technology plan.

Although there is agreement that technology support is a critical component of any successful technology program, in a report published by the Center for Research on Information Technology and Organizations titled *Technology Support: Its Depth, Breadth and Impact in America's Schools,* Ronnkvist, Dexter, and Anderson (2000) found that the term "technical support" is used so inconsistently by educators that it is difficult to determine what it is schools really need. Despite the lack of a clear definition, there is general agreement that teachers must have access to well-maintained equipment along with ready access to a technician when problems arise. They also need assistance from coordinators or trainers who can support the use of technology as an instructional tool. Based upon these agreements, the report recommends close examination of hardware and software issues as well as instructional needs when defining technical support.

Sophisticated computer networks require time and expertise to manage. Many schools acquire technology equipment through grants, donations, and fundraisers without realizing the magnitude of ongoing needs for security, maintenance, and technical support. While businesses generally plan for one technician per 50 computer stations, it's not unusual for school districts to employ one technician per 500 (or more) computer stations. A decade ago, equipment problems were typically handled by school site staff members willing and able to provide assistance; however, because of the amount of equipment now found on most sites and the increase in networked environments, this approach is no longer feasible. According to the Consortium for School Networking (2001), the cost to large districts in terms of lost instructional time as a result of either malfunctioning equipment or teachers providing staff development rather than student instruction is estimated to exceed $16.5 million per year (p. 27). In small districts (35 or fewer teachers), this lost time is the equivalent of one full-time teaching position.

Ongoing systemic professional development is also required for staff members to incorporate effective technology use both personally and instructionally. While a teacher needs to be comfortable with personal use of the computer and software before attempting to use it as an instructional tool, she or he cannot be expected to make this transition without support. Just as the ability to read *Jane Eyre* does not guarantee the ability to teach a literature course, proficiency in personal technology use does not guarantee that a teacher has the skills necessary to teach lessons based on integrated technology use. Once a teacher achieves proficiency in personal use, he or she must then have the time and access to resources to learn how to use technology as an instructional tool.

Staffing at these levels is not cheap; in fact, the cost of technical support is rising. In response to increasing costs, a common next step taken by schools and districts attempting to offer technical support is to hire one full- or part-time technology coordinator to handle both technical and staff development needs. Part-time coordinators generally report spending the bulk of their workday handling technical problems, leaving little or no time to offer staff development training. Full-time coordinators do not fare much better. Most of their time is spent supervising someone else's class when they are using a computer lab or trouble-shooting and installing software. Some schools, particularly those at the secondary level, have developed programs that rely on students to act as technicians, which frees up coordinators to address instructional issues, but these programs have varying degrees of success depending upon the training available and the time students can actually devote to technical assistance. Despite the growing price tag, if adequate support is to be provided, districts and schools must hire both technicians and instructional support personnel for their technology programs.

plan.

This section provides an assessment and implementation strategy for educational leaders as they work to meet Performance Indicator IV.C., assessing current allocations of financial and human resources to implement technology plans fully, determining what changes are needed to increase implementation, and deciding how this can be accomplished.

What Is Already in Place?

Review site and district budgets related to technology and support. In addition to expenditures for equipment and software, examine existing job descriptions, current staffing levels for support, and staff development plans and procedures.

All educational leaders need to:

- Be able to identify the kinds of ongoing support currently in place in their site or office, including personnel, staff development programs, equipment, and software.
- Be able to describe how site or office budgets support existing ongoing support.

Campus Leaders' Additional Responsibilities:	District Leaders' Additional Responsibilities:	Superintendents' and Cabinet Leaders' Additional Responsibilities:
• Review school site plans to find areas where technology purchases and ongoing technical support issues are addressed. • Meet with site staff, students, and parents to discuss needs and successes in ongoing support for technology at the site level.	• Review departmental plans to find areas where technology purchases and ongoing technical support issues are addressed for both sites and district offices. • Gather feedback from sites, departments, and community members regarding the current state of ongoing support. Communicate findings with both campus and cabinet leaders.	• Review comprehensive district plans to find areas where technology purchases and ongoing technical support issues are addressed throughout the district. • Identify existing job descriptions for positions that provide ongoing support for technology, both technical and instructional. • Survey current employees to determine existing ratios for technical support. • Determine school board members' current levels of understanding about ongoing support needs.

What Practices Demonstrate Successful Implementation of This Performance Indicator?

Reach an agreement about a definition of the scope of technical support within the district and guidelines for human resources and budget allocations to provide this support.

All educational leaders need to:

- Develop a common definition for ongoing support that addresses both technical and staff development needs.
- Develop common budget guidelines for TCO needs.

What Steps Lead to Successful Implementation of This Performance Indicator?

Follow through to provide necessary staffing and support for the technology program.

All educational leaders need to:

- Understand that ongoing technology support is necessary and is not a one-person, part-time job.
- Educate staff members and the community about TCO issues.
- Follow established recommendations for support personnel, staff development, and purchases of equipment and software.

Campus Leaders' Additional Responsibilities:	District Leaders' Additional Responsibilities:	Superintendents' and Cabinet Leaders' Additional Responsibilities:
• Involve staff members in the selection of support personnel. • Work collaboratively to design staff development opportunities.	• Define areas of responsibility for ongoing support in both implementation and funding. • Assist campus leaders in offering staff development activities.	• Work with appropriate employee associations to develop job descriptions. • Work with appropriate employee associations to devise effective approaches to staff development. • Offer incentives for campus and district leaders to incorporate adequate ongoing support and staff development at sites and in offices.

resources to ensure complete and sustained implementation of the technology plan.

Activity 3 • Anticipating Total Cost of Ownership

Allocating adequate financial and human resources to ensure complete and sustained implementation of the technology plan requires that you consider all the costs associated with the purchase of any new technology. Use the Activity 3 chart to identify the potential hidden costs of a technology purchase. Answer each question *Yes*, *No*, or *Don't Know*. Although purchasing and installing new equipment and software always entails costs, where you respond *No* or *Don't Know* should alert you to areas where hidden or unanticipated costs may be incurred.

You may also want to review and use ISTE's online tool, the Technology Support Index, available at http://tsi.iste.org/. This framework outlines effective tech-support strategies and allows you to build a profile for your district.

Next Steps: Use the Action Plan at the end of this chapter to identify the steps that need to be taken next to allocate financial and human resources to ensure complete and sustained implementation of the technology plan.

Activity 3 • Anticipating Total Cost of Ownership

Directions: Use the chart below to identify the potential hidden costs of a technology purchase. Answer each question *Yes*, *No*, or *Don't Know*.

Total Cost of Ownership: Computer Hardware			
Ask Yourself	**Yes**	**No**	**Don't Know**
Is the system under consideration compatible with existing equipment?			
Can the new system's configuration support both your immediate and foreseeable needs (e.g., enough memory, built-in CD/DVD-RW drive)?			
Is the manufacturer reliable?			
Is the warranty sufficient for your needs?			
Does the system have an acceptable performance record?			
Have other districts implemented this system?			
Is the price affordable?			
Additional questions:			

Total Cost of Ownership: Network Equipment			
Ask Yourself	**Yes**	**No**	**Don't Know**
Is the equipment under consideration compatible with existing equipment?			
Will the network design support both your immediate and foreseeable needs?			
Is the manufacturer reliable?			
Is the warranty sufficient for your needs?			
Does the equipment have an acceptable performance record?			
Is the price affordable?			
Additional questions:			

Continued

Ask Yourself	Yes	No	Don't Know
Are peripherals (e.g., printers, displays, modified keyboards) readily available for the system?			
Are peripherals for this system affordable?			
Are existing peripherals compatible with this system?			
Additional questions:			

Total Cost of Ownership: Physical Settings

Ask Yourself	Yes	No	Don't Know
Do you have enough furniture (e.g., computer tables, ergonomic chairs) to accommodate the new system?			
Is the space large enough to handle additional furniture?			
Is the proposed location secure?			
Do you have sufficient electrical capacity to add additional systems?			
Do you have sufficient Internet access to add new systems?			
Additional questions:			

Coordinated Planning, Budgeting, and Purchasing

Performance Indicator IV.D.

Educational leaders integrate strategic plans, technology plans, and other improvement plans and policies to align efforts and leverage resources.

Planning school programs has increased in scope and complexity during the last decade. This is at least partially in response to the public's greater demands for accountability and federal mandates. However, it is also a response to the change technology has introduced, not only in schools, but in the way day-to-day business is conducted throughout the world. Thanks to increasingly sophisticated information management systems, educators are able to handle larger amounts of data in shorter lengths of time. As a result, expectation levels about the depth and breadth of plans, reports, evaluation documents, and so forth increase as well, and timelines for producing this material are decreasing. It is not unusual to find that an individual school is expected to generate a technology plan, a program improvement plan, a school safety plan, an after-school program plan, a student performance improvement plan, a school site plan, and so on. District offices are also swamped with various required program reports. While it may be possible for all these different plans to be written and updated regularly, the result is often a lack of continuity and coordination in overall planning.

Performance Indicator IV.D. focuses on aligning various plans to coordinate efforts and leverage resources. How do administrators go about taking this approach? In the article *Toward a New View of Education for the Public Good: Starting the Strategic Conversation,* based on his work with J. Spinks in *Beyond the Self-Managing School,* B. J. Caldwell (1998) suggests that worldwide trends in education make traditional long-term planning difficult, if not impossible, to achieve at this time and that effective school administrators must become strategic thinkers as well as strategic planners. The difference is that strategic thinkers are capable of "seeing ahead, seeing behind, seeing above, seeing below, seeing beside, seeing beyond, and above all, seeing it through. This suggests that strategic thinking should be a continuous activity on the part of leaders and managers." This approach to planning encourages leaders to step back, to take a more global view of the schools and district and the mission for each, and to move forward with strategic thinking and conversations. In this approach, districts and schools generate a shared vision for the organization, strategic intentions, and creativity that enable members to have clear goals, encourage risk taking, and, when appropriate, engage in strategic planning.

The direction in Performance Indicator IV.D., to plan alignment to maximize efforts and resources, works well with Caldwell's recommendations. Consolidated planning in which multiple programs are addressed within one large plan makes sense not only as a timesaver but also as a way to see how individual programs overlap and support one another within individual schools and across the district.

schools within districts, have their own unique approaches to budget development and purchasing, ranging from highly controlled, centralized practices to absolute site-based management. This degree of local control enables districts and schools to respond to the needs of individual students, staff, and community members and to circumvent a certain amount of bureaucratic red tape; however, there are times when group purchasing benefits both schools and districts. Batching purchase orders within a district or purchasing through local consortia formed by multiple school districts or through county and state offices of education allows individual schools to increase their buying power tremendously by taking advantage of large volume discounts. For example, in California, the Cal SAVE program (www.calsave.org) enables educators to purchase electronic learning resources at discounted group rates. One drawback to group purchasing is that sometimes purchase orders are held until a large enough order is amassed. This is problematic when an item is needed immediately, but provisions can be made for occasional emergency orders.

One key to leveraging resources is simply to standardize budget designs and allocations for funding. For example, if TCO guidelines are in place, it becomes reasonable to expect that every budget submitted with technology purchases will include funds for ongoing costs. Guidelines for maximizing the use of categorical and grant funds can also be developed and implemented when administrators at each level are aware of funding regulations, crossover, and the importance of projecting anticipated benefits as well as costs for all projects.

School administrators sometimes fear that increased centralization in planning and budgeting is synonymous with lost autonomy. Using a dynamic planning model and having an understanding of how leveraging resources promotes program growth, along with encouraging ongoing communication among administrators, help allay these fears and make this area of a school administrator's job easier.

Roles and Responsibilities

Performance Indicator IV.D. Educational leaders integrate strategic plans, technology plans, and other improvement plans and policies to align efforts and leverage resources.

This section identifies the roles and responsibilities of educational leaders as they work to meet Performance Indicator IV.D., assessing existing procedures and policies for planning and coordinating resources, determining what changes need to be made to improve these processes, and deciding how this can be accomplished.

What Is Already in Place?

Identify all plans currently required for individual schools and the district as well as procedures for developing budgets and making purchases.

All educational leaders need to:

- Collect and read each plan required for the site or district office.
- Research current budget development and purchasing procedures or policies.
- Learn about the history behind the requirements for the first two items in this section.

Campus Leaders' Additional Responsibilities:	District Leaders' Additional Responsibilities:	Superintendents' and Cabinet Leaders' Additional Responsibilities:
• Research how and when plans were written and by whom.	• Research requirements for plans and reports. • Identify existing funding resources within the district and list all spending restrictions. • Share the information gathered with both campus and cabinet administrators.	• Review existing policies that encourage or deter aligned efforts and leveraging resources. • Discuss policies with campus and district leaders to gain their perspectives. • Identify issues that may require policy changes.

What Practices Demonstrate Successful Implementation of This Performance Indicator?

Incorporate separate plans into one global document for district plans and one global document that integrates all aspects of outcomes, implementation, budgeting, and evaluation for each individual site. Develop or amend policies and guidelines to support coordinated efforts to leverage all available resources.

All educational leaders need to:

- Identify means for consolidating various plans into one global document.
- Research planning and budgeting models that support a consolidated plan.

decision-making groups to explore alternatives to multiple plans and current budgeting practices. • Share ideas and concerns with district leaders.	share this data with cabinet leaders. • Develop suggested templates or models for consolidated plans and share them with campus and cabinet leaders. • Develop suggested guidelines for budget development and share them with campus and cabinet leaders. • Identify existing resources within the district and through county or regional offices of education.	district leaders to work together on planning and budget development. • Review suggested planning and budget models to ensure they conform to policies or assist in revising policies when necessary. • Educate school board members about why planning and budget development must change and how this will positively affect student performance.

What Steps Lead to Successful Implementation of This Performance Indicator?

Create an implementation timeline for developing consolidated plans and aligning budget practices for sites and the district.

All educational leaders need to:

- Meet with staff and community members to provide an overview and rationale for proposed changes.
- Work with existing decision-making groups to begin implementation.
- Develop an action plan and timeline for implementation.
- Provide for regular evaluation and monitoring of implementation.

Campus Leaders' Additional Responsibilities:	District Leaders' Additional Responsibilities:	Superintendents' and Cabinet Leaders' Additional Responsibilities:
• Regularly communicate with staff and other key stakeholders about the progress of implementation. • Support implementation by developing a consolidated plan and following suggested procedures for budget development and purchasing.	• Meet regularly with campus leaders to collect feedback and to monitor implementation. • Provide technical assistance for planning and budget development. • Develop district purchasing procedures to better align resources. • Research existing group purchase consortia and make recommendations about participation.	• Monitor timelines to make certain that implementation deadlines are realistic. • Monitor models and guidelines to ensure that consolidation can be done and makes sense. • Meet regularly with district and campus leaders to provide time for discussion and problem resolution. • Inform the school board about implementation progress.

Performance Indicator IV.D. Educational leaders integrate strategic plans, technology plans, and other improvement plans and policies to align efforts and leverage resources.

Activity 4 • Leveraging Resources and Managing Ongoing Costs

In Chapter 1, Activity 3, you're asked to review various school and district plans to find how these plans are aligned. Funding sources are addressed in this exercise. You may want to use the information gathered for that activity as you explore TCO issues further here.

Use the Activity 4 tables to identify ongoing technology costs currently addressed in your overall budget and the percentage of the budget allocated for these costs. You can use this information to determine whether allocations are reasonable and to consider whether you're efficiently leveraging resources.

The tables can also be used to identify those areas not currently addressed in the budget (almost always hidden costs). Descriptions of how unbudgeted services are provided can then be used to assess the level of hidden costs for the ongoing program.

Next Steps: Use the Action Plan at the end of this chapter to identify the steps that need to be taken next to align efforts and leverage resources.

Total Cost of Ownership: Maintenance				
Does your overall budget include a specific allocation for :	**Yes**	**% of Overall Budget**	**No**	**We Provide This Service by**
Routine maintenance of hardware?				
Regular upgrades of hardware (e.g., additional memory)?				
Making repairs on nonfunctioning equipment?				
Troubleshooting?				
Ongoing technical support?				
Additional questions:				
Total % of overall budget currently allocated for maintenance:				

Total Cost of Ownership: Monitoring and Evaluation				
Does your overall budget include a specific allocation for:	**Yes**	**% of Overall Budget**	**No**	**We Provide This Service by**
Data collection and analysis?				
Reporting findings to stakeholders?				
Planning time to modify and update instructional plans?				
Monitoring software licensing?				
Additional questions:				
Total % of overall budget currently allocated for monitoring and evaluation:				

Continued

Activity 4 • Leveraging Resources and Managing Ongoing Costs

Continued

Total Cost of Ownership: Professional Development				
Does your overall budget include a specific allocation for:	**Yes**	**% of Overall Budget**	**No**	**We Provide This Service by**
Regularly scheduled inservice for certified and classified staff?				
Curriculum and instruction support for classroom technology integration?				
Help desk (or other support) for troubleshooting software problems?				
Additional questions:				
Total % of overall budget currently allocated for professional development:				

Total Cost of Ownership: Recycling And Retrofitting				
Does your overall budget include a specific allocation for:	**Yes**	**% of Overall Budget**	**No**	**We Provide This Service by**
Disposal of outdated hardware?				
Retrofitting buildings to meet increased demands for electricity, and so on?				
Additional questions:				
Total % of overall budget currently allocated for recycling and retrofitting:				

Continued

Does your overall budget include a specific allocation for:	Yes	% of Overall Budget	No	We Provide This Service by
Upgrading software?				
Paying ongoing license and subscription fees?				
Replacing malfunctioning software?				
Additional questions:				
Total % of overall budget currently allocated for professional software:				

Total Cost of Ownership: Supplies and Components				
Does your overall budget include a specific allocation for:	**Yes**	**% of Overall Budget**	**No**	**We Provide This Service by**
Ink and paper for printers as well as supplies such as blank CDs?				
Replacement components (e.g., new mouse, joystick, modified keyboard)?				
Additional questions:				
Total % of overall budget currently allocated for supplies and components:				

Total Cost of Ownership: Utilities and Telecommunications				
Does your overall budget include a specific allocation for:	**Yes**	**% of Overall Budget**	**No**	**We Provide This Service by**
Increased costs for utilities (e.g., electrical)?				
Ongoing costs for Internet access?				
Additional questions:				
Total % of overall budget currently allocated for utilities and telecommunications:				

Ongoing Improvements and Replacement Cycles

Performance Indicator IV.E.

Educational leaders implement procedures to drive continuous improvements of technology systems and to support technology replacement cycles.

In the business world, the life span of a computer system is approximately two to three years, depending upon the original capabilities of the system, its ability to be upgraded, and new demands placed on the system by software or through high-speed communication. Schools seldom replace equipment that frequently, but to run current software and have adequate Internet access, computers and peripherals need to be replaced at least every five years. Thanks to textbook needs, educators are familiar with the concept of cyclical buying, but there are major differences in keeping up with technology costs. First, the replacement cycle for technology is shorter than for books; and, second, technology requires ongoing funding for maintenance, upgrades, and other TCO needs during the cycle, costs not incurred with books.

How are schools and districts going to address these funding requirements? A first step is recognizing that a technology plan is not simply a shopping list. As discussed earlier in this chapter, districts and schools must make provisions for all costs associated with technology, not just the initial cost of the hardware or software. A hidden cost in this area is replacement. When equipment is no longer easily usable or able to be repaired, what do you do with it? How do you decide whether to replace it and, if so, is there a better, more efficient product now on the market?

Educators are trying a variety of approaches to this challenge. One solution is leasing hardware and software with built-in rotation of equipment and programs. Although this ensures ongoing costs, it also provides a system for removing obsolete hardware and software. Another approach taken by districts is to continue making purchases but also to rotate equipment from labs to classrooms or vice versa as new products are installed. Many districts now also politely but firmly refuse donated equipment from various agencies because the cost of upgrading the equipment is not offset by the amount of time it can be used before it is once again obsolete.

It is also important to provide for other infrastructure upgrades and improvements. Integrated services digital network (ISDN) lines were once the envy of any school or district, and T1 lines were considered out of reach. Today, thanks to the federal government's E-Rate program, which provides funding for Internet connectivity, T1 lines are entry-level connections, and schools are considering alternatives, including satellite, wireless, and T3 lines. This trend will only continue to grow with developments in high-speed communication constantly outpacing schools. While it is not necessary to keep up with every upgrade, it is important to realize that it is not possible to avoid upgrading altogether.

replacement cycles.

This section points out the roles and responsibilities of administrators in designing policies and procedures to support ongoing improvements in technology-based programs.

What Is Already in Place?

Assess existing procedures to drive continuous improvement of technology systems and to support technology replacement cycles.

All educational leaders need to:

- Recognize that technology systems must be regularly upgraded and replaced.
- Determine whether the district has existing policies or procedures that provide for improving technology systems and technology replacement cycles.
- Determine whether any existing policies or procedures are being followed.
- Review current budget practices for ongoing expenditures.

Campus Leaders' Additional Responsibilities:	District Leaders' Additional Responsibilities:	Superintendents' and Cabinet Leaders' Additional Responsibilities:
• Examine current site hardware and software inventories and compare what is in place with plans for upgrades and equipment replacement cycles.	• Examine current hardware and software inventories for the district and all sites, and compare what is in place with plans for upgrades and equipment replacement cycles.	• Provide current board policies and regulations regarding equipment upgrades and replacement. • Obtain sample policies for upgrading and replacement cycles from other school districts.

What Practices Demonstrate Successful Implementation of This Performance Indicator?

Implement and follow procedures to drive continuous improvement of technology systems and to support technology replacement cycles.

All educational leaders need to:

- Implement and monitor policies or procedures that provide for improving technology systems and technology replacement cycles.
- Implement budget practices consistent with cyclical purchasing.
- Commit the financial and human resources needed to implement this type of policy and procedure.

Campus Leaders' Additional Responsibilities:	District Leaders' Additional Responsibilities:	Superintendents' and Cabinet Leaders' Additional Responsibilities:
• Follow the action plan and timeline for implementation. • Monitor and evaluate the implementation of this policy. • Provide ongoing feedback to district and cabinet leaders regarding site-level implementation of the policy.	• Coordinate with campus and cabinet leaders to monitor the ongoing effect of policy implementation at both the site and district levels. • Provide support to campus leaders in policy implementation. • Follow the action plan and timeline for district implementation. • Monitor and evaluate the district implementation of this policy.	• Obtain board approval of policies and procedures for upgrading and replacing technologies. • Inform the school board and community about progress in implementing the policy. • Provide incentives for campus and district leaders to implement this type of policy.

What Steps Lead to Successful Implementation of This Performance Indicator?

Establish policies and procedures to drive continuous improvement of technology systems and to support technology replacement cycles.

All educational leaders need to:

- Review existing policies or procedures that provide for improving technology systems and technology replacement cycles to determine whether they are appropriate and effective.
- Review sample policies and procedures from other districts.
- Develop budget strategies consistent with cyclical purchasing.
- Identify the financial and human resources needed to implement this type of policy and procedure.

Campus Leaders' Additional Responsibilities:	District Leaders' Additional Responsibilities:	Superintendents' and Cabinet Leaders' Additional Responsibilities:
• Work with the staff and school site council to identify the potential effects of this type of policy at the site level. • Make recommendations to district and cabinet leaders regarding site-level implementation of this type of policy. • Develop an action plan and timeline for implementation. • Design a plan for evaluation of the implementation.	• Coordinate with campus and cabinet leaders to determine the effects of this type of policy at both the site and district levels. • Identify strategies for providing support to campus leaders in implementing this type of policy. • Develop an action plan and timeline for implementation. • Design a plan for evaluation of the implementation.	• Revise or develop policies and procedures for upgrading and replacing technologies. • Educate the school board and community about the need to upgrade and replace technologies. • Identify possible incentives for campus and district leaders to implement this type of policy.

technology replacement cycles.

Activity 5 • Ongoing Improvements and Replacement Cycles

How does your school or district make plans for improving technology systems and monitoring technology replacement cycles? Use the questions in Activity 5 to review current practices.

Next Steps: Use the Action Plan at the end of this chapter to identify the steps that need to be taken next to implement procedures that both support continuous improvement of technology systems and monitor technology replacement cycles.

Activity 5 • Ongoing Improvements and Replacement Cycles

Directions: Use the questions below to review how your school or district uses planning for improving technology systems and monitoring technology replacement cycles.

Ongoing Improvements and Replacement Cycles	Circle One	
Does your school or district have a long-range plan to upgrade hardware and software?	**Yes**	**No**
Explain.		
Does your school or district have a long-range plan to replace obsolete hardware and software?	**Yes**	**No**
Describe the policies and guidelines and how they're enforced.		
Describe the funding strategies you use to support the upgrade and replacement of hardware and software.		
Disposal of obsolete hardware falls under Environmental Protection Agency (EPA) guidelines. Does your school or district have an EPA-compliant procedure for getting rid of old equipment?	**Yes**	**No**
Explain.		
How do you fund disposal costs?		
Summarize the current issues surrounding the improvement of technology systems and technology replacement cycles at your school or within the district. What are your program's strengths and weaknesses?		

Directions: Use the Action Plan to identify the actions that need to be taken to implement Standard IV in the school or district.

Performance Indicator(s)	Next Steps	Person(s) Responsible	I Will Know This Step Has Been Achieved When ...	Timeline
IV.A. Educational leaders develop, implement, and monitor policies and guidelines to ensure compatibility of technologies.				
IV.B. Educational leaders implement and use integrated technology-based management and operations systems.				
IV.C. Educational leaders allocate financial and human resources to ensure complete and sustained implementation of the technology plan.				
IV.D. Educational leaders integrate strategic plans, technology plans, and other improvement plans and policies to align efforts and leverage resources.				
IV.E. Educational leaders implement procedures to drive continuous improvements of technology systems and to support technology replacement cycles.				

Conclusion

Unresolved TCO issues can prevent the successful implementation of a technology program. Now that we are aware of the true cost of networks and other higher-end equipment, we must adopt and practice procedures that will build these costs into our overall plans for technology integration. Making this kind of adaptation may require a significant overhaul of the current funding and budgeting processes within a school district. Successful implementation will require support from all sites and the district office.

In addition, the improvements required in technology-based management and operations systems, along with the need to meet growing demands for streamlined data retrieval and operational procedures, make it imperative that administrators work together to evaluate, select, and implement these systems wherever it is practical or necessary to do so.

Resources

Guidebooks and Briefs

Consortium for School Networking. (2001). *Taking TCO to the classroom: A school administrator's guide to planning for the total cost of new technology* [Online guide]. Available: www.classroomtco.org

Consortium for School Networking. (2006). *VOI Backgrounder* [Online brief]. Available: www.edtechvoi.org/resources/VOIBackgrounder.pdf

National Forum on Education Statistics. (2003). *Technology in schools* [Online guide]. Available: http://nces.ed.gov/pubs2003/tech_schools/

U.S. Department of Education. National Center for Education Statistics, National Forum on Education Statistics. (2000, October). *Building an automated student record system: A step-by-step guide for local and state education agencies* (NCES 2000-324) [Online guide]. Available: http://nces.ed.gov/pubs2000/building/

U.S. Department of Education. National Center for Education Statistics. (2001, December). *Student data handbook for elementary, secondary, and early childhood education* (2001 ed.) (NCES 2000-343 rev) [Online guide]. Available: http://nces.ed.gov/pubsearch/pubsinfo.asp?pubid=2000343rev

Tools

Technology Support Index. Available: http://tsi.iste.org

CalSAVE program. Available: www.calsave.org

www.crpe.org/cs/crpe/view/csr_pubs/20

Education Week. (2005). *Electronic transfer: Moving technology dollars in different directions* [Online report]. Available: www.edweek.org/ew/toc/2005/05/05/index.html

Ronnkvist, A. M., Dexter, S. L., & Anderson, R. E. (2000, June). *Technology support: Its depth, breadth and impact in America's schools* [Online report]. The Center for Research on Information Technology and Organizations, University of California at Irvine and University of Minnesota. Available: www.crito.uci.edu/tlc/findings/technology-support/

Articles

Caldwell, B. J. (1998, October). *School Design and Civil Society: Towards a New View of Education for the Public Good.* IARTV Seminar Series. (78): 3–16.

Fickes, M. (2004, May). How much does technology really cost? *School Planning & Management* [Online journal]. Available: www.peterli.com/archive/spm/669.shtm

Fitzgerald, S. (2001, January). What we've learned about TCO. *School Planning & Management* [Online journal]. Available: www.peterli.com/archive/spm/213.shtm

Fitzgerald, S. (2001, March). Are you a TCO-savvy school district? *Technology & Learning* [Online journal], *21*(8). Available: http://archives.techlearning.com/db_area/archives/WCE/archives/tcosara.php

Kaestner, R. (2007, January). The business of schools. *Databus* [Online newsletter], *47*(1). Available: http://cetpa-k12.org/newsletter/index.php?cmd=vi&id=193&typ=art

Kongshem, L. (1999, September). Mining the school district data warehouse. *Electronic School* [Online journal]. Available: www.electronic-school.com/199909/0999f1.html

McIntire, T. (2006, July). Enough to go 'round? *Technology & Learning* [Online journal]. Available: www.techlearning.com/showArticle.php?articleID=190302232

Mieles, T., & Foley, E. (2005, June). School staff and the data warehouse. *Technology & Learning* [Online journal]. Available: www.techlearning.com/story/showArticle.php?articleID=163703320

Seattle School District (2005). *Business to business procurement* v2.0B [Online article]. Computerworld Honors. Available: www.cwhonors.org/Search/his_4a_detail.asp?id=4131

State Educational Technology Directors Association (SETDA). (2007). *2007 State funding report* [Online article]. Available: www.setda.org/web/guest/nationaltrendsreport

Weiner, R. S. (2000, November 29). Educator's approach to technology funding matures. *The New York Times Online* [Online newspaper]. Available: www.nytimes.com/2000/11/29/technology/29EDUCATION.html

Standard V

Assessment and Evaluation

Educational leaders use technology to plan and implement comprehensive systems of effective assessment and evaluation.

Performance Indicators for Educational Leaders

V.A. Use multiple methods to assess and evaluate appropriate uses of technology resources for learning, communication, and productivity.

V.B. Use technology to collect and analyze data, interpret results, and communicate findings to improve instructional practice and student learning.

V.C. Assess staff knowledge, skills, and performance in using technology and use results to facilitate quality professional development and to inform personnel decisions.

V.D. Use technology to assess, evaluate, and manage administrative and operational systems.

Chapter 5 Overview

In their haste to bring technology use into schools, educators often forget that simple access to hardware and software is not enough; as a result, they fail to plan for those elements of a technology-based program or reform that actually affect student learning. This situation is compounded by weak evaluation components in many technology-based program plans, with no mechanism in place that enables educators to review the program, identifying its strengths and weaknesses on an ongoing basis. According to SEIR-TEC's report, *Factors That Affect the Effective Use of Technology for Teaching and Learning* (2001), evaluation often is the weakest component in technology-based programs for several reasons:

- Educators report they lack the necessary expertise to develop a comprehensive evaluation design.
- Evaluation does have associated costs: 10% of the program budget is a typical figure, but no funds have been allocated for this purpose.
- Multiple measures are not identified, and evaluators then fall back on standardized test scores that may not accurately reflect technology's effects on student learning.
- Educators do not have access to readily available tools that can be used to gather and process data.

Although this performance indicator specifically targets evaluation of technology use in learning, communication, and productivity, it is important to remember that effective technology use must be evaluated within the context of overall educational programs or school reforms. This approach is supported in *The Learning Return on Our Educational Investment* report, published by WestEd (Ringstaff & Kelley, 2002), in which the authors state, "The overriding message that can be gleaned from most current research on the implementation of computer-based technology in K–12 education is that technology is a means, not an end; it is a tool for achieving instructional goals, not a goal in itself" (p. 1). Keeping this in mind, the following discussion applies to evaluation of educational programs and reforms in which technology is one of several important tools.

What Gets Measured Gets Done

Performance Indicator V.A.

Educational leaders use multiple methods to assess and evaluate appropriate uses of technology resources for learning, communication, and productivity.

Carefully designed, sustained evaluation is based upon defined outcomes and supported through data we collect, analyze, and report. It enables educators to determine whether educational programs or reforms are effective and why. The steps for designing an evaluation are described in the following steps.

states that there will be an increase in the number of students completing advanced placement courses, the committee can ask questions about what might cause an increase or decrease in this figure and what role technology-based interventions have played. You will develop process questions (What did we do?), outcome questions (What were early effects?), and effect questions (What are the long-term effects?).

3. After questions are developed, the committee identifies the audience for each question by asking: Who needs to know the answer to this question and why? How should this information be reported to the targeted groups?
4. Use the questions to identify the kinds of data that must be collected and analyzed.
5. Review costs that will be incurred while collecting, analyzing, and organizing data into reportable formats to be certain they are reasonable and within budget.
6. Develop a timeline for the evaluation process and follow it.

Helpful Evaluation Tools

Tools are available on the Internet, designed by reliable evaluators and intended for use in formal evaluations. For example, Jim Cox offers a tool called the Analysis of Process (AOP), available in downloadable form in his article, *A Data-Driven Organization's Approach to Assessing the Quality of Program Delivery* and available on the TICAL Internet portal for school administrators at www.portical.org/cox3more.html. This tool identifies 15 elements found in any instructional program and serves as a starting point for program review. The two-page document can be used to facilitate discussions that result in identifying strengths and weaknesses of a program as identified by process and outcome information.

Two additional tools used to gain a broad picture of how technology use is integrated into a program or reform effort are the Technology Integration Progress Gauge, designed by SEIR-TEC (www.seirtec.org/eval.html), and sections of the 2002 Toolkit, from the State Educational Technology Directors Association (www.setda.org/web/guest/toolkits).

Well-designed evaluation will tell you the effects of technology use and other interventions in your programs and reforms and, most important, why. When you know why something is or is not working, you can do something about it. Because evaluation is time consuming and requires ongoing effort, you may want to consider contracting with an outside local evaluator who can work with you and your staff on design, implementation, and dissemination of the evaluation.

Roles and Responsibilities

Performance Indicator V.A. Educational leaders use multiple methods to assess and evaluate appropriate uses of technology resources for learning, communication, and productivity.

This section describes the process administrators use to review current evaluation practices, define desirable evaluation practices, and identify necessary steps to move from what currently exists to desired levels for evaluation design. At the cabinet-leader level much of the responsibility for program evaluation will fall to the head of the instructional division.

What Is Already in Place?

Assess current program and reform evaluation practices.

All educational leaders need to:

- Review current evaluation requirements for existing programs, including timelines.
- Review current evaluation designs.
- Review current procedures for conducting program or school reform evaluation.

Campus Leaders' Additional Responsibilities:	District Leaders' Additional Responsibilities:	Superintendents' and Cabinet Leaders' Additional Responsibilities:
• Review evaluation components of school site plans and programs. • Review previously completed program evaluations to determine the breadth and scope of the process.	• Review evaluation components of district master and program plans. • Review previously completed district program evaluations to determine their breadth and scope. • Meet with campus leaders to discuss strengths and weaknesses of current evaluation procedures.	• Review existing board policies or regulations that address program evaluation. • Obtain feedback from campus and district leaders regarding existing program evaluation issues and concerns. • Determine how each division currently provides support to schools and to individual district departments conducting program evaluations.

All educational leaders need to:

- Meet with standing committees at appropriate levels to design and implement ongoing evaluation models.
- Insist that technology evaluation be implemented within the context of instructional and reform programs.
- Review evaluation timelines regularly and coordinate as much as possible to avoid work overload or repetition.
- Make appropriate budget allocations to cover the cost of evaluation.
- Work with local outside evaluators when appropriate.
- Make evaluation results available to appropriate stakeholders.
- Use the results of evaluations to plan program improvements.

Campus Leaders' Additional Responsibilities:	District Leaders' Additional Responsibilities:	Superintendents' and Cabinet Leaders' Additional Responsibilities:
• Provide support to site committee members through stipends, release time, staff development opportunities, and recognition. • Update school program plans to reflect a strong evaluation component based upon evaluation recommendations. • Conduct information dissemination meetings or make formal presentations about findings as necessary.	• Provide support to district committee members through stipends, release time, staff development opportunities, and recognition. • Provide necessary support to sites to ensure thorough, ongoing evaluation takes place. • Offer campus leaders referrals to county and outside agencies that can assist in evaluation design and implementation.	• Provide support to campus and district leaders through release time, staff development opportunities, and recognition. • Determine how each division will provide support to schools and to individual district departments conducting program evaluations. • Share evaluation policy recommendations with campus and district leaders prior to presenting them to the school board.

What Steps Lead to Successful Implementation of This Performance Indicator?

Identify steps that need to be taken to develop and implement evaluation components in program plans and school reforms.

All educational leaders need to:

- Establish standing committees at appropriate levels to design and implement ongoing evaluation models.
- Ensure that technology evaluation is incorporated within the programs that use it.
- Establish coordinated evaluation timelines to avoid work overload or repetition.
- Explore budgets to find places where allocations for evaluation costs need to be made.
- Decide which evaluations can be done in-house and which need assistance from a local outside evaluator.
- Explore successful methods for making evaluation results available to appropriate stakeholders.

Campus Leaders' Additional Responsibilities:	District Leaders' Additional Responsibilities:	Superintendents' and Cabinet Leaders' Additional Responsibilities:
• Meet with appropriate site leadership groups to discuss ways to support site evaluation committee members. • Meet with the site evaluation committee to identify and discuss strengths and weaknesses of current evaluation designs. • Work with district leaders to bring necessary outside resources on campus to share expertise and provide assistance in evaluation design.	• Meet with appropriate cabinet leaders to discuss ways to support district evaluation committee members. • Provide necessary support to sites as they design evaluation models. • Seek out and develop a database of consultants in the county and outside agencies that can assist in evaluation design and implementation.	• Meet with campus and district leaders to discuss ways to support district and site evaluation committee members. • Explore ways each division could provide support to schools and to individual district departments conducting program evaluations. • Work with school board members to educate them on issues related to the evaluation process.

evaluate appropriate uses of technology resources for learning, communication, and productivity.

Activity 1 • Evaluation Procedures

Evaluation tends to be one of the weakest components of school and district plans. Use Activity 1 to review your current evaluation practices. Indicate to what extent your plans fulfill the descriptions in items 1–9 for Use of Technology as a Learning Tool and items 1–9 for Use of Technology as a Communication and Productivity Tool.

Next Steps: Based on your responses to Activity 1, use the Action Plan at the end of this chapter to identify the steps that need to be taken next to strengthen your approach to evaluating the use of technology resources for learning, communication, and productivity.

Activity 1 • Evaluation Procedures

Directions: Respond to each statement below by marking the appropriate column. Those marked *Disagree* or *Strongly Disagree* indicate areas of the evaluation process that require your attention. Use the reflection questions that follow the statements to explore further the current state of evaluation in your school or district.

Use of Technology as a Learning Tool				
School or District Plans That Address Use of Technology as a Communication and Productivity Tool	**Strongly Agree**	**Agree**	**Disagree**	**Strongly Disagree**
1. Clearly describe desired student outcomes.				
2. Clearly describe how these desired outcomes will be measured.				
3. Include short- and long-term evaluation activities.				
4. Provide well-defined timelines for evaluation activities.				
5. Identify those persons responsible for each evaluation activity.				
6. Allocate funds specifically to cover the costs associated with evaluation.				
7. Identify multiple measures for assessing technology's impact on student performance.				
8. Include technology-based assessment tools that can be used to gather and process data.				
9. Evaluate technology use within the context of overall educational programs or school reforms.				
Describe how your school's or district's current evaluation practices measure the impact of technology as a learning tool.				
Identify the strengths and weaknesses of these practices.				

Continued

School or District Plans That Address Use of Technology as a Communication and Productivity Tool	Strongly Agree	Agree	Disagree	Strongly Disagree
1. Clearly describe desired communication and productivity outcomes.				
2. Clearly describe how these desired outcomes will be measured.				
3. Include short- and long-term evaluation activities.				
4. Provide well-defined timelines for evaluation activities.				
5. Identify those persons responsible for each evaluation activity.				
6. Allocate funds specifically to cover the costs associated with evaluation.				
7. Identify multiple measures for assessing the technology's impact on communication and productivity.				
8. Include technology-based assessment tools that can be used to gather and process data.				
9. Evaluate technology use within the context of overall organizational systems.				

Describe how your school's or district's current evaluation practices measure the impact of technology as a communication and productivity tool.

Identify the strengths and weaknesses of these practices.

Using Technology to Manage and Report Data

Performance Indicator V.B.

Educational leaders use technology to collect and analyze data, interpret results, and communicate findings to improve instructional practice and student learning.

An administrator does not need to be an accomplished statistician or programmer to use technology for data collection and analysis. Several software publishing companies offer student record-keeping systems that can be tailored to meet the needs of individual schools and districts, for example, Schoolmaster Student Information Systems (www.schoolmaster.com) and PowerSchool (www.powerschool.com). The philosophy behind using this kind of software is discussed broadly in Chapter 3, Performance Indicator III.A. The process for selecting this type of software is discussed in Chapter 4, Performance Indicator IV.B.

Identifying and Collecting Data

Once the evaluation design is in place and the committee knows what data to collect, members need to decide how to go about gathering the data. Much of the student outcome information will be available through the student record-keeping system. When this system is automated, collection and analysis are likely to be very easy. You need to talk with the administrator of the student record-keeping system to determine whether existing software modules will permit gathering, analyzing, and generating reports using the existing data. If this capability does not currently exist, it is possible that the software publisher will already have or will be willing to create a module that can do the job for a fee. Also talk with the data processing office to determine the feasibility of moving data from one program to another, if necessary. In cases where student record-keeping is not automated, there are commercial programs that can be purchased for statistical analysis, such as the Statistical Package for the Social Sciences (SPSS) (www.spss.com) or Windows KWIKSTAT (WINKS) (www.texasoft.com). It is sometimes necessary to have the data entered by hand, but once the information is there, it can be manipulated for analysis that can be displayed in various report formats.

Process information and certain student outcomes may need to be gathered through surveys, interviews, observations, or other means and recorded, using both traditional and technology-based methods. You might consider using computer and digital technologies, such as online activities and recorded interviews and presentations, to assess student achievement through electronic portfolios designed to track the development of students' problem-solving skills. In addition, survey results can be scanned into a database if the response sheets have been designed for this purpose or downloaded as spreadsheet files when surveys are conducted online using, tools such as SurveyMonkey (www.surveymonkey.com) or Zoomerang (www.zoomerang.com). Other sources of data can be presented in narrative form.

As mentioned above, data made available through the student record-keeping system or in a format that can be entered into a database can be analyzed through the use of special program modules that work with the automated system or by using a statistics program. It is also possible to use a spreadsheet program such as Excel to create a workbook to manipulate data, but with other available products, it's probably not worth the time to set up your own files.

Selecting the kinds of tests or comparisons you want to make may require a quick brush-up in Statistics 101, but it is important to ensure that the data analysis and interpretation actually mean something. The district office may have someone in-house who can help or refer you to a resource person at a county office of education or local college or university.

Disseminating Information

An important aspect of evaluation design is determining who needs access to the results of the evaluation and how the results will be presented to various stakeholders. When preparing information for dissemination, think about each audience you need to address. Parents will not want or need the detail educators will expect. Most likely, community members will simply want highlights of the information, and board members will expect a full report. Technology makes it possible to share information using formats tailored for each group.

The evaluation committee may decide to use a newsletter format for parents, a brochure for community members, and a full report for the school site, district, and board. Once the formats are agreed upon, work with clerical staff to translate the ideas into finished products. The evaluation committee also needs to decide when and where the information will be shared. This may happen in person (during staff meetings, at parent meetings, or through a formal presentation to the school board), online via a website, or through the mail. Again, consider the audience and the best delivery method for ensuring they will read and understand the provided information.

Some schools or districts may benefit from using the free online Data-Driven Decision Making Self Assessment tool to gauge their readiness to manage and report data. Launched by CoSN in 2003, the tool is available at www.3d2know.org/assessment/survey.cfm.

Roles and Responsibilities

Performance Indicator V.B. Educational leaders use technology to collect and analyze data, interpret results, and communicate findings to improve instructional practice and student learning.

This section explains the steps school administrators need to take as they determine current capabilities for managing and reporting data, identify the capabilities they want to have, and then plan strategies for reaching their goals.

What Is Already in Place?

Assess current site and district capabilities for managing and reporting data.

All educational leaders need to:

- Review evaluation design recommendations made while working to meet Performance Indicator V.B. to ensure they meet federal and state reporting requirements.
- Research the existing student record-keeping system to identify current capabilities.
- Identify practices in place for disseminating evaluation results.
- Identify staff members who have the background and training to assist with data manipulation.
- Identify staff members who have the background and training to assist with dissemination of evaluation results.

Campus Leaders' Additional Responsibilities:	District Leaders' Additional Responsibilities:	Superintendents' and Cabinet Leaders' Additional Responsibilities:
• Check the site software inventory for programs on campus that could be used for data collection or statistical analysis.	• Check the district software inventory for programs currently in the district office that could be used for data collection or statistical analysis.	• Review existing board policies or regulations that address evaluation design and information reporting.

All educational leaders need to:

- Review recommendations from the district planning committee regarding the tools, training, and timeline.
- Reach an agreement about the recommendations made.
- Support an implementation timeline and use improved data collection and reporting systems.

Campus Leaders' Additional Responsibilities:	District Leaders' Additional Responsibilities:	Superintendents' and Cabinet Leaders' Additional Responsibilities:
• Ensure that data collection, manipulation, and dissemination are performed based upon sound evaluation design. • Make certain that identified site staff members are available to attend training for the student record-keeping system. • Make certain that identified site staff members are available to attend training for a statistics program. • Make appropriate budget allocations based upon district committee recommendations. • Follow through on dissemination plans through meetings, print material, or other agreed-upon actions.	• Ensure that sites and district offices have access to the necessary tools to conduct data collection, analysis, and dissemination based on the agreed-upon evaluation design. • Ensure that staff development is available to identified site and district staff. Coordinate with campus and cabinet leaders to implement a workable schedule. • Make appropriate budget allocations based upon district committee recommendations. • Assist campus leaders in their follow-through on dissemination of evaluation results through planning meetings, designing reports, and distributing print materials. • Participate in site and district dissemination meetings.	• Schedule time for campus and district leaders to discuss ongoing concerns about tools provided for data collection, analysis, and dissemination, and participate in these meetings. • Make certain that identified cabinet support staff members are available to attend training for the student record-keeping system. • Make certain that identified cabinet support staff members are available to attend training for a statistics program. • Make a formal presentation to the school board regarding a district evaluation design that is supported through technology use.

What Steps Lead to Successful Implementation of This Performance Indicator?

Determine steps that need to be taken to reach goals for managing and reporting data as a basis for thorough evaluation and appropriate information dissemination.

All educational leaders need to:

- Establish a representative group that will work with leaders at all levels to develop recommendations for software selection or expansion, training plans, and cost distribution to create a system that will allow for necessary data collection and manipulation. This group also makes recommendations for information dissemination methods.
- Develop a timeline for implementation of recommendations.

Campus Leaders' Additional Responsibilities:	District Leaders' Additional Responsibilities:	Superintendents' and Cabinet Leaders' Additional Responsibilities:
• Develop a list of the kinds of data you need to collect for site-level use. • Identify which site staff members would need training to use an expanded student record-keeping system. • Identify which site staff members would need training to use a statistics program. • Participate on the district planning committee.	• Research the capabilities of the current student record-keeping system as well as the potential for expansion through modules or specially written programs. • Identify which district staff would need training to use an expanded system and the scope of the training. • Determine the costs of upgrading or expanding the current student record-keeping system and make recommendations about how these costs would be distributed. • Research the capabilities of available statistics software. • Identify which staff would need training to use a statistics program and the scope of the training. • Determine the costs of purchasing statistics software and make recommendations about how these costs would be distributed. • Determine the capability of current district software to generate reports for dissemination in various formats. • Make recommendations to the district committee regarding findings.	• Select a cabinet representative for the district planning committee. • Ensure that there is open, frequent communication between campus and district leaders. • Identify which cabinet support staff members would need training to use an expanded student record-keeping system. • Identify which cabinet support staff members would need training to use a statistics program. • Explore ways to provide financial support to sites and district offices for software upgrades or purchases and staff development through reallocation of district funds or grants. • Educate school board members about the importance of well-designed evaluation and the need for technology support for this endeavor.

analyze data, interpret results, and communicate findings to improve instructional practice and student learning.

Activity 2 • Tools for Accessing, Analyzing, and Reporting Data

The series of questions in Activity 2 is designed to assist you in identifying the kinds of data available to you, how you access or collect that data, and how you analyze and report your findings.

Next Steps: After identifying the kinds of data available, how you access or collect that data, and how you analyze and report your findings, use the Action Plan at the end of this chapter to identify the steps that need to be taken next to use technology more effectively to collect and analyze data, interpret results, and communicate findings to improve instructional practice and student learning.

Activity 2 • Tools for Accessing, Analyzing, and Reporting Data

Directions: Answer the following questions to identify the kinds of data available to you, how you access or collect that data, and how you analyze and report your findings.

Automated Student Record-Keeping Systems	Circle One	
1. Does your school or district have an automated student record-keeping system?	**Yes**	**No**
If your answer to question 1 is *Yes*, answer the following questions. You may need to check with the system administrator to answer them. If your answer is *No*, skip to question 8.		
2. List the types of student data (e.g., attendance, discipline, test scores) you can access using the automated student record-keeping system.		
3. List the types of student data analysis that can be completed using the automated student record-keeping system.		
4. List the types of reports that can be generated using the automated student record-keeping system.		
5. Does the system administrator have the capability to write new queries for data analysis? Explain.		
6. Does the system administrator have the capability to write new formats for reports? Explain.		
7. How do you currently use this system for data collection, analysis, and reporting? Explain.		
8. If you don't have an automated student record-keeping system, what strategies do you use to collect, analyze, and report student data?		

Continued

9. Which of the following data collection tools do you use? Circle all that apply and write a sentence explaining when you use each type of tool circled:

Surveys:

Interviews:

Observations:

Student portfolios:

Other (please identify):

10. Have you used electronic versions of the data collection tools circled above?	**Yes**	**No**
Explain.		

11. How do you analyze the data collected using the tools circled above? Explain.

12. Once you've collected and analyzed data, how do you disseminate the information? Explain.

13. What are the current strengths and weaknesses in your ability to access, analyze, and report data?

Technology Use and Evaluation of Personnel

Performance Indicator V.C.

Educational leaders assess staff knowledge, skills, and performance in using technology and use results to facilitate quality professional development and to inform personnel decisions.

An important part of an educational leader's job is to observe and evaluate the performance of certified and classified personnel. Performance Indicator V.C. addresses performance evaluation and professional development as it relates to implementation of technology use. Just as with other forms of evaluation discussed in this chapter, employee performance in technology integration must be viewed within the context of the school plan and outcomes for instructional programs. Although proficiency levels are important, how employees choose to apply these skills is equally noteworthy.

Evaluating Technology Use in the Classroom or Office

The discussions of the change process and stages of technology use in Chapter 2 remind us that accurate evaluation of knowledge, skills, and use is multidimensional. Employees will be at a variety of levels in terms of their concern about technology use and their ability to make technology work effectively for them. Because this is the case, you can make a strong argument for working with individual employees, both classified and certified, to develop individual professional growth plans and objectives that include technology integration skills as applicable.

A variety of tools can be used with employees to help them identify their present level of use with technology integration and what their next steps might be. In addition to CBAM and the stages of technology integration identified in ACOT research (see Chapter 2), you may want to review SETDA's 2002 Toolkit (www.setda.org/web/guest/toolkits) and SEIR-TEC's Technology Integration Progress Gauge (www.serve.org/seir-tec/publications/ProgressGauge2000.pdf). Both of these instruments ask users to look beyond basic computer proficiency when gauging their technological skills in an educational environment. The Learning with Technology Profile Tool, designed by North Central Regional Technology in Education Consortium (www.ncrtec.org/capacity/profile/profwww.htm), is also a good resource. In addition, some states now have online self-assessments district staff complete annually.

Technology Standards (NETS) for Teachers (www.iste.org). The standards can serve as a model for practicing teachers wanting to increase effective technology use in their classrooms.

Once an employee's plan and goals are in place, they can be used for ongoing discussion about how technology use fits into his or her workday, specific steps taken by the individual to increase skills and knowledge, and the person's expected level of proficiency as agreed upon in the plan.

Working with individuals at this intense level of planning individual goals and professional development strategies enables you to make educated personnel decisions. Your expectations are clearly defined and realistic, based upon mutual input and agreement, tied to expected outcomes for programs, and designed to allow for gradual, measurable growth.

Roles and Responsibilities

Performance Indicator V.C. Educational leaders assess staff knowledge, skills, and performance in using technology and use results to facilitate quality professional development and to inform personnel decisions.

This section is designed to identify the responsibilities of educational leaders at all levels as they review current procedures for evaluation of employees' integration of technology into the workday and plan for future practice. At the cabinet level, most of the responsibility for this standard will fall to the head of the personnel or human resources division. Refer to the roles and responsibilities section for Performance Indicator II.E. in Chapter 2 for specific recommendations regarding the development of or redefinition of professional growth plans.

What Is Already in Place?

Assess existing methods for evaluation of employee technology use and development of professional goals.

All educational leaders need to:

- Review current employee evaluation procedures.
- Review current procedures for identifying professional goals.
- Identify areas of contractually-defined employee evaluation and goal development.

What Practices Demonstrate Successful Implementation of This Performance Indicator?

Utilize procedures that enable employees to structure goals and be evaluated based upon individual needs and experience with technology integration.

All educational leaders need to:

- Use knowledge of the change process and stages of technology integration to assist employees in developing reasonable goals.
- Provide to employees appropriate technology integration self-assessment tools that can be used in developing appropriate goals.
- Provide professional development support to help employees meet their goals.
- Review budgets to identify funds that can be used to assist employees in meeting their goals.
- Meet regularly with employees to discuss professional goal implementation.
- Regularly observe employees using technology.

Campus Leaders' Additional Responsibilities:	District Leaders' Additional Responsibilities:	Superintendents' and Cabinet Leaders' Additional Responsibilities:
• Meet with employees before and after formal observations to discuss how what you see during your visit relates to professional goals. • Make frequent informal classroom and office visits. • Review lesson plans for increased sophistication in technology integration.	• Assist campus leaders in employee development of professional goals. • Follow through on evaluation of district employees as they integrate technology use into the workday.	• Work with employee associations to reach agreements concerning an evaluation design that allows for gradual growth in expertise levels. • Obtain necessary board approval for updates in policies and procedures related to goal development and evaluation. • Meet regularly with campus and district leaders to monitor implementation of evaluation procedures.

All educational leaders need to:

- Use knowledge of the change process and stages of technology integration to create revised goal-setting and evaluation procedures.
- Adopt or develop appropriate technology integration self-assessment tools that employees can use in developing professional goals.
- Allocate funds that can be used to assist employees in meeting their goals.

Campus Leaders' Additional Responsibilities:	District Leaders' Additional Responsibilities:	Superintendents' and Cabinet Leaders' Additional Responsibilities:
• Meet with staff to discuss issues pertaining to writing professional goals and evaluation of technology use. • Communicate staff input with appropriate district and cabinet leaders.	• Seek out and share employee evaluation models for technology integration. • Meet with staff to discuss issues pertaining to writing professional goals and evaluation of technology use. • Communicate staff input with appropriate campus and cabinet leaders.	• Meet with employee association representatives to explore revisions in professional goal-setting and evaluation procedures. • Develop a proposal for revised policies and procedures related to professional goal-setting and evaluation. • Educate school board members on issues related to employee evaluation and technology integration.

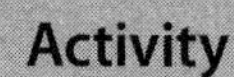

Activity

Performance Indicator V.C. Educational leaders assess staff knowledge, skills, and performance in using technology and use results to facilitate quality professional development and to inform personnel decisions.

Activity 3 • Measuring the Impact of Professional Development Programs

Use the questions in Activity 3 to consider both the quality of the overall professional development program available to you and your employees and the way you currently measure its impact.

Next Steps: Use the Action Plan at the end of this chapter to identify the steps that need to be taken next to ensure that you and your staff have opportunities to take part in high-quality professional development that will have a positive impact on student learning and employee performance.

1. What kinds of professional development opportunities are offered to you and your staff?
2. How are these opportunities selected?
3. Are professional development opportunities based on clear goals and stated outcomes related to school or district plans? Explain.
4. Which staff members take advantage of professional development opportunities, and how is this tracked?
5. What kinds of incentives are offered to staff members who pursue professional development?
6. Who provides professional development programs for your school or district, and how are they selected?

Continued

Activity 3 • Measuring the Impact of Professional Development Programs

Continued

7. Are the implementation strategies suggested by professional development providers research based and linked to academic standards whenever appropriate?

8. How is professional development funded?

9. How do you measure professional development's impact on students?

10. Which of the following evaluation activities are used? Circle each used, and write a brief explanation, including how often it's used.

Training evaluations:

Records of participants:

Formal observations of employee application of new learning:

Informal observations of employee application of new learning:

Staff meeting minutes:

Personal professional-development journals:

Written action plans:

Interviews with students and parents:

Performance Indicator V.D.

Educational leaders use technology to assess, evaluate, and manage administrative and operational systems.

No doubt you have read or heard horror stories about school districts that have adopted technology-based administrative or operations systems only to discover months or even years into implementation that the system has produced faulty data, causing serious problems for students, or has cost the district millions of dollars in lost revenue because funds have been misspent or misplaced. How can you avoid this kind of situation?

Whenever a district opts to purchase and implement technology-based administrative or operations systems, it is imperative that a comprehensive monitoring and evaluation mechanism be in place. As mentioned in Chapter 4, Performance Indicator IV.B., many districts initially run parallel accounting systems as a precaution, but more needs to be done. Form an evaluation committee that will design and implement a plan for monitoring the effectiveness of the system and ensure that if the projected savings in cost or time are not produced, that the problem can be identified and remedied quickly.

When implementing a new or enhanced student record-keeping system, maintenance of data quality is an important issue. Every adult who accesses student records must take responsibility for the accuracy of those records; this means that users must understand why the information is being collected and why accurate information is important. Schedules for regular data entry must be established and adhered to, and those people responsible for data entry must have ongoing, effective professional development training.

Reporting procedures must also be monitored. While it is prudent to use predesigned reports to make good use of employee time, these formats must be reviewed and updated regularly to ensure the proper information is being reported to each agency. You also must determine when it is appropriate to use dynamic (changing) or static databases as your data source. Inaccurate data reporting can result in the loss of large sums of federal and state monies, a consequence most districts can ill afford.

School districts may save significant amounts of money by automating administrative and operations functions such as purchasing, transportation scheduling, and work orders. However, just as with student record-keeping systems, procedures for monitoring and evaluating this automation must be in place to ensure that savings are realized. Regular audits must be conducted to identify strengths and weaknesses of the automated system so necessary corrections can be made. Staff members at sites and within the district office need to be trained in using the system, and then they must track transactions, checking for accuracy and timely implementation. It is also helpful to communicate with other nearby school districts going through this process to share information and solutions to problems encountered along the way.

Roles and Responsibilities

Performance Indicator V.D. Educational leaders use technology to assess, evaluate, and manage administrative and operational systems.

This section explains the responsibilities of educational leaders at various levels as they monitor and evaluate technology-based managerial and operational systems.

What Is Already in Place?

Assess current site and district levels for automation of administrative and operations tasks.

All educational leaders need to:

- Review existing automated administrative and operations tasks to identify current capabilities.
- Review effectiveness of current automation capabilities.

Campus Leaders' Additional Responsibilities:	District Leaders' Additional Responsibilities:	Superintendents' and Cabinet Leaders' Additional Responsibilities:
• At this stage, additional responsibilities fall to district and cabinet leaders.	• Check district automation software agreements for information about expansion and compatibility issues. • Gather data from sites regarding strengths and weaknesses of current systems.	• Review existing board policies or regulations that address reporting format requirements.

All educational leaders need to:

- Review recommendations from the district monitoring and evaluation committee regarding automated administrative and operations systems.
- Reach an agreement about the recommendations made.
- Support an implementation timeline and follow through on identified tasks.

Campus Leaders' Additional Responsibilities:	District Leaders' Additional Responsibilities:	Superintendents' and Cabinet Leaders' Additional Responsibilities:
• Ensure that automation modules are appropriate for site use, accessible, and used properly by targeted staff members. • Make certain that identified site staff members are available to attend training for automated systems. • Make appropriate budget allocations based upon district committee recommendations.	• Ensure that sites and district offices have access to the necessary tools for automation and that these tools are being used properly based on the agreed-upon design. • Ensure that staff development is available to identified site and district staff. Coordinate with campus and cabinet leaders to implement a workable schedule. • Make appropriate budget allocations based upon district committee recommendations.	• Schedule time for campus and district leaders to discuss ongoing concerns about tools provided for automation and participate in these meetings. • Make certain that identified cabinet support staff members are available to attend training for automated systems. • Make a formal presentation to the school board regarding the monitoring and evaluation of district automation systems. • Obtain necessary board approval for updates in policies and procedures related to reporting formats that may be affected by automation.

What Steps Lead to Successful Implementation of This Performance Indicator?

Determine steps that need to be taken to monitor and evaluate implementation of automation of administrative and operations systems.

All educational leaders need to:

- Establish a representative group that will work with leaders at all levels to develop recommendations for monitoring and evaluating automation, training plans, and cost distribution to create a system that will allow for streamlined managerial and operations systems. This group also makes recommendations for methods to use for information dissemination.
- Develop a timeline for implementation of recommendations.

Campus Leaders' Additional Responsibilities:	District Leaders' Additional Responsibilities:	Superintendents' and Cabinet Leaders' Additional Responsibilities:
• Develop a list of the automated managerial and operations systems that are implemented at the school site. • Identify which site staff members have been trained to use the expanded automation system and the type of training they have received. • Participate on the district planning committee.	• Identify the capabilities of the current automation systems as well as the potential for expansion through modules or specially written programs. • Identify which district staff have been trained to use the expanded automation system and the scope of the training. • Determine the ongoing cost of upgrading or expanding the current automation system and make recommendations about how these costs would be distributed. • Make recommendations to the district committee regarding your findings.	• Select a cabinet representative for the district planning committee. • Ensure open, frequent communication between campus and district leaders. • Identify which cabinet support staff members have received training to use an expanded automation system and the type of training provided. • Explore ways to provide financial support to sites and district offices for ongoing software upgrades or purchases and staff development through reallocation of district funds or grants. • Educate school board members about the importance of automated managerial and operational systems and how technology will support this endeavor.

and manage administrative and operational systems.

Activity 4 • Evaluating Administrative and Operations Systems

Use the questions in Activity 4 to identify how you currently monitor and evaluate administrative and operational systems.

Next Steps: Now that you have explored current practice for monitoring and evaluating administrative and operations systems, use the Action Plan at the end of this chapter to identify the steps that need to be taken next to improve these procedures.

Activity 4 • Evaluating Administrative and Operations Systems

Directions: Use the questions below to identify how you currently monitor and evaluate administrative and operational systems.

1. List the various technology-based administrative or operations systems available at your school or within your district (e.g., automated student record-keeping, transportation, purchasing).
Note: It may be helpful to answer the following questions individually for each existing administrative and operations system.
2. Who's responsible for data entry?
3. How is the accuracy of the data ensured?
4. Who receives training on the system and how often?
5. Who checks reports for accuracy prior to their release?
6. What procedures are in place to monitor how well the system is operating?
7. Who is responsible for regular monitoring of the system?
8. How often is the system evaluated to determine whether its performance meets expectations?
9. Who is responsible for regular evaluation of the system?
10. How effective is this system in automating daily tasks?

Directions: Use the Action Plan to identify the actions that need to be taken to implement Standard V in the school or district.

Performance Indicator(s)	Next Steps	Person(s) Responsible	I Will Know This Step Has Been Achieved When ...	Timeline
V.A. Educational leaders use multiple methods to assess and evaluate appropriate uses of technology resources for learning, communication, and productivity.				
V.B. Educational leaders use technology to collect and analyze data, interpret results, and communicate findings to improve instructional practice and student learning.				
V.C. Educational leaders assess staff knowledge, skills, and performance in using technology and use results to facilitate quality professional development and to inform personnel decisions.				
V.D. Educational leaders use technology to assess, evaluate, and manage administrative and operational systems.				

Conclusion

Evaluation enables educators to determine the effectiveness of program or reform innovations. If you can identify success, you can reward it; if you can identify failure, you can correct it. However, without going through the process of gathering and analyzing data, we simply make a "best guess" about the quality of programs or reform innovations. Evaluation of technology integration within instructional programs helps us learn how to do a better job with students. Using technology to facilitate the evaluation process makes it more likely we will maintain a high standard in our evaluation design.

Resources

Assessment Tools

Cox, J. (n.d.). *Analysis of process* [Online tool]. Available: www.portical.org/tools/cox_aop.html

Consortium for School Networking (CoSN). (2003). *Data-Driven Decision Making Self Assessment* [Online tool]. Available: www.3d2know.org/assessment/survey.cfm

North Central Regional Technology in Education Consortium [Online tool]. (1997). Available www.ncrtec.org/capacity/profile/profww.htm

SouthEast Initiatives Regional Technology in Education Consortium (SEIR-TEC). (2000). *Technology integration progress gauge* [Downloadable site profile instrument]. Available: www.serve.org/seir-tec/publications/ProgressGauge2000.pdf

State Educational Technology Directors Association (SETDA). (2002). *2002 Toolkit* [Online tool]. Available: www.setda.org/web/guest/toolkits

Online Survey Tools

SurveyMonkey. Available: www.surveymonkey.com

Zoomerang. Available: www.zoomerang.com

Information Management Software

PowerSchool (SASI). Pearson. Available: www.powerschool.com

Schoolmaster Student Information Systems. Olympia Computing Company, Inc. Available: www.schoolmaster.com

Guidebooks

Bracey, G. (2000). *Thinking about tests and testing: A short primer in "assessment literacy"* [Online guide]. American Youth Policy Forum. Available: www.aypf.org/publications/braceyrep.pdf

U.S. Department of Education. National Center for Education Statistics, National Forum on Education Statistics. (2000, October). *Building an automated student record system: A step-by-step guide for local and state education agencies* (NCES 2000-324) [Online guide]. Available: http://nces.ed.gov/pubs2000/building/

Reports

Apple. (1995). *Changing the conversation about teaching, learning & technology: A report on 10 years of ACOT research* [Online report]. Available: www.apple.com/education/k12/leadership/acot/library.html

Ringstaff, C., & Kelley, L. (2002). *The learning return on our educational technology investment* [Online report]. WestEd. Available: www.wested.org/online_pubs/learning_return.pdf

SouthEast Initiatives Regional Technology in Education Contortium. (2001). *Factors that affect the effective use of technology for teaching and learning.* [Online report]. Available: www.seirtec.org/publications/lessondoc.html#contents

Articles

Alternative assessment and technology. (1993, December). *ERIC Digest* (ERIC Identifier: ED365312) [Online journal]. Adapted from an article by Dorothy Bennett and Jan Hawkins. (1992) *News from the Center for Children and Technology and the Center for Technology in Education, 1*(3). Available: www.ericdigests.org/1994/technology.htm

Bushweller, K. (2000, March). The Smarter Office. *Electronic School* [Online journal]. Available: www.electronic-school.com/2000/03/0300f2.html

Cox, J. (2001). *A data-driven organization's approach to assessing the quality of program delivery* [Online article]. Available: www.portical.org/cox3more.html

Darby, R., & Hughes, T. (2005, October). The evolution of student information systems. *T.H.E. Journal* [Online journal]. Available: http://thejournal.com/articles/17446

McIntire, T. (2004, May). Student information systems demystified. *Technology & Learning* [Online journal]. Available: www.techlearning.com/showArticle.php?articleID=19400338

Moore, D.P. (2003, October). Four Cs in office automation. *School Planning & Management* [Online journal]. Available: www.peterli.com/archive/spm/507.shtm

Tucker, E. (2007, June). Improving efficiency with web-native operations tools. *School Planning & Management* [Online journal]. Available: www.peterli.com/archive/spm/1388.shtm

Vecchioli, L. (1999). A process for evaluating student records management software. *Practical Assessment, Research & Evaluation* [Online journal], *6*(14). Available: www.ericdigests.org/2000-3/records.htm

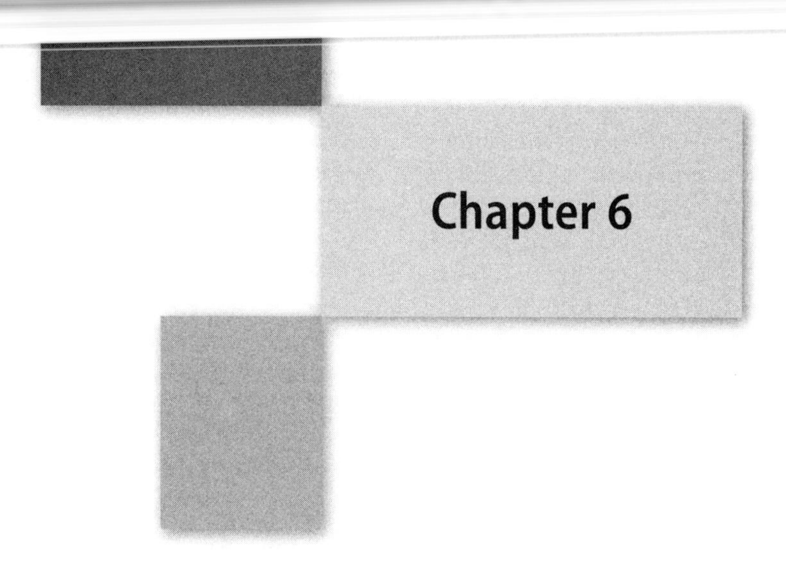

Standard VI

Social, Legal, and Ethical Issues

Educational leaders understand the social, legal, and ethical issues related to technology and model responsible decision-making related to these issues.

Performance Indicators for Educational Leaders

VI.A. Ensure equity of access to technology resources that enable and empower all learners and educators.

VI.B. Identify, communicate, model, and enforce social, legal, and ethical practices to promote responsible use of technology.

VI.C. Promote and enforce privacy, security, and online safety related to the use of technology.

VI.D. Promote and enforce environmentally safe and healthy practices in the use of technology.

VI.E. Participate in the development of policies that clearly enforce copyright law and assign ownership of intellectual property developed with district resources.

Chapter 6 Overview

It is important that educational leaders not underestimate the importance of each performance indicator in this standard, for along with the power and positive potential for technology use in schools comes the possibility for misuse, both intentional and inadvertent. Because administrators are working with so many different, new environments in this Information Age, there are questions and pitfalls they don't even know they should be anticipating, and administrators often find they are on the bleeding edge when it comes to the social, ethical, and legal issues of technology use. For example, Digital Divide issues, once focused on the simple ratio of computers to students, now encompass the kinds of equipment available, the location of equipment, the quality of Internet connections, and the kinds of activities provided for student subgroups. Adult use of school-provided technology has opened a new can of worms as well. Is it OK for teachers to visit eBay during their lunch hour or use an account provided through the district or school Internet service provider (ISP) from home to access a site that would be blocked at school? What are your responsibilities in providing students safe Internet access? Are your staff and students working in environments that might be physically harmful?

This chapter covers four broad areas of concern: equal access; social, legal, and ethical practices; safe and secure online use; and, finally, potential health and environmental issues. In some respects, because of the long-term ramifications of not addressing these areas, this is the most important standard for leaders to understand and address.

In the text of the chapter, Performance Indicator VI.E., addressing copyright and intellectual property rights, is discussed out of sequence because of its close relationship to Performance Indicator VI.B., which covers social, legal, and ethical issues.

The Digital Divide: It Isn't Just about Hardware

Performance Indicator VI.A.

Educational leaders ensure equity of access to technology resources that enable and empower all learners and educators.

There is a persistent belief among some educators and community leaders that equal access to technology is equivalent to the number of stand-alone and Internet-connected computer systems housed at a site. As a result, various data-gathering entities faithfully make yearly reports about the ratio of students to computers of varying configurations. In fact, the ratio is improving, decreasing from 12.1:1 in 1998 to 3.8:1 in 2005, (Technology Counts Report, 2007) but this statistic alone does not tell the whole story. As the amount of hardware increases, administrators find that equity issues are far more wide-ranging than they imagined. When educational leaders of the 21st century look at equal access, they must consider age, condition, and location of the equipment; speed of Internet access; racial and

Age, Condition, and Location of the Equipment and Internet Access

A low student-to-computer ratio is meaningless if the count includes obsolete, little-used equipment, yet schools often include these systems in their reports in the mistaken belief that an improved ratio somehow makes them "look better" to the public. Although the rationale for including obsolete equipment may be that these computers are used for word processing or drill and practice, there are several problems with this reasoning. First, counting these systems as part of the overall ratio gives a false impression about the kind of technology access provided to students. Second, the software and web-based applications that will run on these systems are very limited and do not provide opportunities for students to experience updated technology capabilities. Third, because these systems are often conveniently located in the classroom, where teaching and learning most often take place, their presence may actually inhibit opportunities for students to get to newer technologies less conveniently located.

The condition and location of equipment are also important factors. Older systems often fail and are difficult or nearly impossible to repair, yet educators tend to hang on, hoping that there's a bit of life left in the old computer. Isa Kaftal Zimmerman points out, "Schools need to be able to let go of technology that has outlived its usefulness" (LeBaron & Collier, 2001, p. 110). New equipment is often installed in labs where access is limited and inconvenient; however, it can be difficult to persuade teachers, parents, and other administrators that it might be more instructionally effective to distribute new equipment to classrooms and use somewhat older, though not ancient, equipment in a lab.

As for Internet access, although there are still issues, the picture continues to grow brighter. In a report issued in November 2006, the National Center for Education Statistics states that 94% of U.S. public school instructional rooms now have Internet access. However, this statistic is modified by further explanation that schools located in cities or high-poverty, high-minority enrollment schools still have fewer Internet-connected instructional rooms than schools with more favorable demographics.

Socioeconomic and Gender Factors

Despite the fact that there seems to be some lag in bringing the Internet into classrooms in urban, low-income schools, the overall impact of wealth, or the lack of it, appears to be decreasing when it comes to technological access for students. *Education Week's* Technology Counts 2007 report points out that regardless of race, ethnicity, or income level, student access to school technology is increasingly common. However, this is not the case when examining student access to technology away from school. Data from the National Center for Education Statistics (NCES, 2006), shows a gap of at least 50 percentage points in student use of computers at home between families with the lowest and highest incomes.

According to the Pew Internet and American Life Project report, *Digital Divisions* (2005), the disparity in Internet use that has existed between white and English-speaking Latino students is decreasing. However, African Americans and adults who are disabled, who do not speak English, or who did not complete high school are still least likely to use the Internet. There are several theories about why this is true; however, no single factor is recognized as being the most critical determiner in the extent of technology use with these groups.

One of the first recognized areas of inequity in access—gender—continues to be a factor. Girls and young women tend to shy away from technology-based training and careers. Statistics show that few girls enroll in computer courses during Grades 6–12, and female enrollment in college technology majors is minimal. Again, there are a variety of theories about the causes but few hard facts. Some experts speculate that subtle stereotyping in schools discourages girls from exploring technology careers, while other experts point out that although girls should be encouraged to consider technology careers, pressuring them to do so when they have little interest is another form of discrimination.

Academic Standing, English Language Learners, and Special Needs Students

Often educators still consider technology to be an add-on to "real" education. This is evident in schools where technology is used as a reward for getting work done early or for good behavior. It also is apparent in schools where lower achieving students or those with limited English proficiency use technology for drill and practice or review and higher achieving students use technology for project-based learning and problem solving. Lower expectations for students with academic challenges inevitably lead to lower performance and discourage both teachers and students from capitalizing on the potential of technology use to increase academic performance.

Students with special needs also frequently miss out on using technology because simply having equal access doesn't guarantee these students can use the technology. Visual impairments, physical limitations, and other handicapping conditions can make technology completely inaccessible to these children. There are remedies for these problems, including adaptive devices and software, but few schools currently provide them. An excellent resource for information about this topic is the Center for Applied Special Technology (www.cast.org).

Geographic Location

Most educators are aware that urban schools face unique problems, but few recognize that rural and other isolated settings contribute to the Digital Divide. State and federal funding initiatives may be in place for broadband access to the Internet, but it takes time for companies to provide the necessary connections for Internet access. In some areas, it simply is not possible to lay fiber-optic cable, and consequently, satellite technology must be used instead. While this is feasible, it definitely falls under the heading of "easier said than done." In the meantime, having to rely on dial-up connections means that students do not have access to the kinds of technology experiences their counterparts in suburban and urban schools have.

This section addresses the roles and responsibilities of educational leaders in addressing equal access concerns by looking at the current situation, the ideal, and steps to take to reach the ideal.

What Is Already in Place?

Assess existing methods employed at the site and district levels to ensure equal access to technology for all learners.

All educational leaders need to:

- Understand that equity issues are broad and far-reaching, encompassing multiple issues relating to a variety of factors.
- Meet regularly with staff members to discuss current methods to ensure equity in technology use.
- Include parents, community members, and students when soliciting feedback on equity concerns.
- Model the importance of equal access through their own behaviors, in planning, and through staff development sessions.

Campus Leaders' Additional Responsibilities:	District Leaders' Additional Responsibilities:	Superintendents' and Cabinet Leaders' Additional Responsibilities:
• Review school site plans to see how equal access issues are addressed. • Review discipline plans to determine whether technology use is addressed as a reward or a punishment. • Review existing lesson plans to determine the level of access for students of all academic achievement levels. • Discuss current access issues with special education teachers and specialists. • Review current equipment and software inventories, locations for equipment, and uses for the equipment and software.	• Review district curriculum and technology plans to see how equal access issues are addressed. • Review departmental plans and policies that include equal access issues. • Meet with campus leaders to gather input about equal access and technology. • Review current district equipment and software inventories, locations for equipment, and recommended uses for equipment and software.	• Review existing board policies or regulations that address equal access. • Obtain feedback from campus and district leaders regarding existing equal access issues and concerns. • Determine how each division can provide support to schools and to individual district departments based upon this feedback. • Determine whether existing policies and procedures provide for equal access to technology to all students.

What Practices Demonstrate Successful Implementation of This Performance Indicator?

Ensure that all learners have equal access to available technologies by developing policies and procedures that can be monitored and evaluated.

All educational leaders need to:

- Define groups that currently do not experience equal access to technology.
- Decide whether further action needs to be taken.
- Develop a timeline for research and problem solving.
- Work together to develop recommendations for solutions to equal access issues.
- Identify the appropriate people to contact other districts, the county office of education, vendors, and professional organizations to gather information.

Campus Leaders' Additional Responsibilities:	District Leaders' Additional Responsibilities:	Superintendents' and Cabinet Leaders' Additional Responsibilities:
• Once students, parents, and staff members have been informed of equal access issues, insist that all students have equitable access to the technologies available on site. • Continue to research up-to-date technologies and work with district and cabinet leaders to ensure that your site has equitable access compared to other sites within the district and the surrounding area. • Update school plans and budgets to reflect ongoing costs of technology in all areas covered in Chapter 4 of this book. • Provide yearly training in equity issues.	• Develop and present to both campus and cabinet leaders recommendations for policies to address equal access issues. • Identify support that may be necessary for sites to ensure equal access and make recommendations to the cabinet regarding who would be responsible for providing the support, both technical and financial. • Consider the effects your recommendations will make on sites in terms of cost, training, and ongoing work required. • Communicate with site leaders prior to making final recommendations.	• Schedule time for campus and district leaders to discuss equal access policies and participate in these meetings. • Review recommendations for support and determine the ability of the district to provide this kind of support. • Share equal access policy recommendations with campus and district leaders prior to presenting them to the school board.

All educational leaders need to:

- Bring a representative group together to act as a task force that will make recommendations regarding policies and procedures for equal access.
- Use feedback from sites and the district office to design informational meetings for the educational community.
- Develop an action plan and timeline for implementation of meetings and other steps identified to raise awareness.
- Establish procedures for evaluation and modification of implementation.

Campus Leaders' Additional Responsibilities:	District Leaders' Additional Responsibilities:	Superintendents' and Cabinet Leaders' Additional Responsibilities:
• Provide information regarding equal access to all staff members, parents, and students. • Seek out and share instructional models for offering equal access to technology for all students. • Provide information to all staff members, parents, and students about assistive technologies for students with special needs. • Make provisions for equitable equipment placement and replacement. • Encourage all students to consider enrolling in technology-based courses and design a master schedule that supports their enrollment.	• Assist campus leaders in offering information to staff, parents, and students regarding equal access to technology. • Provide information to district staff, including cabinet leaders, regarding equal access and technology. • Support campus leaders in finding instructional models that demonstrate equitable access to technology. • Assist campus leaders in researching information about assistive technologies for students with special needs. • Include appropriate equal access to technology as a consideration when reviewing curriculum for adoption. • Provide incentives for sites to offer technology-based courses to all students.	• Participate in informational meetings concerning equal access to technology. • Make equal access to technology a goal in the district master plan. • Provide support to sites offering assistive technology to students with special needs. • Support sites that strive to offer technology-based courses to all students through budget allocations, staffing, and other resources. • Educate school board members on issues related to equal access and technology.

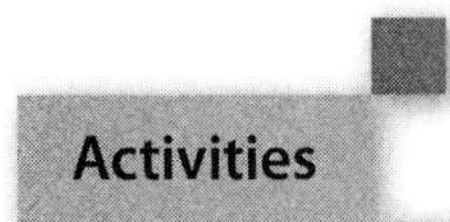

Activities

Performance Indicator VI.A. Educational leaders ensure equity of access to technology resources that enable and empower all learners and educators.

Activity 1 • School or District Profile

A complete analysis of equal access issues requires gathering basic information about the student population being served. Use Activity 1 to create a school or district profile. This profile will be used to complete Activity 2.

Activity 2 • Equal Access at Your School and in Your District

Use the School or District Profile completed in Activity 1 to answer the questions in Activity 2. Site leaders use Activity 2A. District leaders use Activity 2B.

Next Steps: When you have completed Activities 1 and 2, use the Action Plan at the end of this chapter to identify the steps that need to be taken next to ensure equitable access to technology for all students in the school or district.

Number of Students:	Grade Levels:	**District Only**
% Free or Reduced-Price Meals:	Title I School? (School only)	Number of Schools:
Number of Male Students:	Number of Female Students:	Number of Title I Schools:
Ethnicities Served (%)		
African American:	Hispanic:	
American Indian or Alaska Native:	Pacific Islander:	
Asian:	White:	
Filipino:	Multiple/No Response:	
Special Programs (%)		
Special Education Enrollment:	Gifted and Talented Enrollment:	
Language Proficiency (%)		
English Only:	English Learners:	
Fluent English Proficient (FEP):	Students Redesignated FEP:	
Additional Information		
Standardized Test Profile: Attach a school or district summary of test scores in the major content areas tested. Where possible, include disaggregated reports showing performance by special programs, ethnicity, language proficiency, and gender.		
Equipment Profile: Attach a recent school or district equipment inventory (within the last 12 months).		
Technology Plan: Attach a copy of your school or district technology plan.		

Activity 2A • Equal Access at Your School

Directions: The school or district profile completed in Activity 1 can be used by site leaders to answer the questions in the table below.

Site Leaders	Circle One	
Are equal access issues addressed in your school site plan(s)?	**Yes**	**No**
How?		
Is access to technology used as a reward or punishment on your campus?	**Yes**	**No**
How?		
Describe the age and location of computer equipment and peripherals in your school.		
Are students of all ages and academic ability levels offered equitable access to technology-infused learning experiences?	**Yes**	**No**
Describe typical learning experiences for grade levels and student subgroups.		
What access issues exist for students in special education programs?		
What gender-specific access issues exist for students?		
Summarize the current equity issues on your campus. What are your program's strengths and weaknesses?		

in the table below.

District Leaders	Circle One	
Are equal-access issues addressed in current board policies or regulations?	**Yes**	**No**
How?		
Do you solicit regular feedback from school-level leaders about equity issues?	**Yes**	**No**
How?		
How do divisions or departments within the district office provide support to school sites regarding equity issues?		
Do existing policies and procedures provide adequate support for school sites regarding equity issues?	**Yes**	**No**
Explain.		
Summarize the current equity issues in your district. What are your program's strengths and weaknesses?		

Social, Legal, and Ethical Concerns

Performance Indicator VI.B.

Educational leaders identify, communicate, model, and enforce social, legal, and ethical practices to promote responsible use of technology.

Social, legal, and ethical issues are areas where educational leaders need to reach out to experts in various fields for assistance because it is not possible for one person or even one district to keep up with every change. In just a few words, this performance indicator for Standard VI brings up some of the most complex and challenging factors that school administrators are expected to oversee. Social, legal, and ethical issues surrounding technology use become increasingly complex as technologies are more deeply ingrained in daily life.

Although the basis for many concerns stems from familiar territory such as copyright, acceptable use of school or district equipment, methods used for student interaction, and so on, the capabilities of new technologies lead school administrators into uncharted waters as they attempt to apply old understandings to new information environments. The following explanation is written in general terms compared with what might be expected from an expert in these fields. However, it points out concerns school administrators need to consider carefully and refers to resources written by specialists.

Begin with legal concerns. The law outlines for school administrators the minimal level of expectations for behavior and use of technology by students and staff. There are several documents schools and districts can develop and enforce to establish a baseline for acceptable legal use of technology. These documents cover copyright (see Performance Indicator VI.E.) and appropriate use of school and district equipment as well as Internet access provided through education funds. Each document must be written with the advice of an attorney who understands cyber law and must take into account the culture of the community being served by the school district.

Use of School and District Equipment and Services

Educators know that it is not permissible to use a school copier to duplicate invitations to a private party and that school employees may not campaign for political candidates on school grounds. Some uses of advanced technology are as easily defined while others are not so clear. For example, if an employee is at home, using a privately owned computer system but a district-provided e-mail account, does the district still have the right to monitor personal e-mail? To help sort through these types of situations, each school district needs to have an acceptable use policy, or AUP, in place for students and employees. An AUP should be written with the assistance of an attorney. While it does not have to be formally adopted by the school board, doing so ties AUP guidelines to established formal policies concerning student and staff behavior. It provides guidelines for how district-provided technologies may be used and, although originally intended to cover Internet use, can be extended to define all policies and templates, is available on the Virginia Department of Education website www.doe.virginia.gov/VDOE/Technology/AUP/home.shtml/.

Other legal issues include a hodgepodge of items, many addressing disciplinary action and privacy and often related to Internet usage. Recent cases involving schools and technology have focused on disciplining students for Internet misuse, including cyberbullying, censorship of student writing, online groups for adults and public meeting laws, student use of social networks or Web 2.0 tools such as blogs and wikis, and employee use of district equipment for personal reasons. The *eSchool News* newsletters published weekly (www.eschoolnews.com) often highlight articles about legal concerns. *SmartBrief,* a daily online newsletter published by the Association for Supervision and Curriculum Development (ASCD), is also an excellent resource (www.smartbrief.com/ascd/). However, these articles discuss incidents that have already happened. If you find yourself in a situation in which discipline or similar issues are involved, use district and outside resources to work through the problem.

Ethical and Social Issues

Ethical Scenarios

You receive a call or letter from a vendor offering free equipment and/or access to cable or the Internet. The only thing the vendor asks for in return is that you guarantee students will use the equipment a specified amount of time daily or that students watch brief advertisements from their sponsors each time they use the equipment.

Your district uses an Internet service provider that offers comprehensive filtering to protect students from undesirable websites. The company has an excellent reputation and has been in business several years. One morning you read in your local newspaper that this company has been selling aggregated data to marketing companies about how students use the Internet. The data format makes it impossible to identify individual student use, but the collection of data indicates trends in purchasing patterns.

Sometimes technology-based practices that come into question are legal but are considered unethical. The scenarios above fit into this category. Some educators argue that access to equipment or connectivity is worth student exposure to advertisements, while others take the position that we have a higher responsibility to protect students from marketing agencies targeting their disposable incomes.

Other ethical and social issues focus on censorship: Do educators have the right or responsibility to limit the kinds of media to which students have access, and are educators able to censor student output, particularly when it is published on the web? Another concern is privacy. How closely do administrators need to monitor e-mail and sites students and employees visit while online? Recent reports also question whether early technology use and prolonged Internet use encourage children to isolate themselves and create difficulty in forming relationships with others. The Alliance for Childhood's (2000) report, *Fool's Gold: A Critical Look at Computers in Childhood,* and 2004 follow-up report, *Tech Tonic,* elaborate on many of these concerns.

Although legal issues are handled relatively easily through board policies, ethical and social questions are more difficult. You may find general guidance through existing board policies and procedures, but it is important for educational leaders to have ongoing conversations about these issues. Donation policies, guidelines for web publishing, and district-adopted curriculum based on developmental and instructional concerns may be helpful for these situations as long as staff members are aware that they exist and adhere to them.

Roles and Responsibilities

Performance Indicator VI.B. Educational leaders identify, communicate, model, and enforce social, legal, and ethical practices to promote responsible use of technology.

This section addresses the second Performance Indicator for Standard VI, identifying the roles and responsibilities of educational leaders as they assess current policies and guidelines; deciding what modifications need to be made to resolve social, legal, and ethical issues; and determining how this can be accomplished.

What Is Already in Place?

Identify current policies and procedures, how they are communicated to staff and students, and how they are modeled and enforced for staff and students.

All educational leaders need to:

- Be able to identify policies and procedures in place in the district that relate to social, legal, and ethical issues with technology.
- Be able to explain how staff, parents, and students are made aware of these policies.
- Be able to articulate ways educational leaders model the social, legal, and ethical use of technology and provide examples.
- Be able to describe how these policies and procedures are currently enforced.

• Ensure staff, students, and parents are aware of acceptable use policies. • Ensure staff, students, and parents are able to describe how these policies are enforced.	• Provide support to campus leaders in explaining and enforcing current policies and procedures involving social, legal, and ethical issues.	• [illegible] reviewing and updating existing policies. • Support campus and district leaders in enforcing these policies.

What Practices Demonstrate Successful Implementation of This Performance Indicator?

Communicate board-approved policies and procedures to staff, parents, and students; model their use; and enforce them.

All educational leaders need to:

- Become familiar with newly adopted policies and procedures.
- Participate in developing a timeline for introducing new policies and procedures, including inservice, implementation, and enforcement.
- Model use of the policies and procedures regularly.

Campus Leaders' Additional Responsibilities:	District Leaders' Additional Responsibilities:	Superintendents' and Cabinet Leaders' Additional Responsibilities:
• Work with staff to develop procedures for obtaining and filing AUPs. • Use various forms of communication to inform staff, parents, and students about policies and procedures. • Enforce policies and procedures on campus.	• Develop district procedures for obtaining and filing AUPs. • Communicate with campus and cabinet leaders regarding policies and procedures. • Enforce policies and procedures in district offices and support campus leaders in policy enforcement.	• Support campus and district leaders in enforcing policies and procedures. • Keep board members informed about implementation and enforcement of newly adopted policies and procedures. • Inform community members about newly adopted policies and procedures and their enforcement.

What Steps Lead to Successful Implementation of This Performance Indicator?

Develop policies and procedures for board approval.

All educational leaders need to:

- Recognize that legal and ethical technology use requires ongoing education and support.
- Participate openly and frankly in discussions about ethical and social issues related to technology use.
- Keep up with professional reading in these areas through journals, digests, or online services.
- Identify areas where policies and procedures need to be updated or developed.
- Recognize that policies and procedures in this area will be difficult to enforce without support from all educational leaders.

Campus Leaders' Additional Responsibilities:	District Leaders' Additional Responsibilities:	Superintendents' and Cabinet Leaders' Additional Responsibilities:
• Inform staff members about upcoming policies and procedures and their enforcement. • Encourage knowledgeable staff members to share information and ideas for implementation and enforcement of policies. • Share what you are learning with interested staff and fellow campus leaders.	• Research existing policies and procedures in other school districts. • Identify area experts who may be called upon for assistance in developing the policies and procedures. • Develop drafts of needed policies and procedures. • Share this information with campus and cabinet leaders.	• Work with district leaders on drafts of policies and procedures. • Educate school board members about the social, legal, and ethical issues surrounding technology use. • Prepare proposed policies and procedures for board approval. • Communicate your support of these documents to staff and the community.

enforce social, legal, and ethical practices to promote responsible use of technology.

Activity 3 • Acceptable Use of Technology at Your Site and in Your District

Because of the close relationship between staying current with emerging technologies and modeling use, Performance Indicators VI.B. and VI.E. are paired.

Use one of the Activity 3 tables to analyze the existing methods employed at your school or district to identify, communicate, model, and enforce social, legal, and ethical practices that promote acceptable use of technology and enforce copyright law. Site leaders use Activity 3A. District leaders use Activity 3B.

If the school has a website, review it before completing this activity. It's also helpful to have copies of the school's or district's AUP and copyright policy.

Next Steps: Use the Action Plan at the end of this chapter to identify the steps that need to be taken next to ensure that school or district leaders identify, communicate, model, and enforce social, legal, and ethical practices that promote responsible technology use and enforce copyright law.

Activity 3A • Acceptable Use of Technology at Your Site

Directions: The following table is for site leaders to analyze the existing methods employed at your school to identify, communicate, model, and enforce social, legal, and ethical practices that promote acceptable use of technology and enforce copyright law.

Site Leaders	Circle One	
Does your school have a website?	**Yes**	**No**
Does the website address the school's expectations for acceptable use of technology on the part of staff and students?	**Yes**	**No**
If so, how?		
Does the website address copyright issues for both staff and students?	**Yes**	**No**
If so, how?		
Describe methods used to inform staff, students, and parents about the acceptable use policy and copyright policy.		
Describe strategies used to enforce the acceptable use policy and copyright policy.		
Describe ways you personally model compliance with the acceptable use policy and copyright policy.		
Summarize the practices that promote acceptable use of technology and adherence to copyright policy on your campus. What are the strengths and weaknesses of these practices?		

[illegible]

district to identify, communicate, model, and enforce social, legal, and ethical [illegible] acceptable use of technology and enforce copyright law.

District Leaders	Circle One	
Are acceptable use and copyright issues addressed in current board policies or regulations?	**Yes**	**No**
If so, how?		
Do you solicit regular feedback from school leaders about acceptable technology use and copyright issues?	**Yes**	**No**
If so, how?		
How do divisions or departments within the district office provide support to school sites on acceptable technology use and copyright issues?		
Do existing procedures provide adequate support for school sites to enforce acceptable use and copyright policies?	**Yes**	**No**
Explain.		
Summarize the practices that promote acceptable use of technology and adherence to copyright policy on your campus. What are the strengths and weaknesses of these practices?		

Copyright and Technology

Performance Indicator VI.E.

Educational leaders participate in the development of policies that clearly enforce copyright law and assign ownership of intellectual property developed with district resources.

Most educators understand that it is illegal to copy software programs without the publisher's permission and that it is illegal to run a program on more than one computer unless you have purchased a copy of the software for each computer the program is installed on, or have purchased a multiple station license, or have prior permission from the publisher. However, many educators are not clear about laws governing images, audio clips, and text found on websites or other issues that arise when using electronic media created by someone else.

A copyright policy is a document developed at the district level with the advice of an attorney and formally adopted by the school board. Each district needs to have a formal policy in place that is reviewed and updated regularly. Staff, parents, and students need annual notification of the policy, and the policy should be displayed at every site near computers, copiers, or any other device that is used to duplicate or access copyrighted material. Links to copyright resources for schools are available on the Wisconsin Department of Public Instruction website: http://dpi.state.wi.us/lbstat/copyres.html/. This document clearly spells out the district's guidelines for copyrighted material. Two other useful documents found online are the Educators' Lean and Mean No Fat Guide to Fair Use by Hall Davidson, available at: www.techlearning.com/db_area/archives/TL/2002/10/copyright.php/, and a chart developed by the same author, Hall Davidson, available at: www.mediafestival.org/copyrightchart.html.

Intellectual Property

Intellectual property is still primarily an issue at the college and university level, but as K–12 educators develop instructional materials for technology integration, it is possible that questions about the ownership of intellectual property developed with district resources will surface with more frequency. In the business world, when an employee invents or creates something as part of his or her job, the company has a right to use the invention or creation. This is also true when an employee who is hired to carry out general duties creates or invents something on company time, using company resources. The law is not as clear with relation to faculty members.

Under copyright law, courts have allowed teachers to retain their copyright on educational materials they develop. Now the question becomes: Do software or Internet-based materials fall under this same exemption? The answer is "maybe." The National Education Association is working with professional groups to resolve these issues. The University of Texas, Austin, website offers a clear description of the UT system's policies regarding intellectual property in *Who Owns What?* (www.utsystem.edu/OGC/IntellectualProperty/whowns.htm).

of policies that clearly enforce copyright law and assign ownership of intellectual property developed with district resources.

Even though this may not be an issue at your site or within your district, it is wise to begin investigating policies and to consider adopting one. If you have an intellectual property policy that pertains only to print material, an update is in order. This section provides basic guidelines for educational leaders at the site and in the district office for planning and implementing copyright and intellectual property policies.

What Is Already in Place?

Locate and review any current policies that define copyright and assign ownership of intellectual property.

All educational leaders need to:

- Read any existing policies related to copyright and intellectual property.
- Define the scope of the policy (print material, video, software, etc.).
- Research how these policies were developed.
- Review current practices for implementing and enforcing these policies.

Campus Leaders' Additional Responsibilities:	District Leaders' Additional Responsibilities:	Superintendents' and Cabinet Leaders' Additional Responsibilities:
• Ensure staff, students, and parents are aware of the copyright policy. • Ensure staff, students, and parents are able to describe how the copyright policy is enforced. • Ensure staff members are aware of the intellectual property policy and its enforcement.	• Provide support to campus leaders in explaining and enforcing current policies and procedures involving copyright and intellectual property.	• Take responsibility for regularly reviewing and updating existing policies. • Support campus and district leaders in enforcing these policies.

What Practices Demonstrate Successful Implementation of This Performance Indicator?

Implement a policy that defines copyright and assigns ownership of intellectual property created using district resources.

All educational leaders need to:

- Participate in creating a plan to disseminate information about the policy to appropriate stakeholders.
- Follow the timeline for development, approval, and implementation of the policy.
- Enforce this policy.

Campus Leaders' Additional Responsibilities:	District Leaders' Additional Responsibilities:	Superintendents' and Cabinet Leaders' Additional Responsibilities:
• Ensure all computer systems on campus are using legally obtained software. • Ensure that the school's video and software collection includes only legally purchased items. • Include license agreements in budgets for software and video purchases. • Post the copyright policy in appropriate locations. • Provide information to all staff members concerning the provisions of the policy regarding copyright and intellectual property rights.	• Ensure all district computer systems are using legally obtained software. • Ensure that the district's video and software collections include only legally purchased items. • Develop district policies for purchasing license agreements for software and video. • Post the copyright policy in appropriate district office locations. • Publish and distribute information about copyright and intellectual property rights policies. • Organize informational meetings regarding these policies. • Provide support for informational meetings to school sites.	• Prepare and submit a final draft of copyright and intellectual property rights policies for board approval. • Support campus and district leaders in enforcing policies and procedures. • Keep board members informed about the implementation and enforcement of newly adopted policies and procedures. • Inform community members about newly adopted policies and procedures and their enforcement.

ment of ownership of intellectual property.

All educational leaders need to:

- Participate in developing or updating policies related to copyright and intellectual property.
- Work together to create a timeline for development, approval, and implementation of the policies.
- Review possible procedures for implementing and enforcing these policies.

Campus Leaders' Additional Responsibilities:	District Leaders' Additional Responsibilities:	Superintendents' and Cabinet Leaders' Additional Responsibilities:
• The bulk of the development work is a district responsibility because copyright is a legal matter and intellectual property rights in some instances may be negotiated.	• Research existing policies in similar school districts. • Share policy models with campus and cabinet leaders. • Work with cabinet members and other appropriate resources in developing policies. • Share the draft policies with campus and cabinet leaders.	• Work with employee associations while developing or revising policies. • Work with legal counsel on development of the policies. • Make recommendations regarding policies. • Educate school board members about this issue. • Arrange to go through procedures to have the policies formally adopted.

Performance Indicator VI.E. Educational leaders participate in the development of policies that clearly enforce copyright law and assign ownership of intellectual property developed with district resources.

Activity 4 • Appropriate Use of Technology

Because of the close relationship between staying current with emerging technologies and modeling use, Performance Indicators VI.B. and VI.E. are paired.

Use one of the Activity 4 tables to analyze the existing methods employed at your school or district to identify, communicate, model, and enforce social, legal, and ethical practices that promote acceptable use of technology and enforce copyright law. Site leaders use Activity 4A. District leaders use Activity 4B.

If the school has a website, review it before completing this activity. It's also helpful to have copies of the school's or district's acceptable use policy and copyright policy.

Next Steps: Use the Action Plan at the end of this chapter to identify the steps that need to be taken next to ensure that school or district leaders identify, communicate, model, and enforce social, legal, and ethical practices that promote responsible technology use and enforce copyright law.

identify, communicate, model, and enforce [illegible]
technology and enforce copyright law.

Site Leaders	Circle One	
Does your school have a website?	**Yes**	**No**
Does the website address the school's expectations for acceptable use of technology on the part of staff and students?	**Yes**	**No**
If so, how?		
Does the website address copyright issues for both staff and students?	**Yes**	**No**
If so, how?		
Describe methods used to inform staff, students, and parents about the acceptable use policy and copyright policy.		
Describe strategies used to enforce the acceptable use policy and copyright policy.		
Describe ways you personally model compliance with the acceptable use policy and copyright policy.		
Summarize the practices that promote acceptable use of technology and adherence to copyright policy on your campus. What are the strengths and weaknesses of these practices?		

Activity 4B • Appropriate Use of Technology

Directions: The following table is for district leaders to analyze the existing methods employed in your district to identify, communicate, model, and enforce social, legal, and ethical practices that promote acceptable use of technology and enforce copyright law.

District Leaders	Circle One	
Are acceptable use and copyright issues addressed in current board policies or regulations?	Yes	No
If so, how?		
Do you solicit regular feedback from school leaders about acceptable technology use and copyright issues?	Yes	No
If so, how?		
How do divisions or departments within the district office provide support to school sites on acceptable technology use and copyright issues?		
Do existing procedures provide adequate support for school sites to enforce acceptable use and copyright policies?	Yes	No
Explain.		
Summarize the practices that promote acceptable use of technology and adherence to copyright policy on your campus. What are the strengths and weaknesses of these practices?		

Performance Indicator VI.C.

Educational leaders promote and enforce privacy, security, and online safety related to the use of technology.

If any school or school library in your district receives certain federal funding under the Elementary and Secondary Education Act (currently Title II, Part D) or E-Rate monies through the federal Telecommunications Act of 1996, you fall under the provisions of the Children's Internet Protection Act (CIPA), which went into effect in April 2001. This law establishes requirements for Internet safety policies and the use of filtering software or blocking technology to curtail access to online material that is obscene, includes child pornography, or may otherwise be harmful to students (material that falls under the legal definition of "obscene" in regard to children, a stricter standard than for adults). Explanations of the law and steps schools and districts must take to retain funding are available on the Internet. Two resources are the Washington Internet Project's guide to CIPA (www.cybertelecom.org/cda/cipa.htm) and the Universal Service Administrative Company (www.universalservice.org/sl/about/overview-program.aspx). At this time, administrators are free to select the filtering or blocking technology they want to use, but there are specifications within the laws regarding whose access must be filtered and what kind of materials must be blocked.

Internet Safety Policies

Although they are similar in nature, the mandated Internet safety policy is not the same as an acceptable use policy because it covers even more ground than an AUP. CIPA requires that Internet safety policies address several areas, including how the district plans to block access to inappropriate and/or harmful materials on the Internet as defined by CIPA; offers students access to direct communication tools such as chat rooms, instant messaging, and e-mail but safeguards them from unknown users or cyber snoops; protects against unauthorized disclosure of personal information about or by students; prevents illegal behavior by students when using the Internet, including hacking; and allows district employees to monitor student Internet access regularly. The Internet safety policy also requires identification of differentiated filtering levels to be used for students and adults.

Schools Not Covered by CIPA

If your school or district does not receive funds covered by CIPA, you still need to consider Internet security and safety issues. Though the acceptable use policy stands as a first line of defense for many districts, unless the school board formally approves it, you may have problems enforcing it. Consequently, it makes sense for all districts to have formally adopted policies and procedures regarding Internet usage by both students and staff members.

Schools and districts take a variety of approaches to filtering and blocking. At one extreme, no filters or blocks are used; instead, daily logs of sites visited by individuals or on individual stations are monitored, and problems are handled as they arise. At the other extreme, schools or districts choose to block entire categories of information and then filter other sites. Neither approach is foolproof. Monitoring daily logs requires time, and the job often falls by the wayside; filters and blocks are effective but can be bypassed by determined individuals. Many districts respond to the inherent problems with direct communication, such as chat rooms and instant messaging, by not allowing access to them at all.

Internet Safety Classes

Schools also attempt to protect students by offering instruction on safe Internet use, but this can also lead to a false sense of security. The Annenberg Public Policy Center's (2000) report entitled *The Internet and the Family 2000: The View from Parents, the View from Kids* found that although the children ages 10 through 17 who were interviewed stated that it is not OK to give out personal information about themselves or their families on the Internet, 45% of these same children said they would be willing to do so if a free gift were offered. The report also found that even though the majority of parents and children interviewed individually stated that they talk with one another about the dangers of giving out personal information on the Internet, when interviewed in pairs (parent/child) the same interviewees did not agree about whether these conversations had ever taken place. Later studies continue to show that students are often less concerned about Internet safety than adults would like them to be.

The conclusion of researchers is that simple talk is not enough when it comes to safe Internet practices. For schools, the point is that to ensure safe Internet access, teachers and other staff members must be actively involved in what students are doing on the Internet. Many reputable resources for teaching online safety are now available to educators. For example, i-Safe (www.isafe.org)and NetSmartz Workshop (www.netsmartz.org) offer lesson plans and materials for teachers, parents, and students.

Along with online safety classes, educators and parents need to address a relatively new phenomenon called cyberbullying. This is the use of e-mail, text or instant messages, blogs, phone calls, digital images, websites, and other kinds of electronic media to bully or harass someone. In fact, if anecdotal reports are accurate, students are far more likely to become the targets of cyberbullying perpetrated by their peers that they are to be victimized by online predators. School administrators must consider how they will respond to this new, pervasive discipline issue. Websites such as i-Safe and WiredSafety.org (Aftab, 2007) offer extensive information and resources for administrators who are dealing with this thorny problem.

Filtering and other types of blocking, Internet safety policies, and related concerns are on such a grand scale that they become district rather than individual site issues in most cases. It is important for district and cabinet leaders to solicit input from campus leaders and the community because although many challenges to filtering originate with parents or community groups, much of the work to be done will fall to the district office.

security, and online safety related to the use of technology).

This section describes the roles of various educational leaders as they assess existing practices, decide upon what must be in place, and then determine the steps necessary to achieve their goals.

What Is Already in Place?

How does the school district currently work to provide safe, secure Internet access for students and staff?

All educational leaders need to:

- Identify policies and procedures currently in place regarding acceptable use and misbehaviors such as cyberbullying.
- Identify filtering software and other blocking technology presently in use.
- Determine the level of use for AUPs throughout the district.
- Determine the level of use for filtering software and other blocking technology throughout the district.

Campus Leaders' Additional Responsibilities:	District Leaders' Additional Responsibilities:	Superintendents' and Cabinet Leaders' Additional Responsibilities:
• Determine whether current AUPs are on file for all staff and students, and if so, where. • Identify filtering software and blocking technology currently used on site. Determine whether this is used through the district network or is in addition to what the district provides. • Determine whether anyone is using software that circumvents the filtering or blocking technology in place. • Identify methods used to inform staff, students, and parents about safe Internet use and AUPs. • Identify ways Internet use is currently monitored on site.	• Determine whether current AUPs are on file for all staff and students, and if so, where. • Identify filtering software and blocking technology currently in use in the district. • Assist campus leaders in identifying software that can be used to circumvent the filtering or blocking technology and in determining whether this is happening on site or in district offices. • Identify ways district departments inform campus leaders, staff, and community members about safe Internet use and AUPs. • Identify ways Internet use is currently monitored throughout the district. • Communicate with cabinet leaders as they determine the effect of CIPA on district funding and policies.	• Determine the status of the current AUP, including whether it was reviewed by an attorney and board approved. • Determine whether the district has current formal Internet safety policies. • Determine the effect of CIPA on district funding and the need for policies.

What Practices Demonstrate Successful Implementation of This Performance Indicator?

Based upon current technologies, provide safe and secure Internet access to students and staff including policies that can be monitored and enforced.

All educational leaders need to:

- Become familiar with new policies, procedures, and laws pertaining to safe and secure Internet access.
- Implement and monitor new policies and procedures pertaining to safe and secure Internet access.
- Document implementation and monitoring through newsletters, minutes of meetings, signed AUPs, memos, handbooks, and other written data.
- Enforce new policies and procedures.

Campus Leaders' Additional Responsibilities:	District Leaders' Additional Responsibilities:	Superintendents' and Cabinet Leaders' Additional Responsibilities:
• Inform staff, parents, and students about policies and procedures, their enforcement, and potential consequences for violations. • Use the monitoring system developed during planning and follow through on violations.	• Assist campus leaders in planning and presenting information to staff, parents, and students regarding new policies and procedures. • Provide information to district staff regarding new policies and procedures, their enforcement, and potential consequences for violations. • Follow through on violations found during monitoring and support campus leaders in their efforts to enforce policies and procedures.	• Monitor new policies and procedures to ensure they continue to meet legal requirements. If any school or school library in the district falls under CIPA regulations, check policies for compliance. • Make budget allocations for the cost of software, other technologies, and support for sites and district divisions. • Attend informational meetings at the site and/or district levels to demonstrate support. • Work closely with school board members to keep them informed about implementation of policies and procedures. • Support campus and district leaders in their efforts to enforce policies and procedures.

regarding Internet use for staff and students.

All educational leaders need to:

- Understand the effect of CIPA on funding at sites and the district.
- Understand that decisions about filtering, blocking, and Internet safety are sensitive and require community input and support to be successful.
- Develop an action plan and timeline for implementation.
- Provide for regular evaluation and monitoring of implementation.
- Participate in trainings.

Campus Leaders' Additional Responsibilities:	District Leaders' Additional Responsibilities:	Superintendents' and Cabinet Leaders' Additional Responsibilities:
• Meet with stakeholders to discuss filtering and blocking, Internet safety issues, and monitoring procedures to ensure safe use of the Internet. Share input with district leaders. • Develop a system for recording and keeping documentation supporting implementation and monitoring of policies and procedures.	• Assist in gathering information from sites and the community to share with cabinet leaders prior to designing new policies and procedures. • Assist in developing documentation procedures at sites and within district offices. • Research and make recommendations about filtering software or other blocking technologies. If necessary, ensure that recommendations meet CIPA requirements.	• Gather information about CIPA regulations and determine their effects on the district. Share this information with campus and district leaders. • Determine the timeline for meeting legal requirements related to policies and procedures. • Educate the school board about the need for an Internet safety policy and other procedures to continue receiving funding. • If the district is not subject to CIPA, it is still the cabinet's responsibility to review and determine the need for Internet safety policies and AUPs. • Prepare and submit documents for board adoption.

Activities

Performance Indicator VI.C. Educational leaders promote and enforce privacy, security, and online safety related to the use of technology.

Activity 5 • Children's Internet Protection Act Compliance

Despite the potentially serious consequences of not complying with CIPA requirements (e.g., loss of E-Rate or technology funds provided through the No Child Left Behind Act), many administrators are unaware of their responsibilities in this area when their school or district accepts certain federal funds. Answer the questions in Activity 5 to test your knowledge in this area.

Activity 6 • Internet Safety Policies in Your School or District

Use the Activity 6 tables to analyze the existing Internet safety policies employed in your school or district to enforce privacy, security, and online safety for all users. Site leaders use Activity 6A. District leaders use Activity 6B.

It's helpful to have copies of your school's or district's AUP and Internet safety policy (if a separate document exists) while completing this activity. You may need to check with your school or district technician to find out about filtering software or blocking technology currently in use.

Next Steps: After completing Activities 5 and 6, use the Action Plan at the end of this chapter to identify the steps that need to be taken next to ensure that school or district officials promote and enforce privacy, security, and online safety for all users.

Is your school or district currently receiving federal funds that fall under CIPA? If yes, which funds? If no, why?
Briefly respond to the following question, which applies if you're receiving federal funds.
If you are under CIPA requirements, what steps have you taken to be compliant?
If you are not required to comply with CIPA, how do you handle Internet security and safety issues? Does your state have legislation that addresses these issues? How does your school or district ensure compliancy?

If you don't know the answers to the questions above, you can learn more about CIPA by visiting the Federal Communications Commission's website: www.fcc.gov/cgb/consumerfacts/cipa.html/.

 Activity 6A • Internet Safety Policies in Your School

Directions: This table is for site leaders to analyze existing Internet safety policies employed at your school to enforce privacy, security, and online safety for all users.

Site Leaders	Circle One	
Are current signed AUPs on file for all students and staff members?	Yes	No
If so, where?		
What filtering software or blocking technology is currently used at your school?		
Is this filtering or blocking technology provided through the district?	Yes	No
What steps are taken to ensure that staff or students do not circumvent the filtering or blocking technology?		
What steps are taken to ensure that educationally relevant material on sensitive topics (e.g., domestic terrorism, computer security, AIDS, etc.) are not inadvertently blocked by the filtering software?		
What steps do you take to inform staff, students, and parents about safe Internet use and the AUP?		
How is Internet use monitored on your site?		

district to enforce privacy, security, and online safety for all users.

District Leaders	**Circle One**	
Does the district have separate acceptable use policies for staff and students?	**Yes**	**No**
Are staff and students required to sign acceptable use policies annually?	**Yes**	**No**
Why or why not?		
Do district acceptable use policies comply with CIPA?	**Yes**	**No**
Why or why not?		
Did an attorney review the current district AUPs?	**Yes**	**No**
Why or why not?		
Did the school board approve the current district AUPs?	**Yes**	**No**
Why or why not?		
Does the district currently have a formal Internet safety policy?	**Yes**	**No**
Why or why not?		
What is the specific impact of CIPA requirements on your district?		

Ergonomics

Performance Indicator VI.D.

Educational leaders promote and enforce environmentally safe and healthy practices in the use of technology.

Administrators recognize that ergonomics can be a concern for adults and that staff members need to have workstations that are comfortable and not harmful physically, but many do not realize there may be the potential for physical problems for students. The main issues at this time revolve around problems caused by poor posture and eyestrain. Anyone using a computer for a prolonged period of time needs access to a properly placed keyboard and mouse, a comfortable chair that provides back support, a properly positioned monitor, and appropriate lighting. In most office environments these needs can be met by purchasing specially designed furniture.

Even though the same type of furniture can be purchased for classrooms and labs, the challenge is much greater for several reasons. First, to help correct posture problems, the furniture must to be adjusted for each user. There are chairs and desks that allow for this kind of adjustment; however, most teachers realize that the time required for the simple act of doing so for each student user severely limits actual instruction time. Lighting is even more difficult to address. Appropriate lighting for a classroom is not necessarily appropriate for computer use, and school districts are seldom in a position to install sophisticated lighting systems in each classroom and lab.

Fortunately, according to many ergonomics experts, most students are not at computer stations long enough to cause them physical problems. It is also believed that students may be more at risk for physical problems when using a computer at home, where they have access for longer periods of time. The same is true for classroom teachers. However, administrators do need to respond to the needs of employees who regularly spend several hours using computer systems, and steps can be taken to make the environment healthier for students and other employees.

Any employee who uses a computer regularly for lengthy periods needs access to appropriate furniture, and the school or district needs to provide this. Do not ignore a request of this type. Should there still be a problem, it is possible that the employee will need to be assigned other duties.

right next to the keyboard is also helpful, on the right for right-handed students and on the left for left-handed students. Adjustable chairs are the single biggest help, but at $200–$300 each, they simply aren't practical for most schools. Smaller students whose feet dangle when they sit at a computer station can be encouraged to put their backpacks on the floor under their feet for additional support.

Some districts that have attempted to create ergonomically sound environments have also found that furniture solutions for adults are not appropriate for children. At this time, the best course is to take the steps you can for both children and adults, realizing that this issue will not disappear and that you need to stay current on ergonomics and schools. Cornell University maintains a website on ergonomics that is a good resource (http://ergo.human.cornell.edu).

Roles and Responsibilities

Performance Indicator VI.D. Educational leaders promote and enforce environmentally safe and healthy practices in the use of technology.

This section highlights the roles and responsibilities for educational leaders as they examine the issue of ergonomics now and in the future.

What Is Already in Place?

Research the physical computing environment that currently exists in your school or district.

All educational leaders need to:

- Work with appropriate staff to research types of computer furniture currently in use, placement of systems, and lighting.
- Become familiar with ergonomic concerns as they relate to classrooms and offices.

Campus Leaders' Additional Responsibilities:	District Leaders' Additional Responsibilities:	Superintendents' and Cabinet Leaders' Additional Responsibilities:
• Communicate with district and cabinet leaders to identify any health problems that have been reported from your site.	• Review district health records for instances of student health problems related to computer use.	• Review personnel statistics for instances of health problems related to computer use among employees.

What Practices Demonstrate Successful Implementation of This Performance Indicator?

As much as possible, provide ergonomically sound environments for staff and students.

All educational leaders need to:

- Insist that staff members who use computers regularly throughout the day work at ergonomically sound stations.
- Keep ergonomics in mind, particularly lighting, when planning remodeling or new construction.
- Institute a long-term plan to replace old furniture with ergonomically sound furniture.
- Model good work habits and use a safe work environment.

Campus Leaders' Additional Responsibilities:	District Leaders' Additional Responsibilities:	Superintendents' and Cabinet Leaders' Additional Responsibilities:
• Include ergonomically sound furniture as part of the total cost of ownership plan within the site budget. • Follow district recommendations for furniture purchases and computer placement. • Establish incentives for staff to use appropriate placement of equipment for themselves and students and to make modifications in their computer use.	• Develop and adhere to recommendations and guidelines concerning purchases of computer furniture. • Develop recommendations regarding placement of computer equipment. • Include ergonomically sound furniture as part of the total cost of ownership plan within department budgets. • Monitor ongoing instances of health problems related to computer use among students.	• If appropriate, develop and submit policy recommendations regarding ergonomically sound environments to the school board. • Include ergonomically sound furniture as part of the total cost of ownership plan within the district budget. • Establish incentives for site and district staff to use appropriate placement of equipment for themselves and students and to make modifications in their computer use. • Monitor ongoing instances of health problems related to computer use among employees.

during their workday and to improve the environment for other staff and students.

All educational leaders need to:

- Keep current on ergonomics issues in education through professional reading, discussions, and inservice.

Campus Leaders' Additional Responsibilities:	District Leaders' Additional Responsibilities:	Superintendents' and Cabinet Leaders' Additional Responsibilities:
• Work with staff to make adjustments in computer placement for classroom use. • Work with office staff to ensure that workstations are ergonomically sound. • Allocate funds to purchase antiglare overlays. • Allocate funds to upgrade workstations for long-term computer users.	• Meet with campus and cabinet leaders to discuss possible guidelines and recommendations for purchasing computer furniture and placement of computers. • Work with staff to ensure that workstations are ergonomically sound. • Allocate funds to upgrade workstations in district offices.	• Determine whether formal policies or procedures are required in this area. • Work with personnel division and employee associations regarding computer use-related injuries.

Performance Indicator VI.D. Educational leaders promote and enforce environmentally safe and healthy practices in the use of technology.

Activity 7 • Ergonomics Checklist

Use the Activity 7 checklist to analyze your existing policies and facilities from an ergonomics perspective.

Next Steps: Use the Action Plan at the end of this chapter to identify the steps that need to be taken next to ensure that school or district officials promote and enforce environmentally safe and healthy practices in the use of technology.

perspective.

School:		
Completed By:	**Circle One**	
1. Does your technology plan address the issue of ergonomics as it relates to students and staff?	**Yes**	**No**
If so, how?		
2. Visit locations that have adult computer workstations. Which of the following accommodations are being made?		
Keyboard trays are adjustable and at a negative slope to avoid wrist and arm strain.	**Yes**	**No**
The height and back support position of the workstation chair is adjustable.	**Yes**	**No**
The workstation chair has pivoting, adjustable armrests.	**Yes**	**No**
The mouse is placed on a tray or platform that can be positioned close to the body, above the keyboard.	**Yes**	**No**
The monitor is positioned so that the top is 2 inches to 3 inches above the user's line of sight.	**Yes**	**No**
The monitor is placed approximately one arm's length from the user.	**Yes**	**No**
The monitor screen is free from light glare.	**Yes**	**No**
Employees take frequent breaks when using the computer workstation (every 30 to 60 minutes).	**Yes**	**No**
Based on your observations, where do workstation modifications need to be made? What needs to be done?		

Continued

Activity 7 • Ergonomics Checklist

Continued

3. Visit locations that have student computer workstations. Which of the following accommodations are being made?		
Computer monitors are placed so that students don't strain their necks and eyes because they must look up to work.	**Yes**	**No**
Monitor screens are free from light glare.	**Yes**	**No**
Keyboards are placed on a flat surface at elbow level.	**Yes**	**No**
The mouse is located right next to the keyboard.	**Yes**	**No**
Students whose feet do not touch the floor when they're seated are encouraged to place a backpack on the floor under their feet.	**Yes**	**No**
Based on your observations, where do workstation modifications need to be made? What needs to be done?		
4. If students or staff use laptops for more than one hour at a time, observe the settings where the laptops are being used. Which of the following accommodations are being made?		
External keyboards are available to users.	**Yes**	**No**
External mice are available to users.	**Yes**	**No**
External monitors are available to users.	**Yes**	**No**
Users are discouraged from placing laptops on high tables or desks.	**Yes**	**No**
Based on your observations, where do modifications need to be made for laptop use? What needs to be done?		
5. Summarize the current ergonomics issues on your campus. Where are your program's strengths and weaknesses?		

Directions: Use the Action Plan to identify the actions that need to be taken to implement Standard VI in the school or district.

Performance Indicator(s)	Next Steps	Person(s) Responsible	I Will Know This Step Has Been Achieved When ...	Timeline
VI.A. Educational leaders ensure equity of access to technology resources that enable and empower all learners and educators.				
VI.B. Educational leaders identify, communicate, model, and enforce social, legal, and ethical practices to promote responsible use of technology. **VI.E.** Educational leaders participate in the development of policies that clearly enforce copyright law and assign ownership of intellectual property developed with district resources.				
VI.C. Educational leaders promote and enforce privacy, security, and online safety related to the use of technology.				
VI.D. Educational leaders promote and enforce environmentally safe and healthy practices in the use of technology.				

Conclusion

Educational leaders will find that the topics discussed in this chapter will continue to expand and be redefined as technology use in schools grows and becomes institutionalized. The best approach for administrators is to be proactive in researching and monitoring the areas of social, legal, and ethical issues in technology use. Rely upon professional organizations and publications as well as the school district's legal advisors for up-to-date information, and do not hesitate to ask for guidance when questionable situations arise.

Resources

Electronic Newsletters

ASCD SmartBrief: www.smartbrief.com/ascd/

eSchool News: www.eschoolnews.com

Electronic Journals

Converge Online: www.convergemag.com

EDUCAUSE Quarterly: http://connect.educause.edu

Learning & Leading with Technology: www.iste.org/AM/Template.cfm?Section=Publications

T.H.E. Journal: http://thejournal.com

Organizations

Center for Applied Special Technology: www.cast.org

Cornell University: CUErgo: http://ergo.human.cornell.edu

Technology and Young Children: www.techandyoungchildren.org

Bissonette, A. (2006). *Law and technology: Why legal limits don't have to limit teaching options* [Podcast]. Available: www.dangerouslyirrelevant.org/2006/12/ties_technology.html

Davidson, H. (2002). *Educators' lean and mean no fat guide to fair use.* [Online article]. Available: www.techlearning.com/db_area/archives/TL/2002/10/copyright/php/

Davidson, H. (n.d.) *Classroom copyright chart* [Online chart]. Available: www.mediafestival.org/copyrightchart.html

Hunt, A. (2006). *Copyright and fair use* [TrackStar resource]. Available: http://trackstar.4teachers.org/trackstar/ts/viewTrack.do?number=245175

Hunt, A. (2007). *Using technology responsibly* [TrackStar resource]. Available: http://trackstar.4teachers.org/trackstar/ts/viewTrack.do?number=61555

i-Safe. (2007). *Internet safety education* [Online tools and curriculum]. Available: www.isafe.org

Netsmartz Workshop. [Tool for teaching online safety]. Available: www.netsmartz.org

Universal Service Administrative Company. (1997–2008). *Step 10: Children's Internet protection act* [Online guide]. Available: www.usac.org/sl/applicants/step10/cipa.aspx

Virginia Department of Education. (n.d.). *Acceptable use policies: A handbook* [Online handbook]. Available: www.doe.virginia.gov/VDOE/Technology/AUP/home.shtml

Washington Internet Project. (2001). *Children's online protection act* (CIPA) [Online guide]. Available: www.cybertelecom.org/cda/cipa.htm

Wisconsin Department of Public Instruction. (2006). *Copyright resources for schools and libraries.* Available: http://dpi.state.wi.us/lbstat/copyres.html

Reports

Alliance for Childhood. (2000, September). *Fool's gold: A critical look at computers in childhood* [Online report]. Available: www.allianceforchildhood.com/projects/computers/computers_reports.htm

Alliance for Childhood. (2004, September). *Tech tonic: Towards a new literacy of technology.* [Online report]. Available: www.allianceforchildhood.com/projects/computers/computers_reports.htm

Annenberg Public Policy Center. (2000, May). *The Internet and the family 2000: The view from parents, the view from kids* [Online report]. Available to members only: www.and.net/michome1/miccontent/406

Fairlie, R. W. (2005, September). *Are we really a nation online? Ethnic and racial disparities in access to technology and their consequences* [Online report]. Available: www.freepress.net/docs/lccrdigitaldivide.pdf

National Center for Education Statistics (NCES). (2006). *Internet access in U.S. public schools and classrooms: 1994-2005* [Online report]. Available: http://nces.ed.gov/pubs2007/2007020.pdf

National Telecommunications and Information Administration. (2004, September). *A nation online: Entering the broadband age* [Online report]. Available: www.ntia.doc.gov/reports/anol/index.html

Pew Internet and American Life Project. (2005, October). *Digital Divisions.* [Online report]. Available: www.pewinternet.org/PPF/r/165/report_display.asp

Technology Counts 2007. (2007). *Education Week* [Online report], *26*(30). Available: www.edweek.org/ew/toc/2007/03/29/

U.S. Department of Education. (2000). *Digital divide* [Online report]. Available: www.ed.gov/Technology/digdiv.html

Articles

Becker, G. H. (2000, June). Copyright in a digital age. *Electronic School* [Online journal]. Available: www.electronic-school.com/2000/06/0600f2.html

Converge Online News. (2007). *Teach Internet safety and security, says national cyber security alliance* [Online article]. Available: www.convergemag.com/story.php?catid=5&storyid=105772

Davidson, H. (2001). The educator's guide to copyright and fair use. *Technology & Learning* [Online journal]. Available: www.techlearning.com/db_area/archives/TL/2002/10/copyright.php

MacBean, K. B. (n.d.). *Gender equality, computer technology, and the new digital divide.* [Online article]. Available: www.teacherleaders.org/old_site/Resources/members/KMacB_gender_tech.pdf

NetSmartz Workshop. [illegible]
www.netsmartz.org/safety/statistics.htm

Newmarch, J. (2001, June). Lessons from open source: Intellectual property and courseware. *First Monday* [Online journal], *6*(6). Available in archives: www.firstmonday.org/ISSUES/issue6_6/newmarch/

Oregon OSHA. (Accessed: January 1, 2008). *Computer ergonomics for elementary school* [Online article]. Available: www.orosha.org/cergos/index.html

Rasicot, J. (2000, January). Ergonomics 101. *Electronic School* [Online journal]. Available: www.electronic-school.com/2000/01/0100f2.html

Who owns what? (Accessed 2001, September 7). [Online article]. University of Texas, Austin. Available: www.utsystem.edu/OGC/IntellectualProperty/whowns.htm

Print Material

LeBaron, J. F., & Collier, C. (Eds.). (2001). *Technology in its place.* San Francisco: Jossey-Bass.

Concluding Remarks

Imagine a grocery store without scanning devices for check-out and inventory purposes, a bank without computer terminals or ATMs, a travel agent without Internet access, even a gas station without pay-at-the-pump options. While these businesses can function without the technologies named, the lack of technology makes it difficult for them to be competitive or to flourish. Students attending schools that do not have access to information technologies and electronic materials are at a similar disadvantage. Yes, they can still learn, but the lack of access is a handicap. Students are also penalized when they attend schools where the technology is present but the staff does not know how to use it effectively.

Technology use on many school campuses first took root through the work of a few determined teachers who saw its potential as an instructional tool. At that time, the site administrator often assumed the role of cheerleader and fund-raiser but left actual implementation to the classroom teacher. This approach may have worked at one time, but it is no longer sufficient. While teachers are still ultimately responsible for day-to-day delivery of classroom instruction with or without the use of technology, they cannot craft and implement an instructional program using technology as an integral part of the system without the support of their administrators at both the site and district levels. This is the case because of the magnitude of decisions that must be made about curriculum materials selection, professional development, hardware and infrastructure acquisition, technical and instructional support, and policies regarding usage. All of these areas require that technology use become institutionalized and fall beyond the scope of responsibility for the classroom teacher.

For some administrators, gaining personal proficiency in using e-mail, word processing, or working with databases and spreadsheets may be the entry point for learning to manage instructional technology, but their learning cannot stop there. Knowing how to use these kinds of applications can help the administrator streamline personal workload and provide a vehicle for modeling technology use for staff. However, while personal proficiency may help someone become a more efficient administrator, basic proficiency will not make anyone a more effective administrator.

To be a more effective instructional leader of a site or district where technology plays an integral role, a school administrator must be able to look beyond basic proficiency. Essential qualities for leading a school or district to effective use of technology include the following:

- Having a vision and the ability to articulate that vision
- A personal willingness to be a lifelong learner
- Knowledge of a variety of instructional practices
- Knowledge of the change process
- Interpersonal skills

An administrator who possesses this combination of vision, knowledge, and skills will be able to work with the community, staff, students, and parents to research, plan, implement, and evaluate instructional programs that capitalize on the capabilities of technology and result in increased student performance.

An administrator also must take action on certain essential standards and responsibilities where technology is used as a tool for information and effective instruction. These are:

- An administrator's primary concern is student achievement.
- It is imperative to have administrative support through modeling technology use; active participation in planning, implementation, and evaluation; and the ability to locate human and financial resources.
- Program planning must be predicated upon the analysis of appropriate data.
- Program planning must be inclusive and dynamic.
- Staff members must have access to regular, ongoing professional development opportunities in a variety of formats both on and off site.
- Staff members and students must have ready access to up-to-date equipment and an Internet connection that is reliable and well maintained.
- Staff members must have ready access to support personnel for technical problems and curriculum delivery issues.
- Administrators must understand and address concerns about equal access; social, legal, and ethical issues; and system security and use.
- Regular monitoring and evaluation of programs are necessary to move forward.

[illegible] who have not assumed a leadership role in this area now need to do so. The purpose of the Technology Standards for School Administrators, which form the core of the ISTE NETS for Administrators, is to help school administrators become more effective instructional leaders by demystifying the management of technology in education.

However, standards and performance indicators alone are not enough. Administrators also need resources that will assist them in implementing the standards. This book is one resource for administrators, school districts, and institutions of higher learning to use as they begin working with the standards. In addition to the narratives explaining each performance indicator and their roles and responsibilities for administrators as the standards are implemented, a wide range of additional resources are identified in each chapter. The activities provide a variety of tools that can be used to evaluate personal and organizational growth.

Local situations vary, and technology advances rapidly, making it difficult, if not impossible, to develop a definitive profile of the ideal technology-savvy administrator. By using the information provided in this book, along with the standards, performance indicators, and rubrics developed by ISTE and TSSA, within the context of your own situation you will become a more effective technology-using instructional leader.

The NETS committee also recognizes that these standards must be dynamic—updated and revised regularly—to continue to be relevant to administrators. The revised NETS for Students were released in 2007. The revised NETS for Teachers were launched in 2008. The NETS for Administrators are currently undergoing review. There will be opportunities for administrators to provide feedback to ISTE through the website: www.iste.org/Content/NavigationMenu/NETS/NETS_Refresh_Forum/NETS_Refresh_.htm, and you are encouraged to share your experiences and insights through this venue.

Here is one final suggestion for administrators who are working toward developing sustained commitment to the use of instructional technology: Document and share the positive results of technology integration practices using measurable outcomes combined with human-interest narratives. This practice makes educators' efforts more comprehensible and real to members of the school community and the public. For example, it is helpful to know that, based upon discipline records, students' behavior has improved by a given amount in classrooms where technology-based collaborative projects are introduced. When this information is coupled with a brief vignette describing the positive changes in the behavior of a particular student, the significance of the information found in the discipline records becomes more powerful.

Sharing this kind of information takes many forms. Within the school or district office it can be accomplished by asking teachers and other staff members to bring examples of successful projects to meetings to display and discuss. Office bulletin boards can be used as information tools to share highlights of programs with employees and members of the public. Websites of various types, newsletters, newspapers, local access cable television stations, brochures, and special events are all venues for publicly promoting documented positive results based on technology use or other successful innovations.

Service clubs and other organizations are important channels to the community as well. Most of these groups are happy to have education representatives speak about successful programs at their meetings or to bring students to visit as a form of special recognition. In turn, when members of the organizations feel connected to local schools, they are often very generous in their support of education both in time and donations.

Educators are clamoring for examples of best practices in technology integration. A variety of venues are available to educators willing to share their experiences and the materials they have developed. Many Internet portals and print journals also encourage teachers and administrators to contribute writing.

Celebrate your successes and encourage your staff to become active participants by showcasing their work online and in print. In the process, you will find a worldwide network of educators all working toward the same goal: helping students prepare themselves to be self-sufficient, productive citizens in the 21st century.

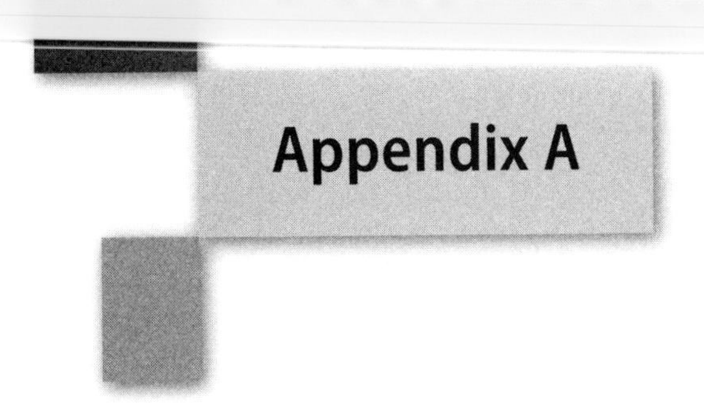

What's in a Name?

Technology Standards for School Administrators and National Educational Technology Standards for Administrators

In November 2001, the Technology Standards for School Administrators Collaborative released the final draft of the TSSA. At the same time, the International Society for Technology in Education (ISTE) released the National Educational Technology Standards for Administrators (NETS•A). So, does this mean there are two sets of standards out there for school administrators to adopt? No. In terms of the actual standards and performance indicators, the TSSA and the NETS•A are identical. However, it is the long-term goal of ISTE to expand upon the TSSA document to include other important information for administrators. This information will include "essential conditions" necessary to implement the standards, profiles for district and campus technology leaders, and position-specific tasks each administrator needs to undertake. However, although ISTE will be offering additional resources to accompany the TSSA, ISTE's NETS•A are the same as the Collaborative's standards.

A significant beginning to the NETS•A phase of ISTE's NETS Project has already been completed with the release of the Technology Standards for School Administrators document. ISTE participated in the TSSA Collaborative and had a lead role in managing the inclusive, broad-based development process. As a result, the ISTE NETS•A initiative confidently integrates and builds on the work of the TSSA Collaborative. Those who embrace NETS•T and NETS•S will appreciate a comfortable compatibility with the TSSA and the expanded NETS•A.

The vision of the TSSA Collaborative is that the TSSA document identifies knowledge and skills that constitute the "core"—what every PK–12 administrator needs regardless of a specific job role—and then extends the core to include the specific needs of administrators in each of three job roles:

- Superintendent or executive cabinet member
- District leaders for content-specific or other district programs
- Campus leaders, including principals and assistant principals

NETS•A embraces that vision and extends it to additional administrative job roles. These standards are indicators of effective leadership for technology in schools. They define neither the minimum nor maximum level of knowledge and skills required of a leader and are neither a comprehensive list nor a guaranteed recipe for effective technology leadership. Rather, these standards are a national consensus among educational stakeholders of what best indicates effective school leadership for comprehensive and appropriate use of technology in schools. Although created as a result of a national consensus building process, these standards should not be viewed as constraining nor construed as a rationale to inhibit new development, innovation, or progress for schools or for school leadership.

During the process of developing the TSSA, the writing team members, the NETS Leadership Team, and members of the collaborating organizations identified several areas in which these leadership guidelines could be enhanced. The initial TSSA phase of this effort does not address the specifics of some administrative positions. ISTE's NETS•A extends the outstanding TSSA work to two new specific job roles:

- District technology director or coordinator
- Building technology facilitator

These two leadership roles for technology correspond with the district technology director who facilitates technology integration system-wide and the technology facilitator for a campus who leads and supports teachers and other campus instructional staff members, as they grow in the appropriate use of technology in teaching, learning, and instructional management. These two additional profiles appear in the full NETS•A document.

Additionally, NETS•A includes an expanded look at the system-wide conditions that must be in place for even accomplished leadership to realize the full potential of technology. Documentation of authentic case studies of the effects these standards are having in real school districts is a part of this project, as is support for assessing administrators' progress toward achieving these standards. As with other NETS projects, current practitioners significantly influence support features that are an important part of NETS for Administrators.

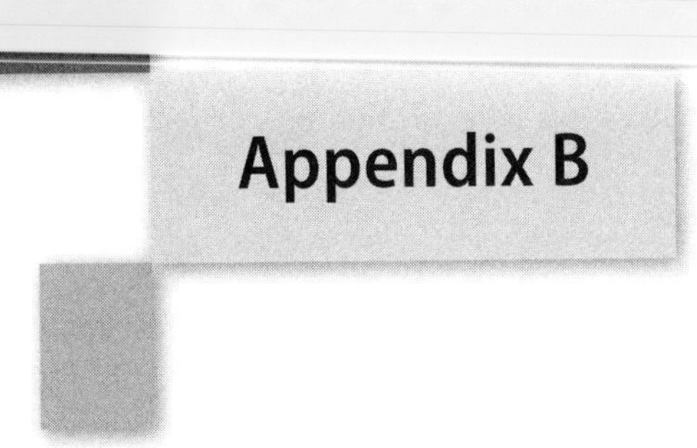

Appendix B

National Educational Technology Standards for Students (NETS•S)

All K–12 students should be prepared to meet the following standards and performance indicators.

1. Creativity and Innovation

Students demonstrate creative thinking, construct knowledge, and develop innovative products and processes using technology. Students:

- **a.** apply existing knowledge to generate new ideas, products, or processes
- **b.** create original works as a means of personal or group expression
- **c.** use models and simulations to explore complex systems and issues
- **d.** identify trends and forecast possibilities

2. Communication and Collaboration

Students use digital media and environments to communicate and work collaboratively, including at a distance, to support individual learning and contribute to the learning of others. Students:

- **a.** interact, collaborate, and publish with peers, experts, or others employing a variety of digital environments and media
- **b.** communicate information and ideas effectively to multiple audiences using a variety of media and formats
- **c.** develop cultural understanding and global awareness by engaging with learners of other cultures
- **d.** contribute to project teams to produce original works or solve problems

3. Research and Information Fluency

Students apply digital tools to gather, evaluate, and use information. Students:

- **a.** plan strategies to guide inquiry
- **b.** locate, organize, analyze, evaluate, synthesize, and ethically use information from a variety of sources and media
- **c.** evaluate and select information sources and digital tools based on the appropriateness to specific tasks
- **d.** process data and report results

4. Critical Thinking, Problem Solving, and Decision Making

Students use critical-thinking skills to plan and conduct research, manage projects, solve problems, and make informed decisions using appropriate digital tools and resources. Students:

- **a.** identify and define authentic problems and significant questions for investigation
- **b.** plan and manage activities to develop a solution or complete a project
- **c.** collect and analyze data to identify solutions and make informed decisions
- **d.** use multiple processes and diverse perspectives to explore alternative solutions

5. Digital Citizenship

Students understand human, cultural, and societal issues related to technology and practice legal and ethical behavior. Students:

- **a.** advocate and practice the safe, legal, and responsible use of information and technology
- **b.** exhibit a positive attitude toward using technology that supports collaboration, learning, and productivity
- **c.** demonstrate personal responsibility for lifelong learning
- **d.** exhibit leadership for digital citizenship

6. Technology Operations and Concepts

Students demonstrate a sound understanding of technology concepts, systems, and operations. Students:

- **a.** understand and use technology systems
- **b.** select and use applications effectively and productively
- **c.** troubleshoot systems and applications
- **d.** transfer current knowledge to the learning of new technologies

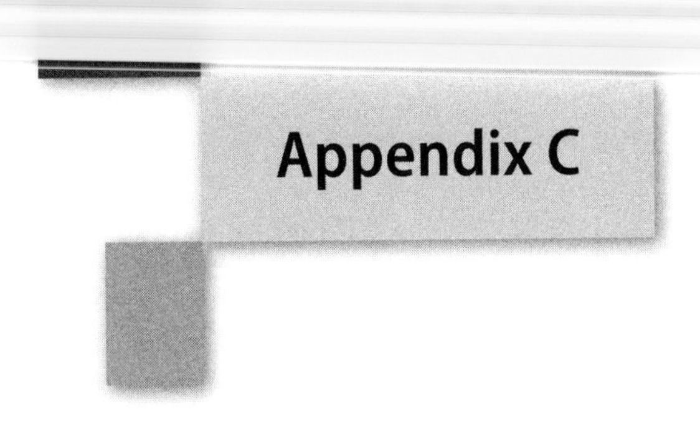

National Educational Technology Standards for Teachers (NETS•T)

All classroom teachers should be prepared to meet the following standards and performance indicators.

1. Facilitate and Inspire Student Learning and Creativity

Teachers use their knowledge of subject matter, teaching and learning, and technology to facilitate experiences that advance student learning, creativity, and innovation in both face-to-face and virtual environments. Teachers:

a. promote, support, and model creative and innovative thinking and inventiveness
b. engage students in exploring real-world issues and solving authentic problems using digital tools and resources
c. promote student reflection using collaborative tools to reveal and clarify students' conceptual understanding and thinking, planning, and creative processes
d. model collaborative knowledge construction by engaging in learning with students, colleagues, and others in face-to-face and virtual environments

2. Design and Develop Digital-Age Learning Experiences and Assessments

Teachers design, develop, and evaluate authentic learning experiences and assessments incorporating contemporary tools and resources to maximize content learning in context and to develop the knowledge, skills, and attitudes identified in the NETS•S. Teachers:

a. design or adapt relevant learning experiences that incorporate digital tools and resources to promote student learning and creativity

b. develop technology-enriched learning environments that enable all students to pursue their individual curiosities and become active participants in setting their own educational goals, managing their own learning, and assessing their own progress
c. customize and personalize learning activities to address students' diverse learning styles, working strategies, and abilities using digital tools and resources
d. provide students with multiple and varied formative and summative assessments aligned with content and technology standards and use resulting data to inform learning and teaching

3. Model Digital-Age Work and Learning

Teachers exhibit knowledge, skills, and work processes representative of an innovative professional in a global and digital society. Teachers:

a. demonstrate fluency in technology systems and the transfer of current knowledge to new technologies and situations
b. collaborate with students, peers, parents, and community members using digital tools and resources to support student success and innovation
c. communicate relevant information and ideas effectively to students, parents, and peers using a variety of digital-age media and formats
d. model and facilitate effective use of current and emerging digital tools to locate, analyze, evaluate, and use information resources to support research and learning

4. Promote and Model Digital Citizenship and Responsibility

Teachers understand local and global societal issues and responsibilities in an evolving digital culture and exhibit legal and ethical behavior in their professional practices. Teachers:

a. advocate, model, and teach safe, legal, and ethical use of digital information and technology, including respect for copyright, intellectual property, and the appropriate documentation of sources
b. address the diverse needs of all learners by using learner-centered strategies and providing equitable access to appropriate digital tools and resources
c. promote and model digital etiquette and responsible social interactions related to the use of technology and information
d. develop and model cultural understanding and global awareness by engaging with colleagues and students of other cultures using digital-age communication and collaboration tools

a. participate in local and global learning communities to explore creative applications of technology to improve student learning

b. exhibit leadership by demonstrating a vision of technology infusion, participating in shared decision making and community building, and developing the leadership and technology skills of others

c. evaluate and reflect on current research and professional practice on a regular basis to make effective use of existing and emerging digital tools and resources in support of student learning

d. contribute to the effectiveness, vitality, and self-renewal of the teaching profession and of their school and community